T0332008

Equity, Evaluation, and International Cooperation

CRITICAL FRONTIERS OF THEORY, RESEARCH, AND POLICY IN INTERNATIONAL DEVELOPMENT STUDIES

Series Editors

Andrew Fischer, Giles Mohan, Tanja Müller, and Alfredo Saad Filho

Critical Frontiers of Theory, Research, and Policy in International Development Studies is the official book series of the Development Studies Association of the UK and Ireland (DSA).

The series profiles research monographs that will shape the theory, practice, and teaching of international development for a new generation of scholars, students, and practitioners. The objective is to set high quality standards within the field of development studies to nurture and advance the field, as is the central mandate of the DSA. Critical scholarship is especially encouraged, within the spirit of development studies as an interdisciplinary and applied field, dealing centrally with local, national, and global processes of structural transformation, and associated political, social, and cultural change, as well as critical reflections on achieving social justice. In particular, the series seeks to highlight analyses of historical development experiences as an important methodological and epistemological strength of the field of development studies.

Equity, Evaluation, and International Cooperation

In Pursuit of Proximate Peers in an African City

GABRIELLA Y. CAROLINI

OXFORD
UNIVERSITY PRESS

OXFORD
UNIVERSITY PRESS

Great Clarendon Street, Oxford, OX2 6DP,
United Kingdom

Oxford University Press is a department of the University of Oxford.
It furthers the University's objective of excellence in research, scholarship,
and education by publishing worldwide. Oxford is a registered trade mark of
Oxford University Press in the UK and in certain other countries

Published in the United States of America by Oxford University Press
198 Madison Avenue, New York, NY 10016, United States of America

British Library Cataloguing in Publication Data
Data available

Library of Congress Control Number: 2022930622

ISBN 978–0–19–286548–9

DOI: 10.1093/oso/9780192865489.001.0001

Printed and bound by
CPI Group (UK) Ltd, Croydon, CR0 4YY

Cover image: © maloff/shutterstock.com

For Ottavio

Acknowledgments

In researching this book, I have learned from a wealth of conversations—both formal and informal. I especially benefited from generous feedback and opportunities to share and refine the research presented here in different forms and forums over several years. Many thanks for such opportunities and for helpful exchanges go to Sumila Gulyani, Garth Meyers, Carlos Nunes Silva, Ananya Roy, Colin McFarlane, Dan Chatman, Jeff Chusid, Mildred Warner, James Connolly, Heather Campbell, Neema Kudva, Natasha Iskander, Kian Goh, Diana Mitlin, Sai Balakrishnan, Charisma Acey, Vanessa Watson, Akbar Noman, Joseph Stiglitz, James Essex, Daniel Esser, and the community of scholars within the Global Planning Educators Interest Group.

I'm also very grateful for the enduring support and energies put into this book's publication by Oxford University Press's Adam Swallow. In addition, I was very fortunate to receive productive feedback on earlier iterations of this work from Oxford University Press's series editors for *Critical Frontiers of Theory, Research, and Policy in International Development Studies*. The product is much improved because of their guidance. On this score, I owe special gratitude to Dr. Giles Mohan, both for his model of scholarship, and his faith in mine.

The first time my flight arrived in what is now Maputo's old international airport, the electricity was down, and with it, my hope to use an ATM to secure some *meticais* for a taxi into town. The experience, however, spurred my first introduction to this tightly-woven, growing city and the incredible generosity of its residents. I do not recall the name of the couple that saw my situation and offered to give me a ride into town that day over a decade ago, but I will always remember how welcomed they made me feel. That initial warmth was extended exponentially as my time in Maputo grew. Among my friends and family, I am perhaps infamously known as someone who does not particularly enjoy cars, and does not, for the most part, attempt driving. And so there are many roads in Maputo's core and peripheries that I came to know intimately by foot as I traveled about for my research. One road in particular became a kind of second home to me: Rua da Argélia. There, at the Department of Architecture and Physical Planning within the University of Eduardo Mondlane,

I met a cadre of inspiring colleagues whose work influences so much across the neighborhoods I walked and beyond. I am forever indebted to them for their willingness to engage with and teach this native New Yorker, whose Portuguese was admittedly tinged with a strange combination of Brazilian, Italian, Spanish, and American accents. Professors Anselmo Cani, João Tique, Julio Carrilho, Luis Lage, and, last but not least, Catarina Torres Cruz shared their expertise and more with me over many years. To know them is to know Maputo, its history, and its future. I am so very grateful for the hours they spent taking in my many questions and helping me see their city a little more clearly. Cani and Caty were especially core to my time in Maputo; they were treasured stewards of my initiation across its many offerings. I further thrived in the great friendship and support of a diverse and open community in Maputo, including the inimitable Roberta Pegoraro, Amalia Mepatia, Ivan Laranjeira, David Morton, Valentina Zuin, and Celia Ruth. I can't wait to meet the youngest addition, Tiyamika! I know New England gets cold, but I still hope for and await their visits.

Over the years of my research in Mozambique, visiting KaTembe's district office, Maputo's City Hall and directorates, and so many other spaces in the city, I made the habit of sitting, observing, and waiting for my turn to speak with those whose knowledge of international cooperation and infrastructure projects I hoped to tap. I am immensely grateful to all the dedicated professionals working in Mozambique, as well as in Brazil and Argentina, who took ample time out of their day—repeatedly, and habitually, for several years—to entertain my questions, my visits with them to sites, my curiosities, and more. I am also especially thankful for the time and acceptance of residents in the communities I frequented across KaTembe, Chamanculo C, and Maxaquene A in Maputo. They allowed this researcher into their neighborhoods, homes, and often lives, always with grace.

Finally, I am ever grateful to my family of families. In Cambridge, the Department of Urban Studies and Planning (DUSP) at MIT has provided a deep trove of support and inspiration. I am so thankful for the enduring encouragement and care of an amazing group of DUSP colleagues who took interest in and supported my progress on this book in many different ways, including Eran Ben-Joseph, Christopher Zegras, Amy Glasmeier, Bish Sanyal, Lawrence Susskind, Lawrence Vale, Xav Briggs, Brent Ryan, Balakrishnan Rajagopal, Janelle Knox-Hayes, Sarah Williams, Mariana Arcaya, and Justin Steil. I entered DUSP at a transition point, but was lucky enough to engage, even if briefly, with a significant treasury of scholars who led so much in their respective fields—from Judith Tendler, Alice Amsden, and Karen Polenske to Judy

Layzer and JoAnn Carmin. My work is indebted to their tremendous legacies in different and critical ways. This ecosystem is beyond any ideal I could have imagined when I first considered becoming an academic—it is, as I've said before, the city on the hill, but one not willing to simply rest.

Both in Cambridge and Maputo, often younger and always brighter minds have lifted and sustained me during the course of researching, writing, and completing this work. I have been fortunate to engage so many student/teachers during my time across both cities, including students in my Southern Urbanisms, water and sanitation, and practicum classes. I'm especially grateful to have found Isadora Cruxên, Jenna Harvey, Prassanna Raman, Daniel Gallagher, Winn Costantini, Silvia Danielak, Dorothy Tang, Haleemah Qurechi, Ben Bradlow, Daniela Cocco Beltrame, Mechi Bidart, Yasmin Zaerpoor, Fizzah Sajjad, Sara Lynn Hess, Tania El Alam, Toral Patel, Chris Rhie, Sarah Dimson, Nene Igietseme, Laura Martin, Fitsum Gelaye, Kadeem Khan, Samra Lakew, Bridget Burns, Milousa Ibraimo António, Idélcia Mapure, Nurdino Manjate, Priscila de Oliveira Ramgi, Milton Botão, Pedro Emanuel, Jorge Américo Ramos, and Arsénio Nhanombe. Their minds—and those of so many others who have trusted me in the classroom and field—have so often given me the energy and feedback I needed to stay the course on this work. It has been a special source of pride to see Idélcia matriculate in the city planning graduate program at MIT after we met so many years back at the University of Eduardo Mondlane. I smile knowing the bridges between our two cities continue to grow with her. Finally, a very special thank you to the brilliant Isa, Daniel, Laura, Jenna, and Milousa for their meticulous work in the field whilst pregnancy and early motherhood kept me grounded. I could not have completed the research for this book without them.

I'm still uncertain how or why I was fortunate enough to be born into a family of such immutable bond, but to them and their unfailing love, I know I owe almost everything. My parents, Alfonso and Maria, and my siblings, Patricia, Herman, and Maryann, together raised and fortified me in ways too numerous to recount. This work is nothing their collective support and patience did not aggregate or manifest. Grace Han, Cindy Kruger, Hannah McCollum, Åsa Frostfeldt, Balkees Jarrah, Janet Reilly, and Sappho Xenakis kept me much saner and happier than I would have been without them. I'm grateful too to my mother- and father-in-law, Yvonne and Ken, in Vermont, for having often and graciously entertained their grandson (and son) on a weekend so that I might work a little more in Massachusetts. At home, Tom has anticipated and endured the research and completion of this book for almost as long as I've known him. Here at last it is, and with it my greatest gratitude for the marathon spirit of pacing and pushing through long journeys he carries. There aren't woods in New England that have not welcomed his hiking feet or heard his fiddle while I researched and wrote—and so I thank the trees and conservation lands too. I dedicate this book to our son, moon, and stars, Ottavio, who has been generously offering to write it for me since he could talk. Perhaps his would have been better, and perhaps the next one, we write together. From these depths of family and friends come any strength I can claim; to and for them, every love I carry.

Cambridge, MA
September 2021

Contents

List of Figures

List of Tables

List of Maps

List of Abbreviations

3Rs	Reduce, Reuse, and Recycle
ABC	Agência Brasileira de Cooperação (Brazilian Cooperation Agency)
AFECC	Anhui Foreign Economic Construction Corporation
Aguas del Norte	Compañía Salteña de Agua y Saneamiento S.A.
AIIB	Asian Infrastructure Investment Bank
ALBC-TCP	Alternativa Bolivariana para las Américas y el Tratado de Comercio de los Pueblos (Bolivarian Alternative for the Americas and the Peoples' Trade Agreement)
AMDEC	Associação Moçambicana para o Desenvolvimento Concertado
ASCHA	Associação Sócio-Cultural Horizonte Azul
AURA	Autoridade Reguladora de Água (Water Regulatory Authority)
AVSI	Association of Volunteers in International Cooperation
BASIC	Brazil, South Africa, India, and China
BRI	Belt and Road Initiative
BRICS	Brazil, Russia, India, China, and South Africa
Caesb	Companhia de Saneamento Ambiental do Distrito Federal
CBA	cost-benefit analysis
CMM	Conselho Municipal de Maputo (Maputo Municipal Council)
CRBC	China Road and Bridge Corporation
DAC	Development Assistance Committee
DFID	British Department for International Development
DIME	development impact evaluation
DIRCO	South African Department of International Relations and Cooperation
DPA	Indian Development Partnership Administration
DUAT	Direito do Uso e Aproveitamento de Terra (Right to Land Use and Benefit)
DUSWMH	Directorate of Urban Solid Waste Management and Health
EDM	Electricidade de Moçambique (Electricity of Mozambique)
Embrapa	Empresa Brasileira de Pesquisa Agropecuária (Brazilian Agricultural Research Corporation)
EWB	Engineers without Borders
Exim	Export-Import
FDI	foreign direct investment
Frelimo	Frente de Libertação de Moçambique (Mozambican Liberation Front)
GAS	Grupo de Água e Saneamento

GDEI	Gabinete de Desenvolvimento Estratégico Institucional (Cabinet of Strategic Institutional Planning)
IACD	Italian Agency for Cooperation and Development
IBSA	India, Brazil, and South Africa partnership
IEG	Independent Evaluation Group
IMF	International Monetary Fund
INEFP	Instituto Nacional de Emprego e Formação Profissional (National Institute of Employment and Vocational Training)
ITEC	Indian Technical and Economic Cooperation
JICA	Japanese International Cooperation Agency
LVIA	Associazione Internazionale Volontari Laici
MZN	meticais novos
NAM	Non-Aligned Movement
NDB	New Development Bank
NEPAD	New Partnership for Africa's Development
NGO	non-governmental organization
NIEO	New International Economic Order
NPM	New Public Management
ODA	official development assistance
OECD	Organization for Economic Cooperation and Development
PAR	Programme Analysis and Review
PGTF	Pérez-Guerrero Trust Fund
PPBS	Planning, Programming, and Budgeting System
RCT	randomized-control trial
Renamo	Resistência Nacional Moçambicana (Mozambican National Resistance)
SADC	Southern African Development Community
SADPA	South African Development Partnership Agency
SDI	Slum/Shack Dwellers International
SENAI	Serviço Nacional de Aprendizagem Industrial (Brazilian National Service of Industrial Training)
SIGEF	Sistema de Gestão Fundiária (Land Management System)
SSC	South–South Cooperation
SSF	South–South Facility
UN	United Nations
UNASUR	Union of South American Nations
UNCTAD	United Nations Conference on Trade and Development
UNDP	UN Development Programme
UNGWOPA	United Nations' Global Water Operators Partnership Association
UNILAB	University of International Integration of Afro-Brazilian Lusophony
UNOSSC	UN Office for South–South Cooperation
USAID	US Agency for International Development
USD	United States dollars
WOP	Water Operators' Partnership
WSUP	Water and Sanitation for the Urban Poor

Introduction

From Rhetoric to Verdict on South–South Cooperation

1. A Harbinger of Possibility

The newspaper article sprawling over the desk of the Brazilian Vice Ambassador to Mozambique ran across two pages of print. Its title, in large, bold font, read: *O NEOCOLONIALISMO BRASILEIRO EM MOÇAMBIQUE*, or "Brazilian neocolonialism in Mozambique."[1] The Vice Ambassador, Mr. Nei Bitencourt, had freshly arrived in the Mozambican capital Maputo following another high-ranking diplomatic appointment in Washington, D.C.[2] I was there to interview him about Brazil's growing portfolio of cooperation projects with Mozambique in the urban landscape, and more widely its role as a global "model" of urban development reform. Clearly, however, I was not the only one interested in this subject. In his short time in Maputo, it seemed Mr. Bitencourt already had been fielding many questions about Brazil's intentions in Africa, and more specifically in Mozambique.

Unsurprisingly, my interview with Bitencourt was a testament to this statesman's political savvy and foreign-policy experience. He said all that a development idealist could hope to hear—making intelligent, frank arguments about Brazilian motivations in Africa widely and in Mozambique especially. In Bitencourt's telling, Brazil represented a harbinger of possibility, not a "model" of urban development (carefully correcting my terminology) and certainly not a neocolonial force. Instead, Brazil was something like a friend or relative of other developing countries. Importantly, this "relative" was one who intimately understood and wanted to help, but also made no attempt to disguise proprietary self-interests. Bitencourt juxtaposed this Southern community to what he called a more troubled historical relationship of hostility and

---

[1] The article in question was published by the newspaper *O País* in August 2011 (Rafael, 2011).
[2] Mr. Bitencourt's appointment trajectory, from an established international relations center in D.C. to a growth pole in Africa, one could reasonably argue, was evidence of his strong performance from the Brazilian perspective. He was later moved to the Brazilian Embassy in Congo, but I interviewed him in the Brazilian Embassy in Maputo on September 15, 2011.

Equity, Evaluation, and International Cooperation. Gabriella Y. Carolini, Oxford University Press.
© Gabriella Y. Carolini (2022). DOI: 10.1093/oso/9780192865489.003.0001

admiration between countries of the global South and their Northern industrialized development partners. Clearly, he was a master of the art of rhetoric, but what Bitencourt espoused in our conversation about Brazilian–Mozambican cooperation that day seemed like more than mere shop talk or political ideology. I wanted to understand whether his hard sell about South–South Cooperation (SSC) was based on realities on the ground. This line of inquiry begs for empirical attention, but rarely receives it at the project level, and even less so within the urban environment.

Provoked by the newspaper lying open in front of him and hoping to expand my study of Brazilian engagements in SSC, I asked the Brazilian Vice Ambassador to suggest projects between the two countries at the urban scale that I might include in my analysis. Surprisingly, he demurred from recommending a major project I had repeatedly heard about from others, a slum-upgrading project with Brazilian technical assistance in one of Maputo's oldest neighborhoods, Chamanculo C. Instead, he suggested I visit the National Institute of Employment and Vocational Training (*Instituto Nacional de Emprego e Formação Profissional,* or INEFP). Vice Ambassador Bitencourt seemed convinced that Brazil's cooperation with INEFP in constructing a new training facility and curriculum for the city's unemployed youth would well represent the success of Brazil's approach to working with other countries in the South. When I visited INEFP, however, its director made clear to me that he did not share Bitencourt's opinion. Instead, he lamented the slow pace of SSC work with Brazil and announced that if the project were to have been in partnership with China—in his telling a country much advanced compared to both Mozambique *and* Brazil—the work would already be complete.[3] I heard similar complaints from some Mozambican municipal practitioners working with Brazilian partners in the aforementioned upgrading project in Chamanculo C, who felt that turnover among Brazilian staff and a lack of information-sharing created delays and therefore difficulties in working with residents who had become skeptical of the project's capacity to deliver change.[4] And yet a very different, more positive picture was emerging from another set of discussions I eventually had with Mozambican municipal practitioners working with partners from the Brazilian city of Guarulhos on the mobilization of waste-picker collectives akin to Brazilian *catadores* in Maputo. These diverse narratives of frustration, satisfaction, and optimism reflect why today there is still more

[3] Interview with Eduardo Chimela on August 13, 2012 at INEFP in Maputo.
[4] Interviews with Cesar Cunguara from the Maputo Municipal Council (CMM) planning office on August 21, 2012 and two Mozambican technical staff hired by an NGO working with Brazil in Chamanculo C on July 4, 2013 (in a project detailed in Chapter 3 of this book).

rhetoric than verdict on the utility of labels such as the "South" and whether SSC is an improvement over other forms of cooperation for development.

2. Plan and Methods for this Book

This book represents my attempt to make sense of the fuzziness around SSC. Specifically, I examine SSC within, as opposed to separately from, the ecosystem of international cooperation stakeholders at the project level and, relatedly, explore the implications of project partnerships for local governance and capacity-building in cities like Maputo. An interrelated set of questions guides my enquiry. Does it matter—as SSC proponents might have us think— if a city partners, with whom it partners, and what their financial backing may be? If so, why and in which ways? The specific outcome of interest in my work is equity—or the distribution of benefits related to an infrastructure project's materiality (i.e., distributive and procedural justice) and the knowledge recognized and produced among stakeholders (i.e., epistemic justice) from the project's planning and delivery. In this way, my research on international cooperation projects fills a critical gap. While procedural justice in project management and governance is well studied, anticipating precisely how international cooperation partnerships influence distributive and epistemic equity is not an object of empirical and scholarly focus. Organizational-learning and project-management literatures provide insights into how partnerships in infrastructure projects influence learning and material outcomes. Those analyses, however, tend to relate more to efficiency rather than equity as in distributive justice. Urban planning and geography scholarship on urban governance offer perspectives on how power relations between infrastructure project stakeholders matter for how urban development is envisioned and materialized. Rarely, however, do these perspectives focus on the context of an African city, like Maputo, where the international development community and aid are major influences. And, of course, critical development and postcolonial studies provide insights into the historically situated political, economic, and cultural influences on cities like Maputo. But these offer few, if any, inter-scalar project-level analyses in an African urban context. The varieties of thinking and the incomplete fit of each of these diverse academic bases vis-à-vis my work convinced me that my initial questions could only begin to be fully fleshed out and answered by an inductive research approach. Inductive research, such as a grounded theory, allows for the exploration of possibilities where a clear explanatory path is not already evident. This was certainly the case I encountered in studying international cooperation—and the presumed specialness of SSC therein—within Maputo's infrastructure project world.

My research methods were also strongly influenced by a vein in critical planning theory, informed by postcolonial scholarship, that deftly demonstrates the epistemic vulnerabilities of universalist explanations for how urban development unfolds (or should unfold) across cities. The latter narratives, shaped by the experiences of cities across North America, Europe, and some parts of Asia, seemed especially misaligned with realities of urban development in Maputo—where the mainstay of planning power sits not with city planning offices nor even private-sector developers, but in national government, a political party, and the diverse and dense cadre of bilateral and multilateral partners. With these theoretical and methodological perspectives related to understanding complex development processes in cities like Maputo, I began spending time in the city in two-, three-, and occasionally four-month blocks. Cumulatively, this amounted to about eighteen months in the field between 2009 and 2015—time spent listening, gathering data and narratives, and beginning to code themes from my encounters with professionals involved in infrastructure cooperation projects. Within the world of infrastructure cooperation, I chose to focus on water-and-sanitation-related projects—in part because water and sanitation were the most enduring challenges where I most often resided within Maputo, namely in KaTembe. KaTembe is one of seven municipal districts in Maputo, and is characterized as rather rural. It lacks an extensive network of sewerage lines, has limited access to treated water, and only partially hosts an electricity grid. Nonetheless, the projects I focused on spanned a wide and diverse landscape across the city of Maputo and captured a range of water-and-sanitation-related projects with different international partners. In each of the projects, the Maputo Municipal Council was an important arbitrator, stakeholder, and participant.

In taking a grounded approach to understanding how cooperation projects, and their partnerships, functioned, I engaged with various qualitative research methods, including: direct observation; in-depth and repeated semi-structured interviews (N=74) with development and municipal professionals involved across the five infrastructure projects; community-based meetings (ranging from one to four per month); and, discourse analyses of documents from infrastructural project practitioners and sponsors, including their evaluations and assessment guidelines. In addition, I led the design and deployment of a rapid household survey (N=261) and an in-depth household survey (N=82) in Guachene, one of five large neighborhoods in the KaTembe district of Maputo, which had the least available background information and current analyses on households and project-level work. These surveys sought to improve information available on intended beneficiaries, their access to water-and-sanitation-related services, and to gather community-based perspectives on project participation, project-related progress, and community-based infrastructure and service priorities. This work in Mozambique was complemented by further qualitative research in Brasília, Brazil and Salta, Argentina, where I also used semi-structured interviews (N=14) with practitioners (e.g., general managers, project, and logistic specialists) working across two water utilities within a technical cooperation project I studied under a United Nations (UN) platform for such partnerships.

This book's findings reflect how multiple scales of organizational nuance in international cooperation influences project-level work and potentialities for equity therein. In surprising ways, what I found explicitly challenges the geopolitical primacy of approaches to international cooperation advanced in SSC. Nonetheless, in the tradition of the aspirational, within which planning (despite all its faults) and my own academic path are squarely situated, my work also points to the potentiality of a different strategy for organizing partnerships promoted in the name of equity and solidarity. As the urban planning and legal scholar Peter Marcuse[5] wrote, it is not enough to simply expose that which does not work. In seeking out change, we must also propose and politicize new modalities of practice. For me, this meant moving beyond my ultimate disappointment with how SSC played out on the ground. It also forced me to think reflectively and critically about the implicit shaping power of project evaluation methods in which I had been trained and which still dominate the development industry. The journey of that reflection, woven into the pages of this book, ultimately helped me to reconcile discrepancies between the distributive, procedural, and epistemic justices which *are*, and those which *ought to be*, in international cooperation projects.

3. Promoting Proximate Peers and Equity

In this book, I reject the simple notion that a combination of similar histories or struggles and the new availability of capital make SSC leaders such as Brazil, China, India, or South Africa especially—or universally—preferred development partners for lower-income countries. Orthodox accounts of SSC would expect projects in Mozambique with Brazil or with China to be equally

---

[5] Marcuse, with whom I studied, has spoken and written about this extensively, but his thoughts are well summarized in Marcuse (2009).

compelling for building equitable development. I show that this is not the case. Indeed, my analysis highlights how even different SSC projects between the same countries are not similarly operationalized on the ground.

With SSC not holding up as a fair general proxy for equity and solidarity in development, what, then, are partnerships that can? Based on my close study of the cooperation landscape in Maputo, my response centers on a *heterarchical* conceptualization of "*proximate peer*" partnerships. These comprise proximities beyond just partners' geopolitical identity and the technologies they use, and toward project governance, embeddedness, and professional theories of practice among cooperation project staff. Advocates and organizers of SSC already point to the relevance of historical geopolitics, and often also use technical proximities as a rationale for expecting that Southern partners are better situated to cooperate around shared development challenges. However, my study of projects in Maputo found that these other characteristics of cooperation work—project governance, embeddedness, and theories of practice—enable a deeper theorization of what types of proximity matter in development partnerships, and *why*.

Critically, this theorization positions Southern actors with a potential relative, but not absolute, advantage over Northern ones in promoting equity and solidarity. Two out of five proximities—namely geopolitical position and technological use—largely, but not universally, afford Southern partners a conceivable advantage over other cooperation partners as proximate promoters of equitable development. Yet I also submit that traditional cooperation "emitters"—or partners from higher-income countries in the global North—can foster solidarity with equitable learning and outcomes. However, this requires that they strategically prioritize and support heterarchical partnerships between practitioners in project governance, encourage embeddedness in host environments through co-locating staff with local partners, and consider the theories of practice their staff bring to projects.

In searching for how attention to such "proximities" might enter and shape projects, I call attention to the utility and governmentality of evaluations in development work. Financial trajectories of aid, trade, and investment are major empirical windows through which SSC and other international development partnerships are traditionally studied and understood.[6] Project-level evaluation is another foundational lens to assess the delivered impacts of

---

[6] The number of publications that reference financial figures is significant, and include: Manning, 2006; Kragelund, 2008, 2015; Brautigam, 2009; Corkin, 2012; Dreher et al, 2011; Patel, 2011; Sato et al, 2011; Tierney et al, 2011; Bhattacharya, 2011; Agarwal, 2012; Chaturvedi, 2012; Herbert, 2012; Humphrey & Michaelowa, 2013; Mawdsley, 2012; Roque & Alden, 2012; Cirera, 2013; Fuchs & Vadlamannati, 2013.

development cooperation partnerships. Yet neither macro-level nor project-level evaluative practice pays attention to some of the primary aspirations of development partnerships such as SSC, rooted in notions of equity and solidarity. Like their macro-level counterparts, project evaluations center on a logic of efficiency rather than a logic of equity. Cost-benefit and cost-effectiveness analyses, performance-based indicators, and even program-level evaluations like randomized-control trials ultimately seek to empirically establish how *efficiently* and how *widely*—but not how *equitably*—objectives are or could be met. While such practices have helped to elevate and leverage the use of expert knowledge in shaping public policy and taming what Cass Sunstein calls "expressivism," or opinion as opposed to information-based decision making,[7] they also raise the false assurance that evaluations are an apolitical exercise.

In contrast, this book shows how project evaluations in development are historically used to both raise and suppress different political priorities. I trace the evolution of evaluation practices and trends therein to demonstrate how a culture of evaluation advanced in the development industry. I find that the widely promoted values of SSC (namely of Southern ownership, leadership, and equity) do not—indeed cannot—register in the orthodox project evaluations that have dominated development work throughout much of the development industry's history. Such evaluative orthodoxies necessarily find that the most fruitful cooperation partnerships are those characterized by efficiencies created by capital availability, predictability, and stability. Thus, projects with traditional multilateral development partners, Northern donors, and most recently China—all partners with relatively greater capital availability and stability—are poised to secure most favorable reviews. Here I contend that assessments of development practice require a critical postcolonial lens as well, or a perspective that emphasizes epistemic justice and a high quality of knowledge, and the criticality of distributive and procedural justice as orienting objectives in projects.[8] Toward this end, my study of international cooperation projects sited in Maputo forwards a framing of project evaluation which positions the logic of *equity* as equally relevant as the logic of efficiency for assessing development cooperation partnerships and projects. This reframing of project evaluation openly embraces the governmentality of the assessment exercise. In accepting the fundamentally political nature of

<hr/>

[7] See, for example, Cass Sunstein's recent book, *The Cost-Benefit Revolution* (2018) for a narrative of how cost-benefit analyses have helped public policies improve well-being.

[8] Even Sunstein (2018), in his celebration of cost-benefit analyses, rightly recognizes that the evaluative practice raises concerns around distributive justice, the criticality of welfare (as opposed to cost efficiency) as an objective, and the lack of full information or knowledge about all costs and benefits of a potential policy. I focus on how to address these concerns within project evaluations in the context of development work.

evaluation, I promote an explicit accounting of equity in material outcomes (i.e., examining the distributive justice of project benefits on the ground), in knowledge production (i.e., assessing who learns *and* what is learned), and in decision-making processes. In short, *both* efficiency and equity can serve as governing principles for projects, as opposed to efficiency alone.[9]

The normative objectives behind international cooperation demand assessments and partnerships that explicitly make room for—indeed elevate—considerations of equity, both within project management as well as in project outcomes. Evaluation exercises are no strangers to rewiring. Major international financial institutions such as the World Bank and bilateral aid agencies like the Japanese International Cooperation Agency (JICA) and US Agency for International Development (USAID) periodically revisit and revise their internal guidelines for project evaluation. These efforts reflect the political zeitgeist and the rising criticisms about the international development industry globally, as well as within national political chambers where budget allocations for aid are made. Thus, we see organizations move from a concern with performance to an interest in output, and from "monitoring and evaluation" toward "monitoring, evaluation, *and* learning." In practice, however, I argue that the changes do little to improve how equity is operationalized and evaluated in development project processes and outcomes.

For example, even evaluations that include efforts to promote knowledge sharing and learning among "beneficiaries" remain concerned with spreading what I position here as basic-level knowledge types: technical knowledge (i.e., understanding basic functions) and conceptual knowledge (i.e., knowledge of interrelationships). A consideration of how well projects foster higher-level knowledge typologies, such as procedural knowledge (i.e., knowledge of different methods and of when to use them) or metacognitive knowledge (i.e., awareness of one's own cognition and self-reflection) is not evidenced in the typical project evaluation, although these typologies are arguably most critical for the successful implementation of highly discretionary development projects (Pritchett and Woolcock, 2004). Furthermore, project evaluations seek to ensure partners work toward effective project implementation, as opposed to engaging in a political concern with the distribution of project benefits. This apolitical stance is a ruse; historically, project evaluations have

---

[9] There has been some interesting recent work to introduce equity considerations into the planning and assessment of transport systems, which is an infrastructure shaped and evaluated historically by measures of efficiency. For example, see Karel Martens's (2016) book, *Transport Justice*. However, the practice of international development planning, and project evaluation therein, are still largely dominated by efficiency concerns across infrastructure sectors.

done much to promote the politics of donors. I argue that they can also better prioritize and politicize distributive, procedural, and epistemic justice through the institutionalization of an explicit concern for equity in development projects.

4. Scaling up: The Implications of Proximate Peer-led Development

If, as I found, heterarchical "proximate peer" partnerships hold promise for equitable development, how might such prioritization of high-level learning, and procedural and distributive justice in cooperation projects be realized across other water-and-sanitation-related international cooperation work? Given the longstanding presence of the UN in water and sanitation advocacy, this question perhaps points most directly at the organization's efforts on the ground. To that end, I examine the UN Global Water Operators Partnership Association (GWOPA), a platform established in the 2006 Hashimoto Action Plan of the United Nations' Water and Sanitation Advisory Board to promote peer learning and basic service improvements among different water utilities and stakeholders in an effort to increase service performance and reduce the proportion of the world's population underserved by treated water and sanitation systems. By examining partnerships promoted by GWOPA, I show how equity is (and is not) manifested across the design and practice of different cooperation partnership projects. I argue that heterarchical proximate peer partnerships demonstrate a greater capacity than SSC, as currently construed in GWOPA, to promote equity by facilitating high-level knowledge production that translates into operational improvements.

From interviews with practitioners in a partnership between Argentine and Brazilian municipal water utilities, for instance, I relate how and why the Argentine utility chose to work with a Brazilian partner over a Dutch one that was proposed through GWOPA. I identify the nature of proximities between these utilities—including, but moving beyond, their geopolitical characteristics—and show how high-level knowledge production was fostered in the South American partnership.[10] Practitioners successfully shared and adapted political strategies to identify and then gain financial support for improvements in project operations, namely the adoption of advanced technologies in water metering and in a digitized customer management system.

---

[10] Some of this argument was recently published in Carolini et al (2018).

These strategies and their success also allowed practitioners to work toward more equitably distributing costs and material improvements on the ground. Indeed, the Argentine utility's success in this work was scaled upwards: it spearheaded further peer partnerships within Argentina.

5. Shaping the Future of International Development Cooperation in Cities

Given the current expanding environment of international financial support for peer-to-peer and SSC aid programming, my book bears particular relevance for how international aid and technical assistance should be deployed. Beyond the UN system, several other financial players and thought-leaders in the development industry like the World Bank, the Chinese-led Asian Infrastructure Development Bank, and the Bill and Melinda Gates Foundation have fully embraced the messaging and advocacy of SSC. Most recently, the Gates Foundation launched a new Global Sanitation Graduate School that will "will transfer new curricula and course materials on non-sewered sanitation to at least 30 universities worldwide, fostering especially South-South cooperation."[11] Yet beyond geographic and technical affinities—or a funding organization's own history of professional experiences across countries—little is typically offered to explain why particular partners are (or should be) paired together for project work.

Whom cities like Maputo work with matters for equitable urban development. The growing density of international stakeholders—from the Southern "rise of the rest," the philanthropic community, as well as the private sector—is intensifying a landscape already well populated by traditional donors. This densification holds implications for urban governance and development because of the way different partnerships govern their projects and because of how well they support high-level knowledge production among local urban practitioners. Urban infrastructure is a bellwether in this landscape of international cooperation projects within cities. The rise of infrastructure as an asset class of interest for a broadening international development community of investors and partners means that much is to be gained or lost in how well cities plan, finance, and implement basic urban infrastructures like water and sanitation *for all*. The incentives and partnerships behind infrastructure development in water and sanitation are particularly important in cities with

---

[11] IWA Network News—accessed November 19, 2018: http://www.iwa-network.org/news/capacit ate-and-professionalise-the-sanitation-sector-iwa-and-ihe-delft-join-forces/

a rapidly growing urban (and poor) population, such as those in many countries across Africa. I argue that heterarchical relationships between proximate peers best supports the type of discretionary decision-making and capacity development required to meet this challenge at the local level.

6. Organization of the Book

The book's first chapter, *Hierarchies in the South*, argues that the continued neat references to geographical and hemispheric labels like the "South" in describing international cooperation work fail to capture the more complex place-based experiences at the project level. On the ground, there is often significant turbidity across time and among project stakeholders, with different international partners coming in and out of focus. Further, between Southern partners, the same hierarchies advanced under South–North partnerships can remain present. Such realities complicate and compromise the claims of solidarity and equity of SSC on the ground. I then introduce my research in the water and sanitation project space in Maputo as a demonstrative case for exploring what types of international cooperation actually do to foster equity. The chapter also situates my study of international cooperation at the urban scale within the broader framework of scholarship on the subjects of Southern urbanisms and planning, particularly in Africa, and the new geographies of development, which positions South–North binaries as antiquated and SSC as a continuation of extant global orthodoxies in the development industry.

In the next chapter, *"We don't refuse money": The Crowding-in of International Footprints*, I provide an empirical account of why so much attention within development arenas has focused on the growing interest in Africa, highlighting the broad strokes of the rise of a diversified international public-sector and private-finance portfolio of development commitments and financing in Africa overall, and in Mozambique specifically. I close the chapter with a question regarding the implications of such investments and cooperation commitments—particularly across infrastructure projects—for cities like Maputo. In Chapter 3, *Anything but Basic: Navigating Turbidity in Water and Sanitation Cooperation*, I provide a more micro-level analysis of the specific expansion of international cooperation projects in Maputo's water-and-sanitation-related infrastructures, relating the details of the five projects I studied during the course of my fieldwork. Here I show that the growth of cooperation commitments in Maputo, from both Northern and Southern partners, has not always translated into lesser material inequalities in the city.

Critically, I also find that the overlapping (though not coordinating) of actors within and across projects on the ground gives us serious reason to question why the macro narrative of development cooperation—as neatly driven by "Northern," "Southern," "bilateral," or "multilateral" stakeholders—persists and continues to occupy space in the imaginary of international development debates.

In Chapter 4, *Looking for Learning in Cooperation Projects*, I reexamine evidence of learning processes and the quality of knowledge production in the project-level work I studied in Maputo. Here, I present the argument that heterarchical cooperation between what I term "proximate peers" offers a more effective categorization for the types of relationships producing high-level capacity development and epistemic equity than SSC writ large, as currently formulated. Critically, I argue that proximities *beyond* technical capacities and geopolitical status—the major rationales typically employed in SSC programming—are key in the day-to-day implementation and to the high quality of learning within international cooperation projects. Chapter 5, *Recognizing Potentials: Moving from Mentorship to Proximate Peers*, extends my analysis to the wider network of cooperation partnerships in the water and sanitation sectors. In particular, I examine another nominally Southern partnership promoted by UN GWOPA to understand whether the nature of partnership proximities that mattered in Maputo would be found elsewhere.

Chapter 6, *The Governmentality of Evaluation*, situates my inquiry in a more reflective mode by interrogating the major orienting tool generally employed by international (including bilateral and multilateral) stakeholders and local agents to determine the success of their efforts: project evaluation. Building on postcolonial and organizational learning theorists' contributions to the study of epistemologies of expertise, as well as more recent work on learning assemblages in the urban environment, this chapter discusses why and how evaluations have been used as a political tool. I then suggest a more heterodox approach to evaluation, centered on integrating a logic of equity to balance the logic of efficiency currently dominating project assessments. I argue that such a rebalancing of evaluations holds particular importance for understanding the value of partnerships forged in the name of equity and solidarity.

In the conclusion, *Anticipating Proximate Peer Partnerships*, I emphasize how indiscriminate claims about SSC—both in reference to the outcomes SSC supports and in terms of SSC's actual composition—injure the strength of the Southern community's challenge to orthodoxy in the development industry and the international economic order it helps maintain. I propose that the development industry can and should begin to codesign partnerships by examining the potential for the proximities I identify as bolstering high-level learning on the ground. I also consider how project evaluations deployed by the international community engaged in development projects might better incorporate questions aimed at understanding the distribution of project benefits and the quality of knowledge production among project staff, both international and domestic, as a means of promoting more equitable urban development on the ground.

1

Hierarchies in the South

1.1 The Flattening Labels of Development Cooperation

The twentieth century saw a political drive to create spaces within the UN for international development leadership by Southern countries, giving birth to Bandung,[1] the Non-Aligned Movement (NAM),[2] and the United Nations Conference on Trade and Development (UNCTAD).[3] This effort differs greatly from the twenty-first century's initiatives to *de*-politicize Southern cooperation. Insisting upon coherence and consensus where there are fault lines, the UN today invokes triangular cooperation just as often as SSC as a critical mechanism for advancing development agendas. The former is considered cooperation between two Southern entities (typically including a large Southern "mentor") with financial support from a Northern donor or multilateral.[4] However, the emphasis on both SSC and triangular cooperation—in addition to the UN insisting that they complement rather than substitute for North–South partnerships—represents such a widely inclusive perspective about who should be involved in—and who should lead—the work of the international development industry in this century that who does what barely seems to register or matter. Instead, in every conceivable official UN

---

[1] In the midst of Indonesia's rapid, post-independence urbanization, its West Javan capital, Bandung, hosted a gathering of Asian, Arab, and newly independent African leaders. The famed 1955 Bandung Conference brought much hope for an effective alliance to address common grievances against colonization and the arms race, as well as to promote cooperation across regions in the global South. Quickly thereafter, Bandung became a mobilizing reference, but as several scholars have noted, the solidarity among Southern countries was more aspirational than practiced (Braveboy-Wagner, 2008; Hurrell, 2013; Prashad, 2007, 2012; Rajagopal, 2003; Ul Haq, 1980).

[2] It took almost a decade before the seeds of Bandung began to germinate into organized forms. The post-Bandung follow-up conference of largely African, Arab, and Asian leaders in Belgrade saw the birth of the NAM in 1961 and, shortly thereafter, UNCTAD in 1964.

[3] UNCTAD amplified the G77 countries' concerns about the structural straitjacket on trade benefits for lower-income, raw material exporters at the periphery of major, high-income, industrialized economies. However, even that augmented voice did not translate successfully into reforming the international economic order. Instead, much of it came across as a cacophony of distinct demands (Arezki & Sy, 2016; Prebisch, 1950; Singer, 1950).

[4] According to the UN, "Triangular cooperation involves Southern-driven partnerships between two or more developing countries supported by a developed country(ies)/or multilateral organization(s) to implement development cooperation programmes and projects." http://ssc.undp.org/content/ssc/about/Background.html.

Equity, Evaluation, and International Cooperation. Gabriella Y. Carolini, Oxford University Press.
© Gabriella Y. Carolini (2022). DOI: 10.1093/oso/9780192865489.003.0002

statement on development, a common reference is that the UN system supports South–South, North–South, and triangular cooperation, seeing these
as non-mutually exclusive and uncontradictory. As former UN Development
Programme (UNDP) Associate Administrator Rebeca Grynspan expounded,
they are "convinced of the important contribution of South–South Cooperation and triangular cooperation to advancing development and tackling global
challenges."[5] Indeed even former Secretary General Ban Ki-moon alerted the
UN community in 2011 that:

> We have yet to gauge the volume and impact of the welcomed impetus
> provided by South–South Cooperation and triangular cooperation. The chal-
> lenges ahead are daunting. In responding to them, let us ensure that all voices
> be heard and that all stakeholders participate actively in building a broad
> consensus on the governance of international development cooperation.[6]

Such all-embracing views neatly afford a place not only to Northern countries and the multilateral organizations they dominate, but critically to the
largest Southern economies as "new" development leaders in SSC as well as
in triangular cooperation.

Led by China, Brazil, India, and South Africa, the largest economies in the
G77[7] are now indeed far from challenging orthodox institutions of the global
economy as they had in the twentieth-century call for a New International Economic Order (NIEO).[8] Among earlier Southern leaders, there was at the very
least an explicit awareness and guard against the flattening of differences—
within the South as well as vis-à-vis the North—in the politics of SSC. This
attention to difference is well captured in the work of the South Commission, a group established in 1987, after years of informal discussions in UN
fora among Southern political leaders, to promote cooperation among Southern economies. In its report, the South Commission described SSC as a call

---

[5] Excerpt from speech in UNOSSC video: South–South Cooperation: An Introduction, 2011.
http://ssc.undp.org/content/ssc/library/videos/introductoryVideos/south-south_cooperationan
introduction.htm.

[6] Excerpt from speech in UNOSSC video: South–South Cooperation: An Introduction, 2011.
http://ssc.undp.org/content/ssc/library/videos/introductoryVideos/south-south_cooperationan
introduction.htm.

[7] It should be noted here that while China participated in the G77 caucus, it did not consider itself to
be a member, hence the peculiarity of all official documents published by the G77 bearing the closing
signature of "G77 and China."

[8] While much effort was put into preparing the first UNCTAD meeting, by 1970 the UN General
Assembly bemoaned the slow pace of UNCTAD's work. That same pace was rather welcomed by North
America, Europe, and the Soviet Union, whose UN member states were unwilling to let go of their
dominance in international economic affairs easily (Braveboy-Wagner, 2008; Prashad, 2012; Rajagopal,
2003).

"towards collective self-reliance, solidarity, regional integration, and effective organization in support of these objectives" (South Commission, 1990: 18). However, it also warned:

> South–South links must avoid reproducing within the South the exploitative patterns which have characterized North–South relationships. As economic levels vary greatly within the South, special arrangements have to be made for the benefit of the least developed and poorest countries and of others in special situations, e.g. landlocked or small island states.
>
> (South Commission, 1990: 18)

Three decades after the South Commission's historic report, a draft agenda for the Second UN High Level Conference on South–South Cooperation in March 2019 repeated that commission's earlier sentiments, delivered this time by the permanent representatives from Uganda *and* Lithuania. This latest report stresses that SSC is "guided by the principles of respect for national sovereignty, national ownership and independence, equality, non-conditionality, non-interference in domestic affairs and mutual benefit."[9] While the 1990 report of the South Commission critically identified the potentiality of power imbalances between Southern economies in their efforts to organize a political and economic voice, the 2019 statement does not give much consideration to how power imbalances between Southern countries complicate "equality" or "mutual benefit" in practice, nor to how the actual composition of SSC matters for distributive justice and equity. Instead, their discussion of SSC appears to be centered on rather apolitical presumptions of cohesion among Southern countries and their shared vision of economic inclusion. Meanwhile, countries like China are creating organizations that re-produce and compete with some of the old lending models and neoliberal governmentalities established under the Washington Consensus.[10] It is be-cause of this reordering of power in international aid and cooperation that many have begun to interrogate the very idea of the South.

---

[9] UN Draft outcome document of the Second United Nations High Level Conference on South–South Cooperation to be held in March 2019. E-reference: https://www.un.org/pga/73/wp-content/uploads/sites/53/2018/12/12-Dec-18-LPGA-0302_Zero-draftSouth-SouthCooperation_12Dec.pdf

[10] Brazil and India, for example, have long lobbied for a permanent seat on the UN Security Council, and a Brazilian national, Roberto Azevêdo, is currently the Director-General of the World Trade Organization. Meanwhile, China—and, to a lesser extent, Brazil, India, and South Africa—have helped to bankroll new international development banks (e.g., the New Development Bank and the Asian Infrastructure Investment Bank), aspiring to compete with old-guard organizations such as the World Bank for infrastructure development loans within the global South.

1.2 The "South" as a Place and as an Idea

The consistently explicit, if frayed, practice of leveraging the Southern solidarity label in international relations and the development industry gives little hint of the deep questioning and implicit politics emerging around the notion of Southern-ness itself. Probes into the accuracy, utility, and meaningfulness of the hemispheric proclivity of the "South" as a descriptor and mobilizer for anything save a physical geography (if that) is driving current debates in theory and practice. The ambiguities subsumed in the reference to the South are many, with some standing out in current political tensions and others remaining ensconced within research circles. For example, international relations between the United States and China have made clear that the former perceives that a central assumption about how to treat or describe China is due revision. The notion of China as a new and threatening superpower is a popular trope in largely North-American-based news outlets that focus on exploring growing tensions with China around trade and other issues. It is not surprising then that in February 2020, the Office of the United States Trade Representative removed China from its list of "developing" countries, with implications for trade negotiations and agreements under the World Trade Organization. In contrast, within the academy, the debates center less on how specific countries might be subsumed within terminologies of developmental gradients, and more on deconstructing the idea of the "South" and whether Southern-ness is actually a reference to place-based geopolitical histories à la "Third World," a collective linked to recent colonial experiences, a term that can act as a proxy for marginalization in its various forms across geographies, or a semantic that refers to the widening of epistemic references (Bratman, 2011; Dados & Connell, 2012; Lewis, 2015; Pollard et al, 2009; Weiss, 2009).

The headliner of "new geographies of development" situates this set of analytical debates in discussions of aid and cooperation for development. Geographers working under this thesis advance the reconceptualization of Southern countries' strategies and agendas with regard to development. For example, Mawdsley (2018) argues that the "Southernization" of development is evidenced in how Southern countries have asserted their agency and unexpectedly influenced shifts in international discourses from, for example, a focus on poverty alleviation to economic growth. Others have pushed for the rescaling of hemispheric binaries of North and South toward other (often subnational) territorialities and nomenclatures that emphasize different critical readings of fractures within countries and regions—as much as between them (Horner, 2019; Horner & Hulme, 2017; Klinger & Muldavin, 2019).

Such interrogations within geography literatures have a parallel within urbanism debates rooted in rejections of the spatial boundedness of orthodox territorial politics and economies, with pushes to reconceptualize the urban itself in the context of new geographies of human settlements, work, and leisure, as well as in acknowledgment of shifting inter- and sub-national (often neoliberal) governance regimes that dominate across global regions (Amin, 2004; Brenner, 2004, 2014; Brenner & Schmid, 2015; Castells, 1996; Roy, 2009; Scott, 2001; Soja, 2001).

A focus on the de- and re-construction of conceptualizations within the urban arena has seen, for example, terms historically used to describe trends shaping cities in the global North *or* the South now used to relate realities in both (though still inviting postcolonial critiques of terminological extensions therein). Thus we see discourses around "gentrification" enter the vocabulary of works on cities across Africa (Donaldson et al, 2013; Eduful & Hooper, 2015; Tosey et al, 2011), and case studies of "informality" across several urban markets in North America and Europe grow (Banerjee & Verma, 2001; Mukhija & Loukaitou-Sideris, 2014; Portes & Sassen-Koob, 1987). Urbanists also call for the resituating of comparative urban studies toward understanding relationalities across contextually diverse geographies, rejecting analytic constructs that essentialize urban experiences and meanings into reflections of analyses rooted in the global urban North (Robinson, 2011a, 2011b; Roy, 2011a, 2011b; Sheppard et al, 2013). Some of the most piercing representations of this new analytical construct centered on urban relationalities across geographies of the global North and South are accounts that trace the mobility and migration of transnational populations and the resulting reorganization of national and subnational governance systems in labor markets and in political representation (Iskander, 2010; Miraftab, 2016).

Viewed together, these critiques of the neatness of Southern analytical labels couple with the accounts of the complications of SSC in practice to magnify the conceptual and structural shortcomings of the persistent reference to terminologies like the "South" that reinforce existing rules of the game in developmental discourses. Perhaps most critically, they also compromise the claims of solidarity in international cooperation relationships, particularly for those forged under SSC. This book, however, reveals two other unanticipated but equally salient arguments for destabilizing hemispherically bounded and geographically laden assertions about types of international cooperation and which therein promote "development," and more importantly, ideals like equity. Through a grounded analysis of the ecosystem of international cooperation at the project level in the Mozambican capital, Maputo, I argue that the hemispheric labels of cooperation belie how international partnerships and their projects are actually operationalized, but also that there are *other* characteristics of cooperation projects—beyond their geopolitical reference—that matter for learning and knowledge production, core elements of capacity building initiatives in the development agenda.

1.3 Reinforcing Labels and Hierarchies over Heterarchies

Analytical accounts of international cooperation often perpetuate the idea that cooperation projects on the ground have a "single-source" origin or providence. However, the international cooperation activities I studied in Maputo, Mozambique over the course of the last decade, and present in this book, show precisely how projects that in name call attention to SSC or traditional donor brands actually shifted from or into differently constituted partnerships over time. In short, projects and their partners evolve, experience volatilities, and shift responsibilities in the operationalization of objectives. This *production* of cooperation on the ground is typically obscured, even in the aforementioned discourses and debates about what is "Southern" and whether SSC represents a more effective, egalitarian route toward "development."

This book foregrounds a place-based analysis of development cooperation. In doing so, I privilege the contextual insights that emerge from inductive research over analyses that seek to understand the geographies of development cooperation through the lens of their macro-level proponents. I contend that to rest on questions about international cooperation at a high level alone is to effectively favor the vantage point of the foreigner, the researcher, or simply the outsider, as opposed to the resident—be they ordinary citizens or public servants. From the outside, projects may be categorized to suit our analyses and comparison rationales, but from the ground, residents experience international cooperation rather differently.[11] In the context of studying international development, it is easy to forget that the nature and constitution of projects change on the ground—often invoking and resting upon various partners who may not have any direct relation or interaction with one another over the course of time. When I began to search for SSC projects to explore for this book, what I found on the ground was frustratingly imperfect from the researcher's "case selection" perspective—and yet it was the

---

[11] An old quip I heard from elders living in a part of Europe captures nicely my logic here. A woman never left her village in northern Croatia over the course of her 90 plus years on earth. And yet, she had lived in at least four different countries in her life.

reality. Projects started with one international partner's promise of funding often engendered several other partners—Southern, Northern, multilateral, non-governmental, for-profit, community-based, municipal, and national—to reach any realization of material improvements.

This reality is a reflection of the growth of international cooperation stakeholders on the ground in a capital city like Maputo, and I argue that the experiences therein are likely shared by other African capitals hosting an explosion of development interests. Yet when international cooperation is examined within analytical frames of SSC or other macro-level narratives, this evolutionary, place-based character of the production of cooperation and the volatility of experiences therein—what I describe as a *turbidity* in international cooperation well known to residents who remain in place over time—is lost. Their perspective, however, deserves attention, as its grounded-ness could do much to inform us about the nature of questions that still require answering— particularly with regard to the kinds of partnership that "deliver results." What I found in Maputo convinced me that the "single-source" geo-hemispheric myths attributed to cooperation at the macro level reflected very little of the place-based project histories, and further mattered very little to the material outcomes they produced on the ground.

Secondly, in this book I argue that the way partnerships are designed, delivered, and evaluated at the project level *does* matter to the type of learning and the learning environment on the ground, revealing much about the actual intentions, assumptions, and rationales international partners bring to the table. Partnerships among peers—so central to the SSC logic—are heralded as providing highly relevant, more sensitive, and practical learning opportunities in countries experiencing challenges in the provision of basic services and more (Bakker, 2007; Bontenbal & Lindert, 2009; Bradlow, 2015; Campbell, 2012; Hall et al, 2009; Mayaki, 2010; Roy, 2011a; van Ewijk et al, 2015). However, as I detail in my examination of cooperation partnerships in Maputo, as well as other international partnership mechanisms in water and sanitation, international cooperation projects often fail to consider exactly which types of peer relationships matter for learning and instead remain ensconced in orthodox modalities of building partnerships that elevate power-reinforcing notions of mentorship and hierarchy. In Maputo and elsewhere, I often saw the reinforcement of notions of *provider* and *beneficiary* as opposed to the ideals of *reciprocity* and *equality*—with implications for the kinds of learning and service improvements that were or could be fostered. Interestingly, however, the reinforcement of hierarchies was not simply a function of the geopolitical typology of cooperation partners, but whether a project's managerial architecture leaned toward heterarchy as opposed to hierarchy between "peers." The trend in building international learning networks and cooperation between Southern stakeholders, however, ignores such nuances.

Within municipal development, for example, there are now several international capacity-building cooperation networks that capitalize on generalized assumptions about learning through SSC, spanning efforts to improve practice in infrastructure sectors like water and sanitation[12] to more general administrative and financial management.[13] By design, they problematically set up *mentorships*, with negative consequences for the types of high-level, strategic learning sought after by so many pioneers of the twentieth-century Southern leadership movement in international discourses. There are, however, emerging accounts of strong resistance to this presumptive mode of partnerships among local authorities and urban practitioners often positioned as mentees. Moodley (2019) found this tension in a relationship supported by United Cities and Local Governments, an international advocacy organization and union of local public-sector stakeholders. It established eThekwini Municipality, Durban, as a "mentor city" with "mentee municipalities" in Otjiwarongo in Namibia and Mzuzu in Malawi. Moodley's work shows that municipal staff in the latter two cities conceptualized learning quite differently than did the Durban practitioners chosen as "mentors." The diverse characterizations of learning among practitioners in that case—and those in my own examination of cooperation projects in Maputo—bring to task the hierarchical presumptions of many—though again not all—programs and projects advanced under the rubric of international cooperation, including SSC. I argue that this reality also highlights shortcomings in the design and completion of international partners' evaluations of cooperation projects, most of which fail to address the specter of inequalities in the landing of international partnerships. Yet it is the very governmentality of the project evaluation in the implementation of projects that positions this administrative but fundamentally political tool as a lever for either suppressing or advancing equity as experienced on the ground—both in terms of material benefits and of knowledge produced and locally owned.

---

[12] For example, the UN's Global Water Operators' Partnership Alliance—an organization whose work I discuss in Chapter 5—largely supports water-operator partnerships between Southern public water utilities (Beck, 2019).

[13] The work of United Cities and Local Governments has centered on promoting peer-learning networks on financial and administrative management for municipal and local governments across countries in, for example, Southern Africa.

1.4   International Cooperation in the Planning of a "Modern" African City

Shortly after I arrived in the Mozambican capital of Maputo in 2009, I joined a colleague from the faculty of architecture and planning at the University of Eduardo Mondlane in attendance at a funeral service held in Maputo's City Hall for one of Mozambique's most celebrated and important photojournalists, Ricardo Rangel.[14] Rangel's work was censored in the 1970s during the Portuguese colonial regime in Mozambique because colonial administrators feared that his depictions of the poor quality of life suffered by Mozambicans under their rule would spur anticolonial ambitions (Thompson, 2013). His photographs of everyday life in the city's cement core and its *bairros de caniço*, or the poorer peri-urban neighborhoods of Maputo, where homes were traditionally built with reed, captured Mozambican children bathing on the streets and "street children" roaming barefoot in search of odd jobs. These images contrasted sharply with his photos of the Portuguese enjoying leisure time, sitting in Maputo's cafes and swimming in private-membership clubs during the colonial dictatorship. The tensions in Rangel's work spoke directly to what are now the well-documented struggles—in the capital as elsewhere—that would ultimately launch the fight for, and secure, Mozambican independence by 1975 (Mondlane, 1969; Mozambique Liberation Front, 1963; Penvenne, 1983, 2011, 2015).[15]

Almost half a century later, Maputo is both transformed and stubbornly set. In the period following independence, the country experimented with socialist programming in the nationalization of basics like education, land, and housing, which meant that parts of the capital which were once off limits to Mozambicans, both materially and in the imaginary, were now newly home (Morton, 2013; Müller, 2010; Sidaway, 1993). Yet during this period Mozambicans also suffered tremendously from a devastating civil war that lasted for fifteen years and saw indiscriminate violence, drought, and famines rob thousands of lives in the new nation (Finnegan, 1992; Macamo, 2006; Weinstein & Francisco, 2005). With peace declared in 1992 and a late-century turn toward

---

[14] Many thanks for that special experience I still owe to Professor Catarina Torres Cruz.

[15] Mozambique's celebration of freedom from Portuguese rule was quickly dampened by an internal war between the socialist-leaning *Frente de Libertação de Moçambique* (Frelimo), a movement-turned-political party that fought for independence, and the *Resistência Nacional Moçambicana* (Renamo), a rebel group backed by the Rhodesian Central Intelligence and the South African Military Intelligence. The civil war ended in 1992 with a much celebrated peace accord. Since that time, Frelimo has largely ruled over the country at the national level, as well as the local level within Maputo, though Renamo, which also shifted into a political party, maintains strong political power in the country's central provinces.

free-market liberalism, the capital city in the 2000s welcomed a renewal of international interest whose impact saw Maputo further distinguished from the steadfastness of poverty that characterized much of the rest of the country, even as the city itself still suffered from inequalities and segregation (Hanlon, 2010; Morton, 2013, 2019; Pitcher, 2002).

Today, the material legacies of a colonial urban ecosystem designed to extract and impoverish remain. Punctuated by new investments meant to herald Mozambique's turn toward a brighter future with a growing middle class—manifest in new shopping malls, gated housing complexes, and the continent's longest suspension bridge—housing inequalities, segregation, and increasingly, displacement, coupled with uneven employment opportunities, and a lack of quality access to basic services like water and sanitation still feature across much of the urban landscape in which the majority of Maputo's residents live (Barros et al, 2014; Carolini, 2017; Jenkins & Andersen, 2011; V. de P. Melo, 2016; V. Melo & Jenkins, 2019; Nielsen, 2010, 2014). This context—often referred to by local residents as "*a realidade Moçambicana*" (Mozambican reality)—is what the Portuguese were wont to ignore in Rangel's photos of Maputo, and yet later became fodder for the overwhelming, foreign popular narrative of African cities like the Mozambican capital: chaotic, overrun by slums, hardships, and full of confusion. This is the domain of Mike Davis's bestseller, *Planet of Slums* (2006)—based on his earlier essay—and its less influential contemporary, Robert Neuwirth's *Shadow Cities* (2005). Davis's work in particular made clear that the world could no longer ignore the urbanization of poverty, and that the twentieth-century explosion of slums was a product of a corrupt political economic architecture perversely strengthened by some of the international institutions established in the wake of the Second World War.

Concurrent to the success of Davis's book on the academic circuit and beyond, I had begun working for the UN Millennium Project on a task force dedicated to identifying strategies to help achieve one of the Millennium Development Goals' targets, namely to have "achieved by 2020 a significant improvement in the lives of at least 100 million slum dwellers" (UN Millennium Project, 2005). Task force members—among whom were municipal authorities, development practitioners, non-governmental organization (NGO) founders, and leading urban scholars—often wryly noted that 100 million slum dwellers were improving their own lives every day without our support. This critical view has been increasingly reflected in scholarship about urban life in the global South generally, and Africa particularly. Since the early twenty-first century, scholars from and/or working on the African continent have sharpened the interpretation of urban realities both within poorer and wealthier neighborhoods to better reflect the complex systems—local and global, formal and informal, personal and communal—that shape African cities and their residents' lives. The urban sociologist AbdouMaliq Simone's (2004) *For the City Yet to Come* is one of the most referenced and earliest works to argue that the "African city as chaos" theory forecloses an understanding of diverse urban systems and life outside of the delimited Western paradigm of how a municipality and its residents should function. Similarly, urban geographer Jennifer Robinson's (2006) *Ordinary Cities* called on scholars to position their urban research on the continent and across other "Southern" regions as work on cities in and of themselves, as opposed to their relative developmentalist achievements, particularly vis-à-vis "global" cities in Asia, North America, and Europe. These works follow in the tradition of Amin and Graham's (1997) call for a postcolonial, multiplex lens on the study of contemporary cities—i.e., examining cities' relational proximities within global networks and their full heterogeneity.

Indeed, over the past two decades, the scholarly world has witnessed an expanding field of African (and more generally Southern) urbanists who are pushing forward conceptualizations of what is, and what may not be, particularly African (or Southern) about cities and urban growth across the continent. This push has begotten new vocabularies, methodologies, and at times conceptual conflicts about urban research that seek to dislodge Western-centric metrics popularly used to measure and understand urban life and development. For example, Mbembe and Nuttall (2004) position their study of Johannesburg through its "underneaths," or the "extracanonical leakages, lines of flight, borderlines and interfaces" through which ordinary lives are lived. In their description of both African and Asian cities, Simone and Pieterse (2017) too advance the study of the mechanics of the "makeshift"—what in Mozambique would be called *trabalho de biscates*, or the day-to-day hustling—that typifies so much of urban residents' efforts to secure livelihoods and housing. They call for a "re-description" of the grey spaces between binaries like formal and informal to better grasp the reality of these "new urban worlds" evolving across Southern cities. Myers (2011) in turn presents cities like Lusaka, typically off the map of supposedly leading cities, as a "postcolonial, informal, unruly and wounded city, yet a cosmopolitan place full of imaginative, generative and connective synergies internally and across the globe," suggesting that as much as any "global" city of the North, Lusaka's experiences too contribute to urban theory and, most critically, inform practices of urban change and improvement across the world. Together such works join with a growing avalanche of others to cement a veritable school of urban research that has adopted the "relationality" of cities as a rich analytical construct; comparing and detailing, rather than ranking and "hierarchizing" positionalities and roles within world systems (Robinson, 2008; Roy, 2009, 2011a). Unlike accounts that seek to universalize rationales or develop widely applicable standards for understanding what is urban and what is urbanism (Storper & Scott, 2016), this Southern school rejects the uni-rationalist project and instead reflects the pluriverse of epistemologies forwarded by heterodox scholars such as Mignolo (2000), Escobar (2011), and de Sousa Santos (2015), both theorizing and positioning Southern urbanisms as part and parcel of a wide portfolio of critical bases from which to know the city.

Among the leading thinkers on African urbanism, Vanessa Watson's provocations on its implications for urban *planning* bear particular importance for understanding how urban development projects led by the public sector and its partners across African cities is challenging orthodox thinking about how projects ought to be run. She argues that there are often fundamentally "conflicting rationales" between low-income residents and municipal authorities seeking to intervene in poor neighborhoods which ultimately doom urban development projects (Watson, 2003). In her studies of projects in Cape Town and elsewhere, Watson recounts how the different rationales driving stakeholders' behaviors in a given neighborhood intervention are typically ignored or unknown by local planners, making it unlikely that project goals will be realized as intended. Winkler (2018) similarly casts doubt on whether planners who claim deep contextual knowledge of poorer urban neighborhoods in South Africa can effectively lead neighborhood change. In yet another planning intervention in Cape Town, she describes how planners failed to grasp the importance of the epistemologies of knowledge which informed their own perspective and how that differed from the Xhosa philosophical ideas and values of residents with whom planners aimed to work. Sihlongonyane (2015a) positions such planning failures within the South African context as an explicit legacy of apartheid planning. He argues that concepts and practices like participatory planning "gained ideological traction to support Eurocentric and globalist traditions of urban change," but contends that participation in this tradition, translated into African terms and metaphors, still fails to deeply transform the planning experience for Black South Africans (2015a: 83). While these authors speak most directly to South African planning, their texts echo critical analyses of urban development relationships and conflicting rationales in planning within other African countries as well. For example, Bassett (2019) reveals how entrenched corruption and the different incentives or perspectives at play between land reformers, the national elite in Kenya, local physical planners, and other stakeholders ultimately impeded change in land management and planning despite a major reform initiative in the wake of the new 2010 constitution. Myers's work in Tanzania and Zambia also relates breakdowns of communication and power asymmetries between local authorities and the international development organizations with which they worked in Tanzania and Zambia. His *Disposable Cities* (2005) in particular sheds light on the ways in which stakeholders in African cities—in his study, Dar es Salaam, Zanzibar, and Lusaka—struggled against the imported discourses and rationales of sustainable development plans promoted by international organizations and European donors.

Conflicting rationales of course have long been at play between those working for "big D" development organizations and their partners on the ground. While some of the best known accounts of these fractures within Africa relate experiences with development interventions in rural areas (e.g., Crewe & Harrison, 1998; Ferguson, 1994), reports of diverging interests in project-related work within urban planning efforts on the continent have grown alongside the aforementioned literatures on Southern urbanisms. That these conceptual and communication gaps persist over decades, however, is troubling and speaks to how epistemologies of knowledge and perspectives are sticky foundations that are uneasily dislodged. Even as Southern critiques of inherited orthodoxies, the recognition of diverse rationales, and the differentiated epistemologies of urban development and planning knowledges across Africa have gained traction with wider audiences, still another catchy, explicitly developmentalist narrative has arisen about African cities. In the latter, we find economic literatures and development organizations that dominate national planning practices across Africa largely positing political and human geographies as circumstantial rather than defining characteristics in economic development theory and practice. In short, in these works, context only matters in so much that it is an obstacle on a path toward an indisputable and recognizable economic end. In considering urban development, these literatures assume a universalist account of what cities look like, how they should function, and what development therein pertains. The African Union's strategic transformation framework for socio-economic development over the next few decades, *Agenda 2063*, for example, positions the city as the latest vehicle for accelerating industrial progress across the continent. This narrative of the city as an engine of national economic development and growth echoes traditional accounts of the urbanization–industrialization nexus emergent from high-income countries' histories. It prioritizes the city's functionality squarely within the developmentalist arc—in other words, the city's agglomeration economies and labor supply are mechanisms by which higher national levels of gross domestic product can be achieved. Similarly, UN-Habitat's recent report on the *State of African Cities* (UN-Habitat and IHS-Erasmus University Rotterdam, 2018) is entirely dedicated to examining how to improve African cities' integration into global markets via enhanced foreign direct investments. Yet another recent report sponsored by the World Bank notes, "cities in Africa produce few goods and services for trade on regional and international markets … [and] must open their doors to the world" (Lall et al, 2017:12). Unlike Southern urbanists, who position African cities as very much *already* integrated and contributing to global flows of ideas, peoples, and goods, these "city as an engine" narratives present African cities as underperforming yet full of potential for greater growth and market share within the global economy, as opposed to questioning the metrics they use for evaluation or the goals they have established. The narrative also affords little attention to how the governing rationales of stakeholders at different scales might clash with these orthodox views of developmental progress.

It is somewhat unsurprising then to find that several municipal authorities are searching for routes to jump-start their "engines," renewing interests in the power of one such spark plug: the master plan. From Kigali through *Cité du Fleuve* on the outskirts of Kinshasa, the visioning processes and master plans enrapturing city halls across the continent are ones Watson (2014) devastatingly critiques as fantasies, with more relevance for cash-rich cities like Dubai than the fiscally strapped cities where substandard housing remains and infrastructural gaps are more typically present than absent. In Maputo, as elsewhere, the implications of such major urban modernization projects—particularly for essential infrastructures—is a continued financial reliance on international partnerships with bilateral or multilateral partners and donors, whether through direct engagements at the project level or through the medium of intergovernmental transfers. This is especially the case where water-and-sanitation-related infrastructures are concerned. Compared with other economic infrastructure areas, donor funding or concessional loans from organizations like the World Bank for water-and-sanitation-related infrastructures have long been substantially stronger than private capital investments therein (see Figure 1.1).

When even domestically driven projects still face difficulty in translating public-sector goals into realities that do not contradict local communities' priorities, internationally driven projects like those in the water and sanitation sector may be expected to continue facing similar challenges, but with greater

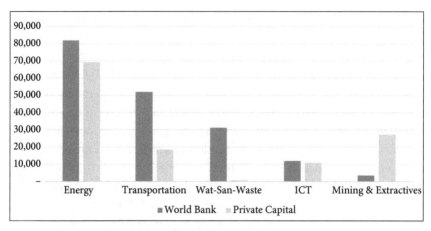

Fig. 1.1 Sources of Infrastructure Investments in Sub-Saharan Africa
2000–2019 (in USD millions)
Sources: Data from World Bank Project Database and Preqin financial database.

orders of magnitude. A recent evaluation of aid across Africa, for example, indicates that there is a nonlinear relationship between increased aid targeting water and sanitation services and actual improvements in access to water and sanitation services (Ndikumana & Pickbourn, 2017). In short, more money from more international donors does not always translate into better services on the ground. Insights from Southern urbanists about how conflicting rationales and knowledge epistemologies shape planning outcomes within African cities then seem especially pertinent for understanding how projects with a prevalence of external funding and international partners might perform differently on the ground depending on the constitution of the partnership. What are the types of conflicting rationalities at work at the local scale when international cooperation is presumably required to deliver basic services like water and sanitation? And, more broadly, how do differences in the identities and the architecture of international partnerships shape conflict, cooperation, and, ultimately, the "benefits" realized on the ground?

This last question sits at the heart of debates around the rise of SSC and the new landscape of international aid. The political call to end colonialism, support independence, and eliminate the arms race that marked so much of the twentieth century's solidarity among Southern countries has given way to a largely neoliberal economic comradery in the twenty-first. Natural-resource extraction and land commodification in the name of infrastructure development, economic growth, and the capture of greater global market depth are today the markers of Southern leadership and the objectives behind some of the most significant efforts at building SSC.[16] This is especially visible in the portfolio of international cooperation advanced by regional leaders like China, Brazil, and India. Each has seen tremendous gains in its own national (aggregated) economic prosperity since the middle of the last century—moving "from recipient to donor" in the international development community (Mawdsley 2012). As development scholars have argued now for almost two decades, SSC forged by these countries and others within the South is similar in incentive, if not always in form, to the cooperation partnerships spearheaded by high-income countries over the past several decades of development work.[17]

For the most part, however, scholarship on SSC has focused on macro-level narratives proffered at the national level of analysis, with much attention centered on the implications of rising powers from the South and the volatility and validity of perceived threats therein for the international architecture of aid and development cooperation. For example, Emma Mawdsley's *From Recipients to Donors: Emerging Powers and the Changing Development Landscape* (2012) provides a rich overview and insights into the implications of the rise of nontraditional donors and the international governance of their emerging partnerships. Other works include several bearing witness to the details of (especially) China's growing presence in African development, with Deborah Brautigam's *The Dragon's Gift: The real story of China in Africa* (2009) followed by many others, including Renu Modi's *South–South Cooperation: Africa on the Centre Stage* (2011); Sachin Chaturvedi, Thomas Fues, and Elizabeth Sidiropoulos' *Development Cooperation and Emerging Powers: New Partners or Old Patterns?* (2012); Fantu Cheru and Renu Modi's *Agricultural Development and Food Security in Africa: The Impact of Chinese, Indian and Brazilian Investments* (2013); and *From Comrades to Capitalists* (2014), edited by Chris

---

[16] For example, Chinese and Brazilian SSC investments in natural resources and the related commodification of especially agricultural lands have been extensively studied on the African continent, and point to familiarities with narratives of extraction by other, higher-income, interventions on the continent (Cheru, 2016; Cheru & Modi, 2013; Mohan & Power, 2009; Power, Mohan, & Tan-Mullins, 2012; Shankland & Gonçalves, 2016; Wolford & Nehring, 2015).

[17] Several scholars have pointed a critical lens at SSC, examining whether its promise of solidarity is more rhetorical than material, the validity of claims about its difference from Northern or high-income aid, its material comparison with OECD members' aid, and deconstructing generalizations about governance, strategies, and decision-making in SSC—particularly involving China, India, Brazil, and South Africa. They include Alden, Morphet, & Vieira, 2010; Alden & Vieira, 2005; de Haan & Warmerdam, 2013; Fuchs & Vadlamannati, 2013; Harmer & Cotterrell, 2005; Kragelund, 2014; Manning, 2006; Martin & Palat, 2014; Mawdsley, 2015, 2010, 2012; McEwan & Mawdsley, 2012; Mohan, 2016; Palat, 2008; Power & Mohan, 2010; Price & Chatham House, 2004; White, 2013; and Woods, 2008. There are of course exceptions to this critical scholarship. For example, Vieira (2012) argues that values such as distributive justice, as opposed to a more materialist account of Southern solidarity, remain a vibrant root of SSC—particularly between India, Brazil, and South Africa.

Alden and Sérgio Chichava, as well as its Portuguese-language equivalent (*A Mamba e o Dragão*, 2012). These books and others like Vijay Prashad's *The Poorer Nations* (2012) challenge apolitical narratives of the global restructuring of international relationships in the North and South. They establish a strong structural foundation for more ethnographically rich, next-generation scholarship on the "rising powers" and cooperation work therein. A recent example of the latter is Ching Kwan Lee's *The Specter of Global China* (2017), which provides a detailed critical accounting of the local and international politics of a diverse portfolio of especially Chinese but also other international investments in Zambia's mining and construction industries. Similarly, Mohan et al (2014) provide rich descriptions of the perspectives of Chinese migrants and their interactions with African counterparts in Nigeria, Ghana, Angola, and Tanzania. Centering on Mozambique, a few recent studies have also made critical inroads into detailing how SSC is locally entangled in place within rural contexts. For example, Shankland and Gonçalves (2016) offer insights into how civil societies in Brazil and in Mozambique have reacted to contentious SSC modeled on the Brazilian experience in Mozambique's agricultural sector, while de Bruyn (2019) provides a comparative look at how Brazilian, Chinese, and Indian health-centered SSC efforts have been received in Mozambique.[18] None, however, look explicitly at the material urban development and municipal governance implications of SSC.

At the urban level, empirical accounts and critical analyses of how SSC lands in place, and why, lag behind. Despite the absence of aid data at the subnational and municipal levels,[19] scholarly neglect of SSC in cities is rather surprising for at least four reasons.[20] First, decentralization reforms have been a centerpiece of the international development community's work over the past four decades, and African *urban* (rather than only rural) development is now widely recognized as central to the continent's growth prospects (UN-ECA, 2017; USAID, 2011). Second, urbanization rates have transformed the world's population into a majority urban one in the twenty-first century. Africa, along

[18] Book-length works on Brazil's interests in SSC have been more limited, and include two Portuguese-language publications, namely Henrique Altemani de Oliveira's *Brasil e China: Cooperação Sul–Sul e parceria estratégica* (2012) and José Flávio Sombra Saraiva's *África parceira do Brasil atlântico* (2012).

[19] Another recent 2017 study from the Overseas Development Institute noted that of the twenty-one countries scoped for a project exploring subnational aid allocation effectiveness, only five countries have sufficient data for study (Desai & Greenhill, 2017).

[20] Beyond Moodley (2019), Harrison's (2015) account of SSC in Johannesburg is the only other urban-specific text I found that examines the emergence of this form of cooperation at an empirically grounded level. Harrison notes, for example, the adoption of Bus-Rapid Transit interventions in Johannesburg, following Bogota's example—which was propounded by its former mayor in his uptake of the presidency of a major international transportation think tank, ITDP.

with Asia, hosts the most rapidly urbanizing population—located primarily in small and medium-sized cities, such as Maputo. Indeed, the UN predicts that the African urban population will triple by 2050 (UN, 2018). Third, leading national advocates of SSC—China, India, Brazil, and South Africa—are also leaders of urban policy experiments within their own countries and related international policy exchange workshops (particularly on the African continent), reflecting their recognition of urban development as a ripe frontier for partnerships. India, Brazil, and South Africa, for example, established a cooperation alliance in 2009 centered on sharing their experiences in housing and urban development practices that address common challenges. Brazil launched its own program for "decentralized" SSC in 2012 to encourage Brazilian cities and other subnational government entities to develop technical cooperation projects with partners in other regions of the global South, especially Africa. African partnerships with China are also transforming urban and peri-urban landscapes through the development of special economic zones, infrastructure projects in (and beyond) China's Belt and Road Initiative (BRI), and even whole cities, such as Kilamba—just outside the Angolan capital.

The fourth reason highlights the aforementioned shifts in urban scholarship over the past two decades. City-focused research in planning, sociology, development studies, and education has produced a powerful critique of Western influences on city-building practices and conceptualizations of expertise in African, Asian, and Latin American cities. Indeed, much has been written about Southern-based epistemologies and, within urban literatures, the need for Southern-informed planning theories that reflect realities on the ground across the cities of the global South (Beard, 2002, 2003; Miraftab, 2009; Roy, 2006, 2011b; Watson, 2016a, 2016b, 2002, 2003, 2006, 2008, 2009). In parallel movement with this scholarship, the philanthropic community has emerged as a major supporter of the "Southern" turn within urban planning. For example, the Rockefeller Foundation was key to the establishment of the Association of African Schools of Planning and the early work of the University of Cape Town's African Centre for Cities, one (if not the) major nucleus of counter-hegemonic thinking that is advancing Southern ways of knowing and planning cities.[21] In light of this scholarly focus and philanthropic support for the distinctions of urban planning and development in cities of the global

---

[21] The African Centre for Cities at the University of Cape Town received a Rockefeller Foundation grant in 2011, for example, to "scale up applied urban research and practice on the African continent" (see https://www.urbanafrica.net/auri/). In addition, channeled through the African Centre for Cities, the African Association of Planning Schools also received three grants from the Rockefeller Foundation between 2008 and 2012 (Watson & Odendaal, 2012).

South, the absence of critical examinations of how SSC is (or is not) challenging Western orthodoxies and promoting solidarity and equity in urban
development in African cities especially is surprising.

Economic geographer Jamie Peck (2011) argues that the acceleration of
global linkages and policy mobility is not apolitical but steeped within the
social construction of policy proponents. He advocates for scholars to pursue
research that "embed[s] mobility [and] explores the ways in which the restructuring of policy regimes and the mobility of fast policy fixes are jointly constituted." While the policy mobility literature that Peck and others launched
largely leverages the experiences of urban restructuring and networks in high-
income contexts, this book takes up Peck's call for embedded scholarship
within African cities like Maputo (McCann & Ward, 2011; Peck, 2011). The
epistemologies behind local planning and policy interventions in African cities
carry the heavy weight of a recent colonial past and the explicit influence
of a growing myriad of international development "experts" and their promotion of "best practices" from other locales. With the recent explosion of
SSC opportunities, those locales are increasingly referencing other cities in
the global South. While international development cooperation has long been
a mechanism for policy mobility and fast (though often inappropriate) policy fixes, SSC has been heralded as a new platform for promoting solidarity
and equity, less encumbered by traditional power imbalances in development
cooperation.[22] As organizational support for it grows, deconstructing SSC's
origins and exploring its impacts on the ground is all the more urgent. This
urgency echoes McEwan and Mawdsley's (2012) call for more studies of trilateral development cooperation, noting that such work "requires a detailed
knowledge of institutions and organizations involved in cooperation, and
asking searching questions about who initiates and negotiates the param-
eters/goals of the projects; what financial managerial and administrative
arrangements are established within and across the different sites of the partnership; what monitoring and evaluation procedures are established, and on
whose terms."

What follows is my attempt to meet this call. In situating my study of SSC
within the ecosystem of international cooperation projects—including trilateral and bilateral cooperation projects with Northern donors—in the urban
water and sanitation sector of work in the Mozambican capital, my objective is to provide grounded insights into the everyday work of international

---

[22] SSC's potential for launching an "emancipatory multi-polarity" in international relations and the
political economic implications of a Southern-led revolution in aid policy are central hopes articulated
in both scholarship and development practice (Gosovic, 2016; Pieterse, 2011; Sorensen, 2010).

cooperation projects and the implications therein for more equitable ends. My emphasis on a grounded analysis seeks first to extricate the misrepresentations and priority of place often afforded to generalized geographic and hemispheric labels, and second, to revise and reposition evaluations of cooperation around equity. The promotion of SSC, and concerns around the rise of China's role therein, provide little insight into how projects forwarded under these broad umbrellas are actually locally constituted and materialized. In this book, I instead cast light on questions around how cooperation's "landing" is shaped, by whom, as well as how it is and should be evaluated, arguing that these inquiries are of far more direct consequence for the communities positioned as "beneficiaries" of cooperation projects as well as the local authorities and partners who serve them.

1.5 Interrogating Indiscriminate Cooperation for Water and Sanitation in Maputo

The rest of this book provides a grounded examination of the implications of the constitution of relationships between international partners at the granular scale of urban infrastructure development in water-and-sanitation-related projects. Water-and-sanitation-related services are fundamentally project-based and one of the most enduring and seemingly technical areas of concern in the development industry. Despite decades of technical cooperation and projects forged among the usual suspects of international development, an avalanche of nonprofit and community-based efforts, philanthropy, and international advocacy, throughout the world almost three times the population of the United States today still defecates openly and lacks basic water services (UN, 2018). The enduring vulnerability of so basic a life need and service, coupled with the rise of climatic liabilities, appears to have translated into a doubling-down of efforts to eradicate water-and-sanitation poverty since the turn of the twenty-first century.

Within Mozambique, these renewed efforts include those promoting knowledge exchanges within the wide community of international and local organizations, governments, sector practitioners, and scholars working across the country in the water and sanitation sectors. The Grupo de Água e Saneamento (GAS) is a collective of these stakeholders that meets usually once a month to share experiences in both rural and urban settings with efforts to improve water and sanitation services, as well as hygiene.[23] Its overall objective,

---

[23] I have participated in a number of GAS meetings—in Maputo and in Beira.

as a forum of exchange, is to help move water-related policies toward the achievement of strategic development goals, though it has been criticized at times for a heavier sectoral emphasis on rural challenges (Edwards, 2015). Its most significant obstacle, however, appears to be organizational. While GAS is a coordinating group, there appears to be little actual coordination among its wide membership. It functions at the service of the national government's directorship for water and sanitation (i.e., *Direcção Nacional de Abastecimento de Água e Saneamento*), but its programming secretariat rotates—typically among large international organizations working in Mozambique, like UNICEF, or—presently—WaterAid-Mozambique. In a recent survey it conducted in 2018, members complained not only of the repetitive nature of the themes discussed, but that the forum had turned into simple "PowerPoint" opportunities to "show off" what each stakeholder group had achieved in various locations.[24] Further, members noted that the group's capacity to brainstorm and build improved strategies for specified problems was stymied by the fact that they lacked specific, potentially helpful national data and incentives to coordinate action.

The fact that this national group dedicated to coordination in the water and sanitation sectors does not actually coordinate activities on the ground reflects what I also found in Maputo: a missing coherence in the city's strategy for taking on partnerships, particularly in the water and sanitation sector. At Maputo City Council's *Gabinete de Desenvolvimento Estratégico Institucional* (GDEI) or Cabinet of Strategic Institutional Planning,[25] I inquired whether there was a municipal-level review or list of all the different international development projects ongoing in the city, overall or at the water-and-sanitation-sector level. While the head of monitoring there indicated that in fact this was something they were planning to take on, there was no list during my time in Maputo that internally accounted for or evaluated which international cooperation projects and partners were working well in the city, and which required rethinking.[26]

From a purely materialist perspective, it is nonetheless clear why Mozambique remains a hotbed of international donor activity for water-and-sanitation-related projects. The country did not reach the water and sanitation targets set forth in the Millennium Development Goals for 2015, and despite progress in the "urban drinking water" sector, with access to at least basic

---

[24] Unpublished GAS Survey of Membership conducted in November 2018.
[25] Perhaps ironically, this was an office created only because the World Bank required that a coordination office for urban development be established for a major municipal capacity-building project it funded in the city.
[26] Interview with Dr. Alda Saude, Assessora de Monitoria, GDEI, in Maputo, July 18, 2014.

drinking water improving from 59 to 79 percent of the population between 2000 and 2015 (WHO/UNICEF, 2017), Mozambique remains at risk of not achieving the expansion of goals in the water and sanitation sector set out in the Sustainable Development Goals. The devastation wrought by two cyclone hits to the country's Central and Northern provinces in March 2019 only intensifies the urgency of the challenges ahead. And while Maputo fares better than other cities and rural landscapes across Mozambique, the access, affordability, and adequacy of drinking water and sanitation systems there remains an enduring material challenge for the city's growing population.

Within the capital's lower-income neighborhoods, which some estimates place as housing around 70 percent of the population, the physical burdens of the weak reach of the water and sanitation sector are clearly apparent (Sambo, 2016). During my time in districts outside of what is commonly referred to as the "cement" core, I saw how treated drinking water scarcity translated into long lines of unattended jerry cans at water pumps, acting as placeholders while their owners awaited the local water-committee head to unlock water pumps at scheduled access times; the lack of drainage systems often meant flooding and—because roads are often unpaved—muddy streets, making commutes to work and school difficult; further, scarce solid-waste collection challenged neighborhood-level hygiene and health—especially for the most vulnerable populations. It is also in such poorer neighborhoods, or "*bairros*," in Maputo that diarrhea is considered the third leading cause of death for children under 14 years old (Nhampossa et al, 2013). The most recent report for which figures are available indicates that only 9 percent of households in Maputo are connected to a piped sewerage system, with households in the low-income areas that are home to the urban majority instead largely depending on pit latrines, septic tanks, and pour-flush toilets (Hawkins & Muximpua, 2015).

In part, these challenges have been exacerbated by the growth of the urban population in Maputo, which, if estimates are correct, will continue to see another 70,000 people annually call it home over the next twenty years, giving the capital a population of just over four million people by 2040 (WSUP— Water and Sanitation for the Urban Poor, 2018). The lack of up-to-date data, recurrence of extreme climate events, and the political obstacles of securing regular public funding for the improvement of sanitation services make it all the more difficult to address this growing population's network of sanitation needs (World Bank, 2019). To address the current financial needs for sanitation infrastructure investments, efforts to raise own-source revenues for municipally led investments in water and sanitation have led to discussions with the country's Water Regulatory Authority (*Autoridade Reguladora de Água*, AURA) in Maputo as well as other major cities, but were as yet unrealized in the capital at the time of writing. More specifically, the City Council of Maputo and AURA is considering a sanitation tariff to be adjoined as a surcharge on water bills (World Bank, 2019; WSUP—Water and Sanitation for the Urban Poor, 2018). The tariff would fund fecal sludge management, a critical service for poorer neighborhoods where pit latrines that require emptying services remain prominent in the city. Yet the planned tariff is not intended to be sufficient to cover all the financial costs of improvements needed in the sanitation service cycle—from wastewater treatment to waste collection and service extensions—across Maputo's diverse districts.

It is within this wider city backdrop that a number of different neighborhood-scaled international cooperation projects have been launched. Over a decade ago, Paolo de Renzio and Joseph Hanlon (2007), scholars of international budgetary aid and Mozambican development, respectively, estimated that there were probably sixty bilateral and multilateral agencies working in Mozambique. Such agencies typically maintain a local presence in Maputo, even if the majority of their projects are outside the capital. Since de Renzio and Hanlon's 2007 study, the international presence of bilateral actors in Maputo has only grown. This timing, in part, coincides with two phenomena: first, the rise of SSC players, and especially China's growing interests in the country since 2007 (followed by what one might describe as a herd mentality among bilateral donors and their accompanying private sectors, newly interested in the country); and second, the important discovery of natural gas off Mozambique's northern coast in 2010 (after much exploration over a four-year period starting in 2006). Since that time, several other Southern economies in Latin America and Asia have made headway building economic and political relationships with Mozambique, opening physical embassies in Maputo for the first time starting in 2011 (Carolini, 2021). For example, while Turkey had enjoyed diplomatic relations with Mozambique since the latter's independence in 1975, it opened its first embassy in Maputo in 2011; South Korea and Argentina followed suit in 2013. Between 2003 and 2015, Turkey's commercial trade with Mozambique grew over twenty times, reaching over USD 120 million in this period (Redacção, 2017). Similarly, between 2011 and 2014 alone, South Korea increased its investments in the country by seven times to USD 3.5 million (Avril Consulting, 2015). This *densification* of international actors—both in bilateral and commercial terms—matters for urban development and change in Maputo and other African capitals like it. The parameters and preferences for cooperation activities and investments that such "newcomers" bring are shaping local material realities and perceptions therein within the city—and the country overall. Further, the emerging relationships between international stakeholders and local government, and in particular its bureaucrats, are also influencing local governance systems in ways that matter for how equity concerns are treated on the ground in their projects.

2

"We don't refuse money"

The Crowding-in of International Footprints

2.1 Comparative Commitments

On a rather chilly July morning in 2014, I waited anxiously for my chance to squeeze into a *chapa*[1] headed down toward *Museu*, an area around the Museum of Natural History in Maputo's city center. I calculated that it would take me at least another twenty minutes to walk over to the City Hall, where I had scheduled a meeting with Maputo City Council's Head of International Relations, Natacha Morais, and her colleague, Chadreque Massingue. When my ride materialized—a *chapa* full of commuters past the carrying capacity limit—I gladly secured a coveted spot by the door. From my perch en route down to the city's center, I spied the newly built presidential palace on Avenida Julius Nyerere, one of Maputo's most elegant (and guarded) streets. My attention was drawn to something peculiar there that I had not noticed before during many hurried walks and rides up and down the avenue. Peeking out from behind the tall palace walls was the top of a Chinese *paifang*, a distinctively colorful and tiled architectural archway seen in cities around the world as the marker of an entryway to Chinese urban districts. I thought to myself how appropriate this symbol was of the booming relationship between high-level authorities in China and Mozambique, increasingly translated into physical form in Maputo through several key urban infrastructure projects.

Earlier that year, then-president Armando Guebuza's celebration of the new palace's completion competed for media attention with reports of strikes at another newly completed major renovation site—the Maputo International Airport.[2] Both were built and funded with Chinese support. The palace's

---

[1] *Chapa* is the local Mozambican term for one of the minivans ubiquitously used as major transport systems across African cities.

[2] The airport was indeed frequently in the news as a scene of workers' strikes. One in 2013 by a small group of Mozambican workers employed by AFECC was sparked by an on-the-job injury, but generally

Equity, Evaluation, and International Cooperation. Gabriella Y. Carolini, Oxford University Press.
© Gabriella Y. Carolini (2022). DOI: 10.1093/oso/9780192865489.003.0003

renovations were paid for by a mixed credit loan from China's Export-Import (Exim) Bank and the airport renovation funds were provided by the Chinese Embassy in Maputo. Both construction projects were also managed by the Chinese firm, Anhui Foreign Economic Construction Corporation (AFECC).[3] However, the similarities between the sites seemed to end there. While a combative narrative emanates perpetually from Mozambicans about working conditions under AFECC and other Chinese construction companies operating in Maputo, nothing but Guebuza's praise was reported about the Chinese construction work at the palace.[4]

Elites in Maputo from government, the private sector, and civil-society organizations have made no secret of their enthusiasm for China's latest investments, as well as their exasperation with the status quo of the Western-led development machine.[5] At a conference on foreign aid in 2008, former Mozambican president Joaquim Chissano explained the expansive African welcome to growing assistance from China and other non-Western sources. He bemoaned traditional donors' "never-ending litany of seminars and workshops ... of doubtful value ... [and praised new donors'] innovative ways to leverage aid and attract private sector resources in order to nurture and support the emergence of robust entrepreneurial classes that have a strong stake in the national economies" (Brautigam, 2009). This sentiment seemed to resound in how Morais and Massingue described to me capacity-building cooperation projects in Maputo, but interestingly their frustration was with Brazil as opposed to traditional Western donors. Both shrugged in discussing the value of capacity-building work—indicating that, yes, it builds competencies, but that it

---

reflected Mozambican workers' complaints that they were not paid overtime or on equal footing with their Chinese counterparts, worked in insecure conditions, and were badly treated (Chichava, 2014; Macauhub, 2014).

[3] AFECC works in Mozambique under its Mozambican subsidiary's name, Sogecoa.

[4] In Maputo alone, according to Alden, Chichava, and Roque (Alden et al, 2014) over thirty Chinese construction companies have offices and typically outbid other firms on tenders by the Mozambican government or the World Bank. The fact that work relations within these firms is gaining scholarly attention is thus not so surprising. For example, Nielsen has written about the worksite confusion Mozambican workers feel in relation to their Chinese employers in infrastructure projects (Nielsen, 2014), while Wethal writes about tensions reported by Mozambican workers in Chinese construction projects more widely within the country (Wethal, 2017). For an account of Chinese workers' perspective on relations in work sites in Maputo, see (Bunkenborg, 2014), or, for a wider accounting of media representations (and misrepresentations) of Chinese work in Africa, see: Brautigam (2009); Power et al (2012); Mohan et al (2014). Chichava (2014) highlights the higher-level narrative of Mozambican-Chinese relations as well, emphasizing that the Mozambican central government affords a great deal of importance to China's work in the country, particularly given that its conditionality only centers on economic, as opposed to political, terms and its financial support has been tremendous, including loan forgiveness.

[5] China has actually provided aid to African countries since at least the Busan Conference of 1955, and specifically gave Mozambique assistance during its war for independence from Portugal in the 1970s (Alden & Chichava, 2014; Haifang, 2010; Jackson, 1995).

did not have as much impact on problems as cooperation projects that allow for capital investments or purchases of what they considered much-needed equipment.[6] Their perception of the delimited value of capacity-building projects reinforces why China, with its emphasis on physical capital investments, particularly in infrastructure, is such a stand-out among new donors and old in Mozambique as much as other countries across Africa.

Among the commitments to the continent made by Brazil, South Africa, India, and China (BASIC[7]) since the turn of the last century, China is by far the leading source of financial investments (see Figure 2.1). Indeed, even relative to the Organization for Economic Cooperation and Development's (OECD) Development Assistance Committee's (DAC) aid flows, Chinese contributions are impressive. Figure 2.2 demonstrates how China's commitments are converging with that of the DAC's aggregated thirty countries' volume of aid. It further highlights how, without China, leading Southern economies' aggregate volume of aid is far below the USD billions committed by DAC members to African development.

Critically, the volume comparison of commitments in Figure 2.2 also shows that the trends between the three groups are diverging.[8] DAC members and

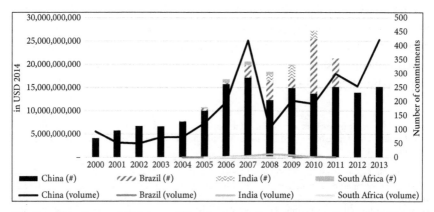

Fig. 2.1 Number and Volume of Development Commitments from BASIC to Africa

Sources: Figure calculated by author based on two datasets from Aiddata.org, published by Strange et al (2015) and Tierney et al (2011).

---

[6] Interview in Maputo City Hall, July 14, 2014.

[7] The BASIC countries—Brazil, South Africa, India, and China—formed an alliance in 2009 urging that higher-income countries honor climate-change agreements, though in this book the acronym is not used to reference their environmental coalition.

[8] Critically, data on Brazil, India, and South Africa for the past six years delimits this trend in number, as data is much less granular than that gathered on China. However, Brazil's aggressiveness on

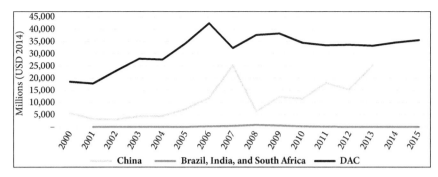

Fig. 2.2 DAC, China, and Brazil/India/South Africa Commitments to Africa

Sources: OECD.stat's dataset on ODA commitments (2017). BASIC data is based on authors' calculations from two datasets at Aiddata.org available from Tierney et al (2011).

Brazil, India, and South Africa have all stagnated in recent years in terms of the volume of their commitments to Africa.[9] Even while levels of aid are greater from DAC members as a group, not even the *Paris Declaration on Aid Effectiveness*[10] in 2005 effectively combated the impact of the global financial meltdown of 2008 on DAC commitments. Only China's volume of development assistance grew in the period following the global financial crisis. As shown in Map 2.1, much of China's official-development-assistance-like (ODA-like) commitments have been directed toward the African continent.

Popular sentiments propagate the sense that the volumetric divergences between China and other donors with development commitments on the African continent are matched by differences in the ethical approaches to aid,[11] but research empirically challenges this framing. Using a new collection of data available about China's portfolio of development commitments, Dreher, Nunnenkamp, and Thiele (2011) argue that new and old donors behave similarly in several respects, arguing that the two groups do not exhibit significant differences in their aid preferences for better-governed countries and that concerns

the continent has diminished since former-president Ignacio Lula da Silva left office in 2010. Furthermore, while both India and South Africa have established their own development cooperation agencies, activities therein have not surged in the same way that China's has on the continent. South Africa's agency is, to this date, barely functional.

[9] The reasons for stagnation in regard to commitments from the DAC as well as countries like Brazil, India, and South Africa are largely related to domestic politics as opposed to a strategic retreat from the African continent. For example, Brazil's political and economic crises over the past several years have refocused the country's attention inward.

[10] The Paris Declaration commits DAC countries to ensure aid shows up on national budgets and works to untie donor aid to specific targets over time (among other aid-effectiveness targets).

[11] Many scholars have worked to correct and historicize the popular visceral reactions to China's aid policy vis-à-vis Africa in particular (Brautigam, 2009; Lee, 2017; Mawdsley, 2012; Taylor & Williams, 2004).

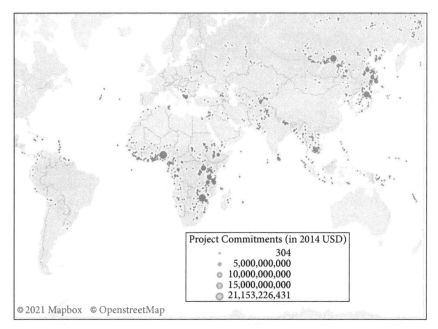

Map 2.1 Chinese ODA-like Project Commitment Volumes 2000–2013 (in 2014 USD)

Source: Author's visualization based on data from Bluhm et al (2018) and from the AidData Research and Evaluation Unit (2017) Geocoding Methodology, Version 2.0. Williamsburg, VA: AidData at William & Mary. https://www.aiddata.org/publications/geocoding-methodology-version-2-0

about the pursuit of commercial self-interest is overblown for both. Nonetheless, the fact that new donor groups exist creates a diverse marketplace for development aid and strategies. China, Brazil, India, and South Africa are far from representative countries of the global South or even of their regions (Alden et al, 2010; Hurrell, 2013; Thakur, 2014), but their financial injections—both in the form of cooperation and through private-sector actors—is creating greater opportunities for choice among so-called beneficiary countries (Abdenur & da Fonseca, 2013; Enns, 2015; Humphrey & Michaelowa, 2013; Mawdsley, 2012).

2.2 A New Marketplace for Aid, Trade, and Investments

Mozambique is one of the lower-income African countries on the "recipient" end of many SSC alliances and traditional donor aid, as well as a party to the trade and private investments that tend to follow from the growth of bilateral loan agreements. Much as with trends across Africa as a whole, Mozambique began to see a rise in bilateral loans after 2006. The country's debt service payments to bilateral partners represented roughly half of its debt service payments to multilateral actors like the World Bank at that time. However, by 2014, debt service to bilateral and multilateral actors was almost equivalent, largely due to a rise in credits from countries like Brazil and China (Chivulele, 2017). It is not surprising, therefore, that after Chinese president Hu Jintao visited the country, Chinese foreign direct investment (FDI) substantially increased in just one year—from 905,000 USD in 2006 to 61.15 million USD in 2007 (Chichava, 2014). During that same year, private investments from other countries with bilateral stakes in Mozambique also began to grow, with ten different multinational corporations, including those with US, Canadian, Australian, and British roots, exploring for oil in Mozambique's north (Hanlon, 2015:18). By 2011, marked by the discovery of natural gas, FDI stock overall grew sharply and has continued to rise since (see Figure 2.3).

The growing foreign portfolio of private interests with direct investments in Mozambique is specified in Table 2.1, where surprisingly, given all the fanfare its investments have received, China's direct investment position ranks

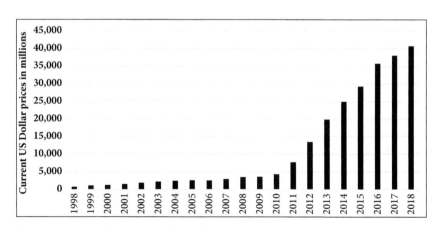

Fig. 2.3 FDI Stock in Mozambique (1998–2018)
Source: Statistical annexes of the UNCTAD *World Investment Report 2019*.

Table 2.1   Inward Direct Investment Positions in Mozambique in USD millions

Investment from:	2009	2010	2011	2012	2013	2014	2015	2016	2017
Mauritius	288	974	931	1,248	1,394	1,884	3,885	6,985	7,345
United Arab Emirates	−45	−455	1,087	2,361	4,418	5,911	7,708	7,393	6,786
Italy	22	78	225	901	1,606	2,076	3,056	4,842	5,398
Portugal	495	819	840	1,233	1,324	1,390	−374	2,774	3,381
United Kingdom	−16	2	485	663	891	952	−286	2,673	2,890
South Africa	1,280	1,309	1,849	2,583	2,951	3,065	2,954	2,021	2,626
Netherlands	37	46	55	205	601	606	818	2,004	2,161
India	85	125	190	423	537	541	2,336	1,607	1,812
Australia	631	661	808	1,229	1,544	1,763	412	1,029	1,148
Ireland			0	0	0	0	4	741	758
France	31	43	120	195	228	238	516	536	576
Tanzania	23	37	64	104	129	129	224	390	438
Brazil	72	80	80	80	85	105	251	270	334
Kenya	−1	0	−3	−8	−1	3	−78	312	332
Austria			0	0	0	14	0	301	287
Germany	38	55	65	134	159	160	289	253	278
Spain	6	7	34	48	56	56	130	207	223
Virgin Islands, British	0	0	28	31	38	80	89	125	141
China		2	8	0	0	44	70	123	138
Norway	10	19	13	27	32	51	77	113	123
Zimbabwe	23	32	22	14	16	17	45	66	70
Botswana	19	21	23	24	25	32	41	54	67
Kuwait	1	1	10	9	11	12	32	50	52
Switzerland	68	307	285	298	314	317	238	49	50
Isle of Man	4	9	5	13	14	14	48	28	29

Source: The IMF's 2018 Coordinated Direct Investment Survey (CDIS). Low and middle-income countries in the table are shaded for emphasis.

rather low.[12] However, this is likely due to definitions used.[13] Excluding Mauritius, whose ranking is perhaps most telling of its own utility as a tax haven

---

[12] Here it is important to note that this data is self-reported from Mozambique to an IMF survey, and that China may be underrepresented in these figures, which do not, for example, also include investments from Hong Kong.

[13] The IMF explains direct investment as that which gives foreign control or a significant degree of influence on the management of an enterprise that is resident in another economy (International Monetary Fund, 2015). It is therefore not surprising to see countries like South Africa, India, and Brazil rank higher on the list of direct investors in Mozambique than China, which is not as significantly involved in shared-control enterprises within the country.

and money-laundering vehicle, South African investments top the list among Southern economies. This is expected given South African activity in the mining sector with firms like Randgold and Metorex, as well as its success in telecommunications, retail, tourism, and financial services within the Southern African region. Indian firms like the Tata Group, Ranbaxy Laboratories, and Kirloskar Brothers, on the other hand, are engaged in building wider market shares on the continent in the energy, mining, and pharmaceutical industries, explaining India's impressive rank as an investor in Mozambique—growing its level of engagement by just over twenty times since 2009 (Besharati, 2013; Prichard, 2009).

Interestingly, even while high-income countries like the United Arab Emirates, Italy, Portugal, and the United Kingdom still top the list of direct foreign investments in Mozambique, the scenario is rather different in terms of commercial trade. Imports of merchandise to Mozambique from other developing economies were growing more rapidly than imports from developed economies, surpassing them in 2012 before dipping briefly in 2015 and regaining a lead in 2016, as seen in Figure 2.4.

Much of the uptick since 2011 evidenced in Figure 2.4 reflects the economic boom Mozambique has experienced because of natural-resource extraction and its corresponding reverberations across major infrastructure development. For example, in 2011 the Brazilian mining firm Vale announced that it would build a railway connecting its mining operations in Mozambique's Tete province with the coastal town of Nacala, the same city in which the Brazilian Development Bank signed a contract with the central government of Mozambique to convert Mozambique's military airport into a commercial one (Hanlon, 2015). The work contract to build Nacala International Airport

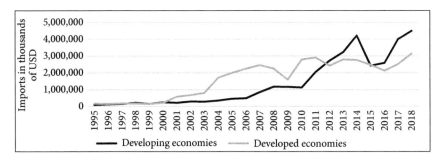

Fig. 2.4 Imports to Mozambique from Developing and Developed Economies
Source: Statistical annexes of the UNCTAD *World Investment Report 2019*: Merchandise trade matrix—detailed products, imports in thousands of dollars, annual, 1995–2018.

was ultimately awarded to Odebrecht, a Brazilian construction company now infamous for admitting to bribing government officials around the world—including Mozambican authorities involved in the Nacala airport case—to win public work bids (Caldeira, 2019a). The Indian firm Jindal Steel and Power was also authorized to build a power plant in 2011, while China more recently signed an accord in October 2017 to provide Mozambique with roughly 14.8 million USD in economic and technical cooperation (as well as debt forgiveness) to build an international airport in the Gaza province just north of Maputo.[14]

This recent surge in imports and foreign investments is of course not unique to Mozambique. In the 2009 book *The New Scramble for Africa?*, Southall and Comninos reported that several top-performing firms throughout the continent were either owned or partially owned by foreign, non-African multi-nationals or investors. Yet while the linkage between donor activities and affiliated private-sector ventures is not surprising, their relative scale is rather indicative of what development anthropologist David Mosse (2005, 2013) has described as the rise of the "business" of development. In Africa, FDI significantly surpasses official development assistance. Figure 2.5 illustrates precisely how much FDI outpaces official assistance in four of the largest recipients of

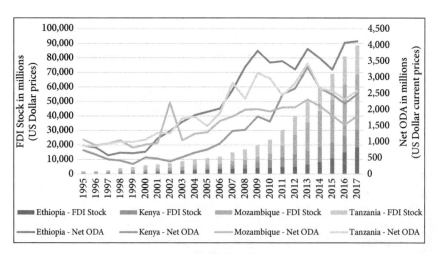

Fig. 2.5 Trends in Net ODA and FDI Stock (1995–2017)

Sources: FDI figures are from the statistical annexes of the UNCTAD *World Investment Report* 2019 and net ODA figures are from OECD (2019), *OECD International Development Statistics* (database).

---

[14] The airport in Gaza province's capital, Xai-Xai, is envisioned as helping to relieve some pressure from Maputo's international airport, according to Mozambican president Filipe Nyusi's statement to the press. See http://www.abola.pt/Nnh/Noticias/Ver/698797.

aid in Africa, according to the OECD. Notably, however, these figures exclude China, whose involvement in all four countries involves a significant amount of funds similar in character to official development assistance as well as FDI.[15]

Private-sector participation—both from domestic and foreign investors—in infrastructure development and/or rehabilitation provides further insights into the rise of private investments in African assets over time and their sectoral particularities. For example, Figure 2.6 provides a snapshot of the rise of private finance investments in infrastructure projects in the sub-Saharan African region, showing the growing dominance of energy project investments since 2000.

Within the investment community, several of the larger Southern economies have been notable players. For instance, of the project finance infrastructure

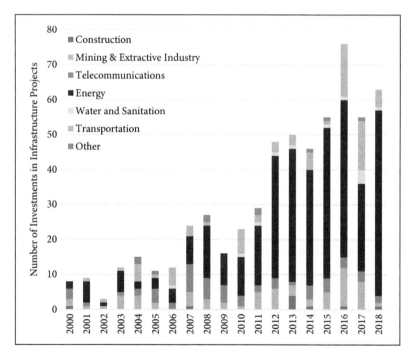

Fig. 2.6 Private Investments in Sub-Saharan Africa by Project per Sector (2000–2018)

Source: Author's calculations based on data from Preqin financial database.

[15] Between 2000 and 2013, for example, China provided more funds for commercial activities in Africa than it provided aid, much in line with the rest of the international community. For more on China's funding on the continent, see aiddata.org and research emerging from their dataset (Parks, 2015; Tierney et al, 2011).

deals in Mozambique for which financial sponsors or investors are known, 58 percent involve investors registered within Mozambique and/or high-income economies, while 38 percent involve investors from other Southern economies, especially Brazil, South Africa, India, and China (or the BASIC countries).[16]

2.3 On Shaky Grounds with South Africa, Brazil, and India

The growth of aid, trade, and private investments among Southern countries will not surprise scholars of industrial policy.[17] What Amsden called the "rise of the rest," regarding how late-industrializing countries developed a novel and successful paradigm of government-coordinated economic growth, has translated into an expansion of the donor class in the twenty-first century (Amsden, 2001). While countries like Brazil, India, China, and South Africa were once major recipients of international aid, today these industrial "latecomers" have also become donors in their own right (Carmody, 2013; Mawdsley, 2012; Mwase & Yang, 2012; Thakur, 2014). As Mawdsley (2012) and

---

[16] Data calculated by author from the SDC Platinum finance database covering all project finance records from 1992 through January 2019, of which forty Mozambican project finance deals list project sponsors or investors.

[17] This financial story of course is highly dependent on the quality of available data, which for the most part remains very convoluted and plagued by some definitional chaos. As a number of scholars remind us, agreement on what constitutes "foreign aid" or "official development assistance," as the OECD calls it, is not forthcoming among DAC members, never mind the new donor class (Mawdsley 2012; Tierney et al, 2011; Dreher et al, 2011). Some of the latter, like Brazil, resist the financial categorizations of aid, insisting that their engagement in SSC is distinguished by the fact that they do not provide financial aid but instead technical cooperation (which is of course still backed up by funding). In several discussions with Brazilian professionals working in Mozambique (from the Embassy through to projects highlighted in this book), this point was repeatedly emphasized as a manner of reiterating how Brazil was unlike the traditional donor community working in the country. Mawdsley reports the same from India, where the term "foreign aid" is replaced by "development cooperation" (2012:81). These differentiations complicate comparisons of SSC with the traditional development community's engagement in Africa. The traditional donors' activities are well represented in the OECD's International Development Statistics and in the World Bank's development indicators database. In addition, websites like AidFlows.org visualize data from regional development banks, the OECD, and the World Bank, while the International Aid Transparency Initiative (www.aidtransparency.net) allows a diverse set of organizations (e.g., foundations, governments, non-governmental organizations, multilaterals, and the private sector) to publish their activities directly on the site. However, none of these data resources boast substantial information on the aid activities of the new donor class. In their stead, a major recent effort was made by researchers to improve accessibility and quality of information available from all donors. A joint effort of researchers from the College of William & Mary, Development Gateway, and Brigham Young University launched the AidData initiative in 2009 to track and collate all aid data and make it publicly searchable (see www.aiddata.org). They have organized and standardized donor datasets at the project-level, including most importantly otherwise dispersed aid data on the new donor community's activities. Perhaps most impressive is their dataset on China, which offers a significant (albeit still incomplete) picture not only of the number of projects or volume of aid, but also the nuances of such aid, including: sources of information and whether these were verified, geocodes of project location, whether loans are concessional or interest-free, loan maturities, and grace periods for non-payment.

others have shown, Southern economies like Turkey and Thailand have also followed suit, establishing their own Southern cooperation programming—often accompanied by private-sector interests. While China remains the clear financial leader among the Southern "donor" class, an institution-building process—with dedicated loan programming for African counterparts and investments on the continent over the past decade—is in evidence across the broader spectrum of Southern economies, especially South Africa, Brazil, and India, but with varying degrees of success.

Mozambique's closest neighbor, South Africa, for example, has been a rather limited propagator of aid therein, despite its efforts to establish the South African Development Partnership Agency (SADPA) (Lucey & O'Riordan, 2014). On the other hand, it has been rather more successful in its efforts to build up the New Partnership for Africa's Development (NEPAD) and the Southern African Development Community (SADC), two major fora through which it has exerted a strong influence on both economic and political initiatives at the continental and Southern regional levels. Though encompassing membership from the whole continent, NEPAD's existence is really due in large part to South Africa's diplomatic efforts and political leadership both among African States and vis-à-vis continental relations with industrialized countries (Alden et al, 2010). Likewise, SADC is very much a product of South Africa's promotion of a neoliberal economic agenda accompanied by a development strategy of infrastructure creation and resource development. Not surprisingly, however, South Africa's dominance in both organizations has been critiqued by neighbors. While SADC was established as a cooperation vehicle for the region to launch mutually beneficial development projects, South Africa's comparative advantages in gaining the bids to implement such development projects and its benefits from the organization's promotion of economic liberalization in the region have been well noted by smaller-sized economies (Alden et al, 2010). Figure 2.7, for example, shows how South Africa alone comprises a substantial portion of sub-Saharan Africa's (SSA) intraregional trade.

Carmody (2013) reports that much of South Africa's African trade expansion has been facilitated by its state-owned Industrial Development Corporation, which has spearheaded investments in over twenty-one African countries. Discounting the country's presence in Mauritius, which often is used as an offshore conduit for investments seeking a tax haven, South Africa's direct private investments sit atop the ranks of the largest foreign direct investors across several African countries. Beside Mozambique, which receives its largest outward investments within the African continent, South Africa is

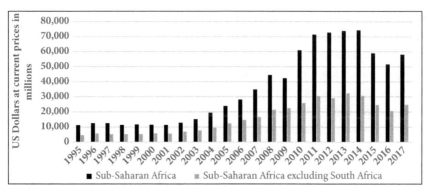

Fig. 2.7 Intra-group Trade in Sub-Saharan Africa, Including and Excluding South Africa

Source: Data from UNCTAD secretariat calculations, based on UNCTAD, UNCTADstat Merchandise Trade Matrix.

also the largest foreign direct investor in Namibia. In Ghana, South Africa's direct investments surpass China and Switzerland, and in Zambia, it sits as the fifth-top source of direct investments.[18]

The timing of South Africa's efforts to establish itself more strongly as a major development and investment player in the region coincides well with Brazilian deceleration therein (Marcondes & Mawdsley, 2017). As highlighted in Figure 2.8, the Brazilian federal government's interest in Africa has slowed

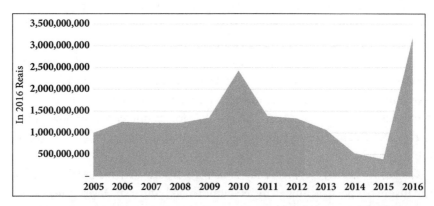

Fig. 2.8 Federal Brazilian International Cooperation Distributions (2005–2016)

Note: The international cooperation distributions from Brazilian federal government here depicted include several branches of federal government involved in cooperation work, not just the Agency for Brazilian Cooperation. Available data is for the 2005–2016 range only.
Source: IPEA/ABC 2018.

[18] Data on South Africa's direct investments come from the IMF's 2018 Coordinated Direct Investment Survey (CDIS), which reports volumes of investments in 2017—the latest year for which countries noted here reported figures.

since the former Brazilian president Luiz Inácio Lula da Silva exited office at the end of 2010. The government itself explains the uptick in its international cooperation costs in 2016 as an aberration and simply a reflection of late payments made in that year to international organizations of which it is a member.

Notwithstanding the decline in financial commitments, by the end of Lula's tenure in December 2010, Brazil had opened nineteen new embassies throughout Africa. In addition, the Brazilian Cooperation Agency or *Agência Brasileira de Cooperação* (ABC) extended its development cooperation activities to thirty-seven African countries (Silva, 2015). This commitment to African engagement translated into Mozambique sitting at the top of Brazil's bilateral aid list for every year since the end of Lula's presidency (see Figure 2.9) (Instituto de Pesquisa Econômica Aplicada & Agência Brasileira de Cooperação, 2018).

Brazilian cooperation in Mozambique targeted a few major areas through various fora, including bilateral SSC, triangular cooperation, and cooperation with international organizations in the agriculture, health, education, urban housing, and development spheres. The majority of funds from Brazil were directed toward work which involved the Brazilian Agricultural Research Corporation, or *Empresa Brasileira de Pesquisa Agropecuária* (Embrapa), followed by the government's support for scholarships enabling Mozambican students to study in Brazilian higher-education institutions (Instituto de Pesquisa Econômica Aplicada & Agência Brasileira de Cooperação, 2018). Some of the more notable projects involving Embrapa reference Brazil's triangular

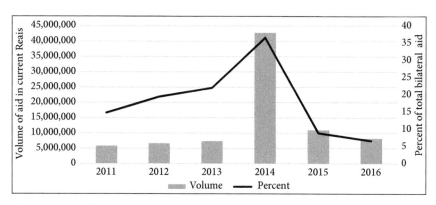

Fig. 2.9 Federal Brazilian Bilateral Cooperation Spending in Mozambique (2011–2016)

Source: Author's calculations from IPEA/ABC 2016, 2018.

cooperation with JICA in ProSavanna, an agricultural development project in Mozambique's Nacala Corridor, modeled on Brazil's agricultural success in its Cerrado.[19]

Brazilian attention within the education sector has been somewhat—though not entirely—less controversial than some of its forays into the agricultural sector. It includes technical education, knowledge transfer, and vocational training. The International Policy Centre for Inclusive Growth, for example, is a partnership between the UNDP and Brazil's Ministry of Planning, Budget and Management and the Institute for Applied Economic Research to promote South–South learning on social policies targeting the reduction of poverty and inequality. The Brazilian National Service of Industrial Training or *Serviço Nacional de Aprendizagem Industrial* (SENAI[20]), a professional education network promoting technological training, services, and innovation for the Brazilian industrial sector, is also actively engaged in several capacity-building and knowledge-exchange programs within Africa with the assistance of ABC. It is building vocational training centers in all African Lusophone states, including Angola, Cape Verde, Guinea Bissau, São Tomé and Príncipe, and Mozambique (Agência Brasileira de Cooperação, n.d.). These efforts are typically in partnership with national vocational training institutes. For example, in Angola, SENAI works with the *Instituto Nacional de Emprego e Formação Profissional de Angola* (or the Angolan Institute of Employment and Professional Training), and in Mozambique, the aforementioned INEFP, whose director first complained to me of the slow pace of progress in cooperation work with Brazil. In addition, much like China, Brazil has encouraged African students to enroll in Brazilian higher-education opportunities. The education scholar Susanne Ress writes about the example of the University of International Integration of Afro-Brazilian Lusophony (UNI-LAB), which was inaugurated in 2010 in the northeast of Brazil as a testament of ties between Brazilians and Africans in the region. UNILAB reserves a significant number—50 percent—of its seats for students from Portugal and

---

[19] The project has received much local and international media attention, prompted by the fear of land-grabbing it evoked and the environmental degradation associated with the commercialization of what have long been smaller farmlands worked by rural families in Mozambique (Amanor & Chichava, 2016; Shankland & Gonçalves, 2016).

[20] Within Brazil, SENAI has 809 mobile and fixed operational units that offer around 3000 courses for workers, covering 28 industrial areas.

Lusophone Africa.[21] However, Ress notes that the university's racialized focus has been criticized for effectively essentializing Africans and confining the continent and its connection to Brazil in the past.

Another highly publicized area of Brazilian cooperation is its health diplomacy. In Mozambique, which receives the largest portion of Brazil's bilateral support in the health sector, Brazil forwarded the construction of the first publicly-owned antiretroviral pharmaceutical factory in Africa just outside of Maputo city (Russo et al, 2014). The promise of pharmaceutical independence from high-priced drug cocktails produced by Northern-based pharma-giants won much praise from both local and international development stakeholders. Likewise, Brazil's promotion of human milk banks across Latin America and Africa—and specifically in Mozambique—has garnered much praise for its innovative approach to building low-cost health interventions to improve natal health and food security (De Bruyn, 2019; Pereira, 2017).

Brazil's engagement in other sectors is relatively smaller than its agricultural, educational, and health projects in Mozambique, as elsewhere, but its influence is also sometimes under the radar of official cooperation records. For example, multilateral organizations and Northern donors alike have referenced Brazilian experiences—and hired Brazilian technical experts—to help roll out reforms in areas like public administration and land management as well. When I spoke to representatives of the International Monetary Fund (IMF) based in Maputo in 2011, they reported that while European donors and multilaterals like the IMF were funding the implementation of a new digitized system of public-sector accounting and financial management in the country, they had borrowed heavily from the financial administration model of Brazil (or *Sistema de Administração Financeira do Estado*) and had hired Brazilian experts to help implement the system in Mozambique.[22] Indeed, the central government of Mozambique had also directly hired Brazilian consultants to this end. Brazil's electronic Land Management System, or *Sistema de Gestão Fundiária* (SIGEF), a cadastral digital platform for land management, represented another window of influence, with Brazilian and Mozambican land-management staff engaged in exchanges directed through the Brazilian Federal University of Pernambuco to understand how SIGEF could be used in the Mozambican context.[23]

---

[21] Carmody (2013) too argues that the long history of Brazilian "affinities" for Africa can be read as a political strategy—both with domestic and international currency.

[22] Interview with Victor Lledo of IMF in Maputo headquarters, September 22, 2011.

[23] Brazil's own National Institute of Colonialization and Agrarian Reform reports on this in 2014. See http://www.incra.gov.br/noticias/funcionarios-do-orgao-de-terras-de-mocambique-conhecem-acoes-do-incrape

Formal and informal Brazilian influence also shapes the country's engagement in the urban-development sector. The formal narrative of Brazilian urban-development cooperation is led by the country's national public bank, the *Caixa Economica Federal* (or Caixa), often in partnership with ABC. For example, in 2007, a cooperation agreement in support of urban development in Mozambique was signed by Caixa and Mozambique's then Ministry of Public Works, Housing, and Water Resources. The main objective of this agreement was to support the transfer of construction technologies in support of low-income housing production in Mozambique, as well as technical cooperation on waste recycling, on monitoring, and on evaluation methods (Instituto de Pesquisa Econômica Aplicada & Agência Brasileira de Cooperação, 2018). However, these types of cooperation agreement and the projects they cover belie the deeper reliance on Brazilian expertise and experiences with urban development and management in everything from slum upgrading and waste collection to participatory budgeting and administrative capacity building.

Finally, although Lula spent an unprecedented total of fifty-five days on African soil and ignited a popular imagination about Brazilian solidarity with the continent, his tone of deep engagement also sought to expand opportunities for the Brazilian private sector. Under Lula's government, the Brazilian Development Bank, BNDES, began to provide subsidies to Brazilian companies expanding their businesses to the African continent (Saraiva, 2012). As a result, Brazil has significant private-investment positions in Angola, South Africa, Ghana, and Mozambique.[24] Vale was one of the larger beneficiaries of Brazil's African diplomacy, but is also one of the companies on international watchdog lists for its treatment of vulnerable populations on the continent (and most recently within Brazil itself). Carmody cites a 2012 report by an international advocacy group that complained of laborers' deaths on Vale's mining project in Mozambique, as well as its displacement and inequitable resettlement policy for families affected by their work.[25]

India too has made headlines for what some criticize as its firms' land-grabbing strategies on the continent (Allan et al, 2014; German et al, 2013). Although India's largely agricultural investments in Ethiopia and to a lesser

---

[24] Data on Brazil's direct investments come from the IMF's 2018 Coordinated Direct Investment Survey (CDIS), which reports volumes of investments in 2017. Investments in Mauritius have been excluded from my analysis here due its typical use as a tax haven as opposed to a site of material investment.

[25] Carmody (2013) cites a 2012 report of grievances by the group "International Movement of People Affected by Vale." In addition, recent deaths from Brazil's own Brumadinho dam disaster in 2019 further highlight questions about Vale's operations and responsibilities (Kowsmann et al., 2019).

extent Kenya are widely written about, India's direct private investments reported on the continent in 2017 were targeted toward South Africa, Libya, Ghana, and Nigeria, and to a much lesser extent Gabon, Zimbabwe, and Kenya (Carmody, 2013; Taylor, 2012).[26] Like Brazil, it has also accelerated its political outreach, with over twenty-five new embassy or high commission openings since a previous period of closings in the 1990s (Naidu, 2009). These efforts have been matched by India's expanding development assistance, which grew from 90 million rupees in 1990 to 1,500 million rupees by 2010 (Chaturvedi, 2012). After the first India–Africa Forum Summit in Delhi in 2008, India committed to opening several new institutes on the continent for research and training in fields as diverse as foreign trade, plastics technology, education planning and administration, telemedicine, diamond polishing, and information technology. Similar to South Africa, India's Ministry of External Affairs finally launched its own cooperation agency in 2012—the Development Partnership Administration (DPA)—notably within its Economic Relations Division. Modeled after the US Agency for International Development, the DPA is an effort to "streamline implementation" of India's varied development agendas first launched in the 1960s with the Indian Technical and Economic Cooperation (ITEC) and the Special Commonwealth African Assistance Programme working across Asia and Africa (Mawdsley, 2012; Patel, N. 2011; Taneja, 2012). ITEC, which is active across forty-seven SSA countries, deploys Indian technical assistance, and provides scholarships for partner countries to send candidates for training workshops in India. For instance, at a 2015 South African function celebrating that country's ITEC trainees, the Indian High Commissioner, Ruchi Ghanashyam, stated, "With Africa having a special place in India's development assistance programme, nearly 50 per cent of the ITEC slots, some 4,300 slots annually, is allotted to this continent" (PTI, 2015).

These examples provide strong evidence that non-DAC donors like China, Brazil, India, and South Africa are creating alternative if sometimes controversial channels for development partnerships while also building influential pathways for private investment. What is less clear, however, is what the widening of the partnership base actually means for development on the ground. Macro-level accounts of financial flows tell us little about the quality of how donor commitments and partnerships affect targeted "beneficiaries." Further, as I've written before, in capital cities where the dense physical and

---

[26] Data on India's direct investments come from the IMF's 2018 Coordinated Direct Investment Survey (CDIS), which reports volumes of investments in 2017.

socio-economic footprint of the aid industry (and its affiliated private inter-ests) typically holds a base, the growing density of international stakeholders has implications for basic urban systems: housing, energy, water, sanitation, transport, and labor markets—not to mention local governance (Carolini, 2021). Yet the growing combined urban footprint of the aid and private-investment community across African cities like Maputo is rarely studied as a factor of urban development in and of itself. Given that such cities are also increasingly inhabited by the poor,[27] and that local authorities must try to ad-dress their basic functional needs at the same time as attending to those of the donor/investment class, this omission requires redress.

2.4 Local Governance and Development's Urban Footprint

Urban development, as an actual target of international development itself, only began to grow at the turn of the last century, alongside the recognition that our global population was by 2007 reported to be a largely urban one for the first time in history.[28] The delayed examination of poverty in cities in the global South up to this point reflects the lingering influence of scholars like Michael Lipton (1977), whose seminal work on urban bias in the late 1970s argued that urban political elites concentrated investments in cities to the detriment of the rural poor majority, adding that donors needed to re-engage with rural poverty through agriculture-led development strategies. Since that time, the urban bias thesis has been widely criticized for not understanding the nature of urban–rural migratory linkages, intra-urban inequalities, miscount-ing what or who is poor in both rural and urban areas, and for overlooking the other reasons for urban economic growth (e.g., production clusters, innova-tion, and job growth) (Jones & Corbridge, 2010; Mitlin & Satterthwaite, 2013; Lucci et al, 2016). Today, urban poverty and inequality are instead widely rec-ognized as pressing challenges in themselves. The UN Millennium Declaration of the Millennium Development Goals, the Sustainable Development Goals, and most recently in the 2016 New Urban Agenda put forth by UN-Habitat, all aim to address the complex nature of urban poverty and inequality.

---

[27] Small- and medium-sized cities like Maputo represent the most rapidly growing urban environ-ments in the world. The UN reports that urbanization is most rapid in low-income countries and in sub-Saharan Africa. In addition, it expects that a further 2.5 billion people will reside in urban areas by 2050, and that 90 percent of that population growth will take place in Asia and Africa (UN, 2018).
[28] Much lobbying went into including urban poverty, for example, as a target in the Millennium Development Goals, which included an explicit effort to address the quality of life of slum dwellers (UN Millennium Project, 2005).

While scholarship on the challenges of urban development in Maputo has grown, the recency of Mozambique's independence from Portugal and the country's post-independence internal war both mean that research on the city under peaceful democratic rule is relatively nascent.[29] The first democratic municipal elections in Maputo were only held in 1998 and the period since that time has been characterized as one of rapid economic growth in the capital city and the country more widely. However, that growth has not been felt evenly. Only two years after its first election, the city was besieged by an epic flood caused by both heavy rainfall and Cyclone Connie (Christie & Hanlon, 2001). By 2005, economists argued that the city hosted (or arguably continued to host) the highest rates of inequality in the country (James et al, 2005). Furthermore, although land is nationalized, this has not stemmed the effects of gentrification, land speculation, and urban infrastructure displacement from the uneven distribution of the much celebrated economic growth in the city and country alike (Barros et al, 2014; Sambo, 2016). With over two decades of post-conflict development work, what has the presence of the international development industry—and the private-sector allies of bilateral development agents—done to help—or hinder—these growing urban inequalities?

The growing physical presence in Maputo of an international private-capital and development industry active in Mozambique, shored in part by the rise of SSC in the last decade, creates what seems like a nominal buyer's market for financial assistance. Peculiarly, however, Maputo's authorities are not (yet) able to take advantage of the choices in such a theorized market. Instead, the *Conselho Municipal de Maputo* (CMM), or Maputo Municipal Council, accommodates international cooperation, much as the national government has, shedding light on the real or perceived precarity of financial interests in the city and country. A 2005 report on donor relations with Mozambique argued that the national government was compliant to a fault with donor requests and mandates, fearing that asserting its own priorities would lead to donor flight.[30]

---

[29] Beyond Mozambican urban scholars like Jose Forjaz and Julio Carrilho—both of whom worked in and closely with the post-independence national government—very few scholars of urban development studied Maputo extensively during the post-conflict era. For example, Paul Jenkins, now the head of the School of Architecture and Planning at the University of Witwatersrand, is one of the very few planner/architects to write about urban development in Maputo for over two decades. The bibliography listed in his early English-language city profile of Maputo published in 2000 largely refers to either his own work on urban planning and development in the city since independence, or official government documents. James Sidaway, a geographer, is another early scholar of Maputo in this era.

[30] The report was—perhaps ironically—commissioned by the Programme Aid Partners and financed by the Swiss State Secretariat for Economic Affairs and the UK's Department for International Development (Killick et al, 2005).

Joseph Hanlon and others have also described the consequences of Mozambique's ready welcome and prioritization of donor-led development strategies,
and largely point to the need for reform in the donor community itself. In
a number of different publications, Hanlon recounts Mozambique's difficult
experiences with accommodating ill-conceived donor policies—with the
World Bank's insistence that it liberalize trade in what had been a strong
domestic cashew-nut industry being perhaps the most notorious.[31]

In a 2010 interview with the Maputo-based newspaper, *Verdade*, Humberto
Zaqueu, an economist at the Mozambican Debt Group (*Grupo Moçambicano
da Dívida*) offered another explanation for the Mozambican government's
acquiescent attitude toward donor requirements. He claimed that because
Mozambique is as a country always in transformation, responding to crises
and changes, it remains dependent on external actors and aid. More specifically, Zaqueu argued that the benefits of independence were not yet being
enjoyed given that the government does not allocate time for evaluation, or
a "cost and benefit study of its decisions" (Sexta, 2010). Harrison too notes
that the persistence of inequalities in the country after the civil war's end was
enabled by the ruling party's (Frelimo) rather passive accommodation of the
traditional donor industry's market-led reforms. He explained the welcoming
reception of international donor demands—as well as of international private-
sector ventures—as being tied to, among other things, the ruling elite's capacity
to profit from corrupt deals largely within the private sector, and the country's
long history of acting as a "service economy" for its larger neighbors (mostly
South Africa, but to a certain extent also Zimbabwe) (Harrison, 2002).

The translation of that service-economy inclination is evidenced in the
municipal government's positionality vis-à-vis the international community
and the central government's aspirations for economic growth via urban
infrastructure development. Despite decades of the promotion of decentralization, a recent joint report from the OECD and UNDP on development
cooperation reveals that traditional (or DAC) donors had not made significant
progress in regularly involving local governments in mutual assessments of cooperation projects. Less than half of donor countries, or 47 percent, reported
involving local governments and non-executive stakeholders in assessments

---

[31] There are several publications from Hanlon that describe both the cashew experience and others
with the international donor community. He also reports that recently the cashew industry in Mozambique has begun to recuperate from the losses it endured when the country was strong-armed into
liberalization. See his website for an extensive accounting of Mozambique's experiences, including these
publications: Hanlon (2004); Hanlon (2006); de Renzio & Hanlon (2007).

(OECD/UNDP, 2016). Given the significance of bilateral development cooperation in Mozambique—and particularly in Maputo—such admissions are devastatingly indicative of the status of city government in driving urban development. When I asked if there were ever a cooperation partner that the city refused or would prefer not to work with, Morais quipped that the Maputo Municipal Council does not refuse money, or *"nós dinheiro não recusamos."*[32] What are the implications of this reality in cities like Maputo, where the density of the donor community has grown with the rise of SSC, and where aid remains a critical resource? In other words, how does a government's social contract with its people fare when in competition with a government's financial contract with lenders, donors, or investors, whose commitment to involving local governments in assessments is equivocal at best? This scenario arguably changes the logic of accountability and the prioritization of equity that are so central to calls for decentralization, democratization, and poverty reduction across Africa and elsewhere. It also challenges the claims of solidarity, equity, and capacity-building typically advanced in international cooperation at the project level.

[32] Interview in Maputo City Hall, July 14, 2014.

3

Anything but Basic

Navigating Turbidity in Water and Sanitation Cooperation

3.1 Of Water and Waste

The ecosystem of urban international cooperation projects in the water-and-sanitation-related space I studied in Maputo included partnerships that authorities working in agencies under the CMM described to me as falling under the rubric of SSC, triangular cooperation, and more traditional cooperation partnerships with donors from the global North (see Map 3.1). Among Southern "donors"[1] active in Maputo's water-and-sanitation-related project space, two were most prominent: Brazil and China. One project, with the Brazilian city of Guarulhos, aimed at improving Maputo's solid-waste management system through efforts at helping to establish waste-picker cooperatives for those working at the city's infamous open dump in the Hulene neighborhood. Brazil was also involved via its agency for Brazilian cooperation (or ABC) in a trilateral cooperation project with the Italian Agency for Cooperation and Development (IACD) under Italy's Foreign Ministry (as well as technical support from the Cities Alliance), which targeted the upgrading of sewerage and drainage systems in Chamanchulo C,[2] one of Maputo's oldest neighborhoods and affiliated with the resistance movement that emerged to

---

[1] Neither China nor Brazil refers to its cooperation projects or state investments abroad as "donor" activities, resisting the typologies used by the broader international development community of donors. Here, I nonetheless include them as donors given the donor-like terms of their engagements, including subsidized loans and technical capacity-building as core elements in Chinese and Brazilian projects in Maputo, respectively.

[2] Within the period of my fieldwork in Maputo, the CMM decreed a change in spelling of all neighborhoods and districts to better reflect the local orthography. In this book, I adopt the orthography most used during the period of the projects I studied—some reflecting Portuguese orthography, and others the local orthography. For example, "Chamanculo" (Portuguese orthography), which I use here, has become "Nhlamankulu" in formal documents, though for the major part of the project I studied there "Chamanculo" was used. Likewise, for another cooperation project, I use "KaTembe" (African orthography), as opposed to "Catembe," as "KaTembe" was the term used for the longest duration of the project I studied.

Equity, Evaluation, and International Cooperation. Gabriella Y. Carolini, Oxford University Press.
© Gabriella Y. Carolini (2022). DOI: 10.1093/oso/9780192865489.003.0004

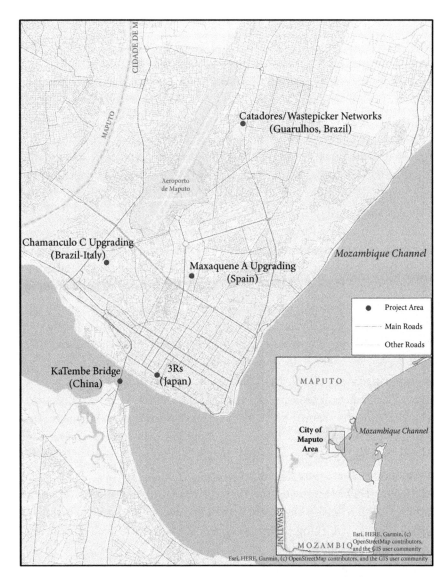

Map 3.1 International Cooperation Projects and Partners Studied in Maputo

challenge Portuguese colonists. Another SSC project was in partnership with China's Exim Bank and the China Road and Bridge Corporation (CRBC), which involved a major bridge and road infrastructure project tied to basic service provision in Maputo's KaTembe district. The project was unlike the others in several respects (as is typical in so much of China's international engagements on the continent), but mostly because it resembled a concessional contract for finance and construction of specific deliverables as opposed to a cooperation project fashioned in a traditional marriage promising both material and capacity-development improvements. A fourth project, which engaged the Spanish Catalonia chapter of Engineers without Borders (EWB) in the Maxaquene A neighborhood, also involved efforts to improve drainage and latrines with funding from the City Council of Barcelona, as well as four smaller municipalities all within the Province of Barcelona (namely Rubí, L'Hospitalet de Llobregat, Manresa, and La Roca del Vallès). The fifth project, supported by the Japanese International Cooperation Agency (JICA), centered on launching a Reduce, Reuse, and Recycle (3Rs) waste-management program, with interventions spreading across the city (though for the benefit of its visualization in Map 3.1, I positioned it in the city's downtown).

Table 3.1 provides a further snapshot of the cooperation projects explored, indicating partner organizations, locations, timelines, budgets, and targets. The projects ranged in funding volumes from a half-million US dollars to over 700 million US dollars. Projects involved at least two years of work on the ground, though this time period does not account for the preliminary explorations and pilot projects often conducted by both local and international partners, nor the evolution of projects under different stakeholders. All, however, were either in progress or in planning discussion when I began exploring cases in 2009. As of the end of 2018, all have officially closed as projects. Critically, all projects also featured the key involvement of Mozambican practitioners from the CMM, or local government, as partners. Two agencies—or "directorates"—were particularly implicated in the cooperation projects I studied, given my particular subject of interest in planning and water and sanitation. These were the Directorate of Urban Solid Waste Management and Health (DUSWMH), and the Directorate of Urban and Environmental Planning. With relatively small staff overall in these offices—and even smaller staff dedicated to working on the projects I studied (for example, there was only one staff planner in charge of overseeing the city's upgrading projects in "informal" settlements)—I was able to build a solid rapport and converse with key Mozambican experts from these two directorates (as well as others) on multiple occasions over the course of my time in Maputo. They—and their international partners—maintained that the projects reflected the needs and visions outlined in Maputo's Master Plan for Urban Solid Waste Management and Maputo's Master Structural Plan—both from 2008—the latter serving as the first physical planning document entirely prepared by Mozambican planning professionals (Andreatta & Magalhães, 2011). The approach I followed takes an expansive view of water and sanitation projects—from recycling and waste-picking to drainage and water supply—in part to ensure variation on

Table 3.1 Snapshot of Cooperation Projects Studied in Maputo

Cooperation	Targets	Site	Partners	Budget/ Dates
SSC with Brazil*	Solid-waste management and waste-picker collectives	Hulene	City of Guarulhos, Brazil; CMM	USD 243 million (2007–2012)
Trilateral cooperation with Brazil and Italy	Neighborhood upgrading of drainage and sewerage	Chamanchulo C	ABC (Brazil); IACD (Italy); Cities Alliance; CMM	USD 2.2 million (2010–2017)
SSC with China	Bridge and roads development with trunk infrastructure including water and energy	KaTembe	China Exim Bank; CRBC; CMM; Maputo Sul (public enterprise)	USD 725 million (2012–2018)
North–South cooperation with Spain	Neighborhood upgrading of drainage and latrines	Maxaquene A	EWB (Spanish chapter from Catalonia); Associação Moçambicana para o Desenvolvimento Concertado (AMDEC); Associação Sócio-Cultural Horizonte Azul (ASCHA); City councils from the Province of Barcelona; CMM	USD 486 thousand (2007–2011)
North–South cooperation with Japan	Reduce, Reuse, and Recycle (3Rs) program	City-wide pilots	JICA; CMM	USD 6.9 million (2013–2017)

* Originally, municipal staff in Guarulhos and Maputo were part of a trilateral cooperation agreement forged in 2011 with the French city of Seine-Saint-Denis, as well as Maputo's neighboring city, Matola, in the launch of a "decentralized" trilateral cooperation program supported by the national governments of France and Brazil. However, staff at the CMM working on the project referenced it as an example of SSC with Brazil to me, and indeed in their final report on the project, highlighted the objective of the project as building a partnership with Guarulhos.

the different types of partnership working on the ground across these sectors in Maputo, but also to ensure coverage of the broad spectrum of services and projects in this sector, where otherwise drinking-water service interventions tend to dominate financially.

3.2 Mobilizing Waste Pickers in Decentralized Cooperation with Brazil

> Lá tem catadores organizados, catadores que praticamente, dizia é uma empresa! Um deles fez uma presentação ... [e] no final falou uma frase: "O quê que seria do municipio ou do lixo sem catadores?" ... Eles lá vêem a questão do catador como uma profissão [no Brasil]. Então realmente a coisa que mais me impressionou e que gostariamos que o municipio de Maputo e de Matola um dia tivesse isso.

> There they have organized waste pickers, waste pickers that are practically a company! One of them made a presentation ... [and] at the end said a phrase: "What would be of the municipality or the garbage without waste pickers?" ... They see waste picking as a profession [in Brazil]. So really the thing that impressed me the most and that we would like to see in the municipality of Maputo and Matola is to one day have this.

> (Florência Francisco Martins, technical professional, Directorate for Urban Solid Waste Management, Maputo)

As detailed in the Master Plan for Solid Waste in 2008, elaborated with the assistance of the German Cooperation Agency, Maputo has long suffered from the lack of a formal comprehensive system for solid-waste management across all its neighborhoods (Conselho Municipal de Maputo, 2008). However, the production of waste therein is uneven. The city's historically wealthiest "cement" core produces twice the volume of waste as that in what are typically referred to as Maputo's suburban areas—in reality, second-ring neighborhoods of Maputo city where Mozambicans resided in largely reed homes, or casas tradicionais, during the colonial period (Conselho Municipal de Maputo, 2008). In the decade since the master plan was introduced, most of the gains in these suburban areas of the city have come in the form of pilot projects or neighborhood-scale efforts to collect waste, improve drainage, or build latrines by private, community-based organizations or NGOs, often with international roots, and of course discreet projects for which the CMM received funding and technical support from bilateral and multilateral partnerships. In some cases, these stakeholders have also worked together. For example, Water and Sanitation for the Urban Poor (WSUP), a British NGO active in the sanitation space in Maputo, has worked in the city since 2008, focusing on the improvement of pit latrines and the introduction of community-based facilities in particular. Its partnerships with the CMM, as well as with the Water and Sanitation Programme within the World Bank, have been highlighted as some of the most successful for implementing effective improvements in the quality of community-level sanitation and hygiene (WSUP—Water and Sanitation for the Urban Poor, 2018). This same narrative of success, however, has largely evaded the solid-waste sector, where the city's dependence on a single, open-air dump site in the neighborhood of Hulene has long proven both insufficient and dangerous given the environmental and health risks it poses for Hulene's residents and the informal waste pickers or *catadores* who work there to find salvageable goods in the accumulating mountains of waste.

Hulene's municipal dump, sitting nearly ten kilometers from the capital's center, was started in 1973. It welcomed waste from across the city with gates open twenty-four hours a day. Originally occupying a space of around two square kilometers, the city's dump site formally employed eleven workers when it opened, but also immediately hosted informal waste pickers (Cuna, 2004). Almost forty years later, despite repeated calls to close the site, it was still receiving roughly 700 tons of waste a day, with some mountains of waste rising up to fifty meters high (Mertanen et al, 2013). It was in this context that the CMM first entered into a partnership on solid-waste management with the Brazilian city of Guarulhos. That partnership was not born of a traditional SSC agreement but from a series of, at first, casual encounters, followed later by the participation of both cities in a broader initiative between Brazil and France calling for decentralized trilateral cooperation, which originally targeted as beneficiaries the country of Haiti as well as countries within the African continent. That initiative was the brainchild of Brazil's presidential office of federal affairs, Brazil's ABC, or cooperation agency, and France's Foreign Ministry as well as its embassy in Brazil. However, the partnership between Guarulhos and Maputo has city-level roots and city-level continuity.

Two years after they first met at a meeting of the international city advocacy group, United Cities and Local Governments, Maputo's then-mayor Eneas Comiche welcomed the mayor of Guarulhos at the time, Elói Pietá, to Mozambique, extending the latter's visit to Nairobi for the Forum for Local Authorities in 2007. When I asked Domingos Paulo Chivambo, head of solid-waste management in the CMM's DUSWMH, about the origins of Maputo's work with Guarulhos, he explained to me that during Pietá's visit to

Maputo, the two mayors established a memorandum of understanding to grow a partnership between their cities.[3] A year later, professionals from the municipal government of Guarulhos first visited Maputo to understand how it was addressing challenges in the areas of transportation, solid waste, and housing. During that same period, staff from Guarulhos also traveled to the French city of Seine-Saint-Denis to learn more about that city's wastewater treatment and sewer systems.

In 2011, the possibility of a formal—and funded—cooperation relationship began to come into view. At that time, the "decentralized cooperation" initiative supported by France and Brazil formally put out a call for proposals from cities interested in working in Haiti or countries within Africa. This also happened to be when technical staff from Maputo first visited Guarulhos— in July of 2011—as part of the intentions first laid out in by their respective cities' mayors years earlier. Responding to a request from Maputo's representatives, the city of Guarulhos invited the city of Seine-Saint-Denis to be part of their proposal to the initiative. The Brazilian federal government—via its Ministry of Foreign Affairs and the ABC—also played a supportive role in the preparation of the proposal, organizing and funding a visit in September 2011 by Guarulhos staff to both Maputo and its neighboring city, Matola, where a new, improved landfill site was set to be built to serve both cities— and enabling at last the closure of the Hulene dump site. The visit was set to help improve the proposal put forth by the cities, which indeed later won funding from the Franco-Brazilian decentralization cooperation initiative to work on solid-waste management challenges (Coordenadoria de Relações Internacionais, 2015). Within the portfolio of the project's initiatives was an effort to institutionalize an intersectoral approach to solid-waste management within the two Mozambican cities and to strengthen capacities toward that end among Mozambican staff. More specifically, the program envisioned the completion of at least two "intersectoral" solid-waste management projects in both the city of Maputo and its neighbor Matola.

Intersectoral efforts in the context of solid-waste management signified projects integrating technical capacity, environmental education, and social mobilization, but also projects that secured the participation of a wide group of stakeholders in their design. Toward this end, technical staff from Maputo's DUSWMH visited Guarulhos to understand how that city had addressed its solid-waste management challenges in recent years. During that visit to Brazil in July of 2012, staff from Maputo also first met with members of the

---

[3] Interview in Maputo, July 8, 2014.

Movimento Nacional dos Catadores no Brasil, or the National Movement of Brazilian Waste Pickers, as well as with COOPERMAPE, a cooperative of waste pickers from the city of Embu, which sits roughly fifty kilometers outside of Guarulhos. Members of COOPERMAPE explained that their work as a cooperative had begun when the dump they worked in individually was closed—a point of interest to staff from Maputo who were aware of the problems with the Hulene dump in their own city and were already working with partner NGOs on how to improve the lives of waste pickers in Maputo. What staff from Maputo learned was that key to Guarulhos's intersectoral approach to solid-waste management was the involvement of the Brazilian federal government as well as the participation of the city's Secretariat for Development and Social Assistance and the Secretariat for Public Services. In short, intersectoral efforts translated into interscalar efforts and cross-agency coordination in Guarulhos. More specifically, Guarulhos' Secretariat for Development and Social Assistance and the Secretariat for Public Services were involved in mobilizing and supporting waste pickers and helping them form a cooperative after the close of the dump from which they worked. They also managed income transfer and social support programs for waste pickers, in addition to providing family assistance and training workshops. The visit of members from a waste-picker collective from the city of São Paulo, the *Rede CataSampa de São Paulo*, manifested the importance of this multi-faceted approach to strengthening actors within the solid-waste management system. They were explicit in explaining how important municipal and federal government cooperation was to them, materially but also in terms of bolstering their self-dignity. In presenting their most significant recent achievements, members of the São Paulo cooperative told the visitors from Mozambique that they were most proud of two wins: their participation in the city's master planning document and the recognition of "waste picker" as a profession in the Brazilian Occupation Classification system, thereby legally guaranteeing waste pickers' social-security rights, such as retirement benefits (Coordenadoria de Relações Internacionais, 2015).

While efforts in Maputo had already been under way to improve the solid-waste management system, the macro context and intersectoral support clearly presented in Brazil's experience was different from the context of Mozambique. Maputo's master plan for solid waste encourages recycling as a major avenue by which to reduce waste that was otherwise flooding the already full capacity of the Hulene dump. The operationalization of recycling, however, was heavily dependent on small-scale operations. The CMM held partnerships with three relatively small private organizations which work at limited scales within the city, including Recicla (which collects hard plastic),

Amor (which collects cardboard and cans), and Fertiliza (which composts organic waste). All three organizations employ individuals who previously worked independently as waste pickers, but all three also have links with non-profit organizations. In addition, Pagalata is a Mozambican company that buys recyclable waste for international export. It was not until staff returned from visiting Guarulhos that they began to make efforts at also mobilizing the self-organization of waste-picker cooperatives in Maputo.

I was very excited about the possibilities of the waste-picker cooperative in Maputo, having witnessed myself how empowered and organized such groups had become in Brazil. Yet Chivambo, who had joined one of the trips to Guarulhos from Maputo, admitted to me that when he first heard that he was to join the mission trip to Guarulhos, it was not made clear to him why staff from Maputo were going. As he told me:

> Many times projects appear; we acquire projects many times without thinking about what it is that we want, at the base.... I knew one week that I had to go to Guarulhos, and asked what is the problem [and why are we going], and the answer was "oh, I don't know—a project about waste pickers." It was not clear what we were going to discuss there, what was the way in which we could reach the results we wanted. And this, many times weakens our projects. We need a clear definition first of what we want. Then we can present what are possible solutions.[4]

Despite his misgivings, Chivambo reported that his directorate organized two public meetings when he returned to Maputo to discuss the possibility of forming waste-picker cooperatives and to explain the potential benefits of cooperative work, inviting waste pickers themselves and nonprofit organizations like *Associazione Internazionale Volontari Laici* (LVIA), an Italian NGO working in Maputo on environmental-education-related programming, and *Meninos da Rua*, an organization that worked with street children in Maputo. From these meetings, LVIA offered to take charge of the next steps in organizing waste pickers, with the directorate taking on a supportive role in facilitating contacts. LVIA launched a pilot project for a waste-picker cooperative in the neighborhood of Sommerschield II. Their mobilization strategy involved offering waste pickers protective equipment for their work as well as equipment that would facilitate the transportation of waste they collected. I tried to understand why, despite all the interagency coordination and leadership that

---

[4] Interview in Maputo, July 16, 2014.

was witnessed in Guarulhos, the directorate did not keep the effort to mobilize waste pickers under its own portfolio. Chivambo explained to me that "we as the government found it difficult to do that, but they [LVIA] were able to advance the organizing process."[5]

Indeed, I later learned that LVIA was critical to the establishment of Recicla and Fertiliza in Maputo, thus explaining their willingness to take on the mobilization of waste pickers on a broader scale for the city. Despite their efforts, however, the waste-picker cooperatives were not working in Maputo. Florência Francisco Martins, a DUSWMH technical professional in Maputo focusing on monitoring and evaluation within the solid-waste sector, further explained the difficulties that they were encountering on the ground in Maputo, noting that while ongoing efforts in Maputo were admirable, there were major structural and individual-level differences between the experience of waste-picker cooperatives in Brazil and those they were trying to mobilize in Mozambique. First, she explained to me that "we [in Maputo] have a lot of waste pickers but ours are very dispersed. They work individually … [and] are not used to working in cooperatives, [so] many abandoned the group. The group still exists, but I don't know how many waste pickers are actually part of it."[6] Luisa Langa, the head of monitoring at Maputo's DUSWMH concurred, adding that while Maputo is advanced compared with other cities in Mozambique, the level of education and mobilization that staff from Maputo saw among the members of waste-picker cooperatives they met with in Brazil was not present within Maputo.[7] Secondly, both Francisco and Langa cited the lack of a national law recognizing waste picking as a formal profession with associated social-security guarantees, as in the Brazilian case.

It was clear by the end of the initial project in 2012 that staff at the directorate in Maputo did not feel they had the proper tools or context in which to help establish the waste-picker cooperatives that were so central to the purpose of their exchange with Guarulhos. As Tvedten and Candiracci (2018) hint, however, the sense of helplessness felt at the level of the directorate may also find root in the lack of political support for the subject of sanitation among the urban poor at higher levels of municipal governance. They argue that the municipal government takes a very neoliberal, technical perspective on waste, noting that a *Vereador*, or political appointee, in the CMM government argued that "the missing link to an effective solid-waste management in the informal settlements [of Maputo] is not the municipal system as such but the need

---

[5] Interview in Maputo, July 16, 2014.
[6] Interview in Maputo, July 15, 2014.
[7] Interview in Maputo, July 15, 2014.

to 'educate the people and make them produce less waste'"(Tvedten & Candiracci, 2018: 637). Together with the broader structural and individual-level constraints facing the effort to mobilize waste-picker cooperatives in Maputo, the municipal political climate is not one likely to see waste pickers as part of a critical solution to solid-waste challenges in the city. As such, it is not surprising that staff in the directorate were, at the end of 2012, looking for other avenues of continuing cooperation with Guarulhos in particular. Indeed, the directorate's internal report on the "decentralized cooperation" initiative to the CMM stated that a partnership with Guarulhos was its main objective, largely ignoring the initial involvement of Seine-Sainte-Denis (Direcção dos Serviços Municipais de Salubridade e Cemitérios, 2012). Chivambo lamented, however, that even while "Guarulhos was the most indicated as the developer of the project with us ... there has been no evaluation—not with Guarulhos, nor with Sainte Denis. It seems like we abandoned them, but it is not the case. We do not want to abandon before knowing the results of the project."[8] Nonetheless, while Guarulhos remained involved in exchanges with Mozambique, its work shifted to cooperation with other cities like Nampula, while Maputo's cooperation was extended to the Brazilian city of Belo Horizonte, both through yet another "decentralized cooperation" initiative focused on urban planning and budgeting, organized between 2013 and 2015 by United Cities and Local Governments, as well as the local municipal administrators' networks in both Brazil and Mozambique (Bennaton et al, 2015). Solid waste, it appears, fell off the decentralized cooperation radar. Indeed, Maputo's dump site at Hulene remains open, with waste pickers still working and living near the site. It is, however, the target of yet another cooperation agreement—this time signed with Japan's Ministry of the Environment in February 2019, aiming to transform the open dump into a semi-aerobic landfill (Ngulela, 2019).

3.3 All the Right Parts: Trilateral Cooperation with Brazil in Chamanculo

Acho que se perdeu uma oportunidade ... se passou muito tempo sem ter feito uma missão [mesmo] com todos os parceiros.
I think an opportunity was lost ... a long time went by without having accomplished the project objectives [even] with all partners.
    (Silvia Cabrita, Municipal Project Coordinator, Chamanculo, Maputo)

---

[8] Interview in Maputo, July 16, 2014.

From a planning perspective, when I began studying cooperation on the ground in Maputo, I harbored the most hope for an upgrading project I had heard about from several different sources. Colleagues in the planning department at University of Eduardo Mondlane, staff in Maputo's planning office, Brazilians I met working in the city, and friends from Maputo all related the particular historical importance of the neighborhood of Chamanculo in Maputo, and those with a connection to planning work noted that a "trilateral" upgrading project with Brazilian and Italian partners was unfolding in the neighborhood. Chamanculo had at one time been home to many of the resistance fighters in the war for independence from Portugal, including for a time a young, pre-presidential Samora Machel. It seemed to me that such historical references would help conjure resources and incentives to effectively implement plans to improve the living conditions in that neighborhood, where drainage, sewerage, and other basic amenities were lacking. The reality of course is always different from the dream, and I found myself half amused and fully intrigued when leadership in the Brazilian embassy in Maputo encouraged me to focus my attention elsewhere. I of course did not.

While the project in Chamanculo C—a subsection of the neighborhood—was formally termed a "trilateral technical cooperation project" in the agreement signed with the CMM, in reality it was more like a quadrilateral (or quinquelateral—depending on how one counts) project on the ground. Beyond the local government and residents in Maputo, the project counted as partners on the Brazilian side the ABC (Brazilian Cooperation Agency), Ministry of Cities, and *Caixa Econômica Federal* (Brazil's economic development bank). In addition, on the Italian side, the Ministry of Foreign Affairs was a sponsor of the project, and while not formally a project signatory, the real Italian presence in Chamanculo C was manifest in the work of the Association of Volunteers in International Cooperation (AVSI), an Italian development and humanitarian NGO. In addition, the Cities Alliance—a global partnership between the World Bank and UN-Habitat with country members, was a strong driving force in setting up the cooperation as well as in the design of an "integrated" upgrading project in Chamanculo. Funding for the project was split between the foreign counterparties, with the Italian government covering 58 percent, the Brazilian ABC 25 percent, and Cities Alliance 17 percent. Given the project's focus on upgrading, it also aligned well with and received financial support from the World Bank's *ProMaputo* program, which was supporting the CMM with major investments in financial administrative reforms and basic service provision. The origins of the project, however—much like the others I studied in Maputo—involved a deeper history with a wider network of actors than those immediately apparent.

In 2006, during the first meeting of the Council for Brazilian-Italian Co-operation (*Conselho de Cooperação Brasil-Itália*) in Rome, the parties agreed to work together in trilateral cooperation with another lower-income country (Ministério do Desenvolvimento Regional, 2016). Mauricio Monteiro Vieira, a Brazilian working as a consultant to the Political Director (or *Vereador*) of Urban Planning and the Environment, explained to me that around the same time, the Cities Alliance began pursuing a pilot project in Maputo, banking on its successful work with AVSI, the Italian NGO, on slum up-grading in Brazil. The Cities Alliance provided the CMM with a preparatory grant to develop a project in Maputo based on the experience it supported in the Brazilian state of Bahia. That upgrading project—launched in 2001 in the informal neighborhood of Alagados in the Bahian city of Salvador—was dear to Cities Alliance as one of the first projects it had undertaken after the organization was established in 1999 (Cities Alliance, 2008). It too was supported by the Italian government, in addition to the Cities Alliance and the World Bank, while also counting on the support of the State of Bahia Urban Development Company and AVSI, particularly to integrate public par-ticipation in slum upgrading plans. In its formal report on the experience in Alagados, the Cities Alliance noted that the "real lessons of Alagados, and the state of Bahia, are those of partnership and consistency ... the consistent sup-port of the government of Italy, the flexibility and the skills displayed by the public authorities, the presence of AVSI in the community, and the political maturity shown by all parties provided the support that the slum dwellers needed" (Cities Alliance, 2008:3). With almost all the same actors and the same approach, Cities Alliance very much hoped to repeat that integrated and consistent, yet flexible and contextually-informed model of slum upgrading in Maputo.

Of course, within the city of Maputo, stakeholders were also independently working on plans to upgrade informal settlements. By 2005, the director and founder of the planning program at the University of Eduardo Mond-lane, José Forjaz, was already conducting a rapid diagnostic survey of water and sanitation needs in Chamanculo for the CMM. By the time Cesar Cun-guara, a planner I repeatedly spoke with in Maputo's Directorate of Urban Planning and the Environment, joined the directorate in 2008, there was a strong push to implement a pilot project in Chamanculo C based on the rapid assessment conducted by the university. This push grew when, in 2009, a new mayor, David Simango, was looking to scale up upgrading efforts in water and sanitation and to leverage a national plan announced that year for all informal settlements in the country, launched by the Ministry for the Coordination of Environmental Action (*Ministério para a Coordenação da Acção Ambiental*) and the National Directorate of Land-Use Planning (*Direcção Nacional de Planeamento e Ordenamento Territorial*). Cunguara noted that having Mozambican national ministries indicated in the effort to upgrade settlements like Chamanculo informed the city's connection to Brazil, whose federal government had also signed an accord with Mozambique's national government in 2007 to support urban development in the latter country. Indeed, eight Mozambicans—including a technical expert on infrastructure development, one community member, and six professionals associated with the Directorate of Urban Planning and the Environment (including Cunguara)—were sent to Brazil in 2009 to learn more about how the latter country organized slum upgrading programs. By June of 2010, Mozambican staff were enrolling in a distance-learning course via Skype offered by Brazil on slum upgrading, and by September of that year, the CMM, with the Cities Alliance's preparatory grant, put forth the proposal for the "trilateral" project in Chamanculo, signed by all partners. The proposal was envisioned as the third phase of work in Chamanculo C, following from the rapid diagnostic survey in the first phase and the pilot project launched by the CMM in the second.

From the perspective of residents, by the time the trilateral project with Brazil, Italy, and the Cities Alliance arrived in 2010, five years had already passed with city-level interventions in the neighborhood. They were beginning to show signs of "development fatigue"—that very particular sense of losing an anticipated hope for change. The expectation of now also receiving international partners and financing for improvements reignited residents' hopes to see material improvements on the ground. At the start of the trilateral project, the neighborhood of Chamanculo C was home to a population of over 26,000 residents and hosted sixteen community water points, but only five of the points were well functioning. Drainage on the unpaved streets was also a major obstacle for the mobility of residents, as when the rainy season arrived, rainfall often left the streets flooded and difficult to pass, especially for vulnerable groups like children and the elderly (Conselho Municipal de Maputo, 2010). For these reasons, the trilateral project's material priorities were to pave streets, introduce drainage systems, plant trees, and build new potable water points (*fontenários*), using the same coupling of physical and socio-economic interventions that had worked so well in Alagados now in Chamanculo C. To do this work, different responsibilities were assigned to two teams: an urbanism team, led by Brazil, would lead the work on physical planning and design interventions, while the social-action team would be led by Mozambicans trained by two Brazilian social workers and Italians working with AVSI in Maputo. The social-action team was to work with AVSI within Chamanculo C in an effort to gain the trust of community members and engage them in the planning process to understand their priorities and help translate those into actionable items under the purview of the project.

Despite the effort to integrate both social and physical outreach objectives within the material goals for Chamanculo C's upgrading, the trilateral project almost immediately began to run into problems. As Flávia Nhassengo, a Mozambican professional working on the AVSI team, related, at first residents suspected that the trilateral project's objective was to relocate them to a different neighborhood—and indeed, that is what technical professionals like herself presumed to be the best choice for residents.[9] However, Nhassengo and others soon learned that residents had no desire to be resettled away from their neighborhood, despite its substandard infrastructures, because their location right next to the "cement" core of the city was ideal for work. The secretary of the neighborhood,[10] Zeferino Chioco concurred.[11] He noted that during the early pilot work in Chamanculo C, the widening of a street to facilitate mobility in the neighborhood required some resettlement of homes. As such, when the trilateral project began, residents presumed more resettlements would be required and were very resistant to the project. It took AVSI's social-action team several attempts in community meetings and door-to-door efforts to better communicate with residents that the intent of the project was to upgrade the neighborhood as opposed to evicting its members, even though further resettlements would be required for the installation of drainage pipes.

The communication challenges between project administrators and residents represented only one of the difficulties of implementing the objectives in the trilateral project. The administrative management of the project was similarly troubled. UNDP managed Brazil's financial contributions to the trilateral project—as is typical in Brazilian cooperation. Indeed, the external management of funds is one of the ways by which Brazil insists it is not a traditional donor, but instead a technical cooperation partner, as it typically does not provide direct funding to cooperation projects, but instead pays for its technical assistants to participate in projects via its contributions managed by UNDP. In the case of Chamanculo C, the CMM's coordinator for the project, Silvia

---

[9] Interview in Maputo, January 13, 2015.

[10] Maputo's local governing system includes seven district secretaries representing each of the districts of Maputo city within the CMM. Within each district are several neighborhoods or *bairros*. The secretary of the neighborhood, or *secretário do bairro*, is the main linchpin between neighborhood residents and the district secretary. Within a neighborhood like Chamanculo C, which is part of the district of Nlhamankulu, there are also further hierarchies of representation. For example, Chamanculo C hosts many quarters, or *quarteirões*, comprised of about fifty houses each, which in turn is split into groups of ten houses, each of which is represented by a *chefe* or leader.

[11] Interview in Maputo, January 16, 2015.

Cabrita, explained that Brazil's arrangement with UNDP translated into long delays and no local ownership over the project when it came to contracting work for qualified professionals.[12] The entire hiring process for planning project professionals essentially transpired outside the auspices and influence of the local government in Maputo. At most, the CMM was involved in writing the terms of reference for the work, which they then sent to Brazil's ABC, which in turn passed on the contract request to UNDP, which held its own selection process independent of Maputo's authorities and local partners. Secretary Chioco also felt the CMM's legitimacy was belittled by the fact that international partners, and in particular the Italian cooperation agency, insisted that feasibility and impact studies needed to be conducted in Chamanculo C, despite the fact that the CMM had already performed such studies in its first-phase intervention in the neighborhood.[13] Thus residents were obliged to again participate in diagnostic studies that delineated their priorities and needs. However, Secretary Chioco expressed frustrations about the ways in which negotiations between the CMM and international partners had similarly ignored the neighborhood-levels of government in Chamanculo C, as well as the potential to train and hire local residents—especially among the youth—to conduct the new surveys required. He recounted how during the initial meetings, the AVSI coordinator from Italy had presumed that the agreement for working in Chamanculo C with the CMM was sufficient, and that further agreement with the secretary himself was unnecessary—noting that in Italy, such hierarchies within neighborhoods did not exist. However, Secretary Chioco explained that "in Mozambique, this exists. We even have traditional leaders!"[14] Unlike the CMM's relationship with UNDP, Secretary Chioco's insistence that the trilateral project better integrate him and other local neighborhood leadership in the process of planning and implementing reforms was eventually honored by AVSI. However, these negotiations delayed project implementation.

The frustrations in building an effective team for the physical planning work in Chamanculo C were further aggravated by financial woes that hit the project. Cabrita bemoaned the fact that the Brazilian planning professionals hired also demanded salaries that were higher than those anticipated in the original budget; as such the project was only able to hire two Brazilian urbanists rather than three.[15] Of the two Brazilian urbanists hired, there was at least one defection—though most of the professionals I interviewed demurred

[12] Interview in Maputo, January 14, 2015.
[13] Interview in Maputo, January 16, 2015.
[14] Interview in Maputo, January 18, 2015.
[15] Interview in Maputo, January 14, 2015.

from explaining precisely why the individual left on negative terms. The ensuing recalibration of the team meant even more time lost. Finally, Brazil's 2013 announcement that it would not be able to meet its financial obligations to the project drove the project to an unanticipated, if temporary, halt. As Cabrita explained, the physical planning element for which the Brazilian team was responsible was one of the two major efforts of the overall trilateral project. In the wake of that announcement, other partners scrambled to raise the funds for the planning work that Brazil would no longer provide. The Italian Cooperation Agency in Maputo eventually stepped in with supplementary financial support. However, the project's financial crisis engendered another loss of time and, most critically, of community confidence in the upgrading work to be done.

In early 2015, five years after the trilateral project agreement was signed, the planning work in Chamanculo began in earnest. During that period, the most significant effort introduced by the project was its "prepping" of residents—or simply the process of getting the community residents to both understand and agree with a set of project objectives. By the end of that time, however, what had been a trilateral project in name had translated into a bilaterally supported NGO project in function. From the original plan, a main entry road to Chamanculo C, Avenida Amaral Matos, was paved, a new drainage channel over one kilometer in length was installed, and the community center was rehabilitated—all largely through the city's partnership with AVSI, supported by the funding from the Italian cooperation. The project's resettlement planning was then outsourced to the Scandinavian engineering, economics, and environmental science consultancy, COWI, which long had a presence in Maputo, while water points were introduced largely in conjunction with the British NGO, WSUP. In addition, AVSI worked beyond the scope of the original priorities envisioned in 2010 for Chamanculo C, rehabilitating public spaces, like a local soccer field, as well as creating new children's playgrounds, with funding from the City Council of Barcelona and in partnership with Architects without Borders.

3.4 A Bridge that Carries Water? SSC with China

[P] Quais sao as mudanças que voce gostaria ver no bairro [em relação à ponte]?
[A] Agua canalizada, mais luz, e transporte.
[Q] What changes would you like to see in your neighborhood [in relation to the bridge]?

[A] Household water connections, more lighting, and transportation.
(Resident, Guachene, KaTembe)

The first time I traveled to KaTembe, one of Maputo's municipal districts sitting across the Maputo Bay from the city's mainland, I joined a long line of residents awaiting the day's last scheduled ferry boat departure from Maputo's *baixa*, or downtown. Once our ferry had docked, what seemed like at least one hundred other residents and I traveled along the dirt roads off the port seeking our way home. We were met by modest food stalls, a few awaiting minibuses or *chapas*, and, for the most part, the darkness of night. I was lucky to have to walk only a mile or so to reach my destination on one of the few main roads where there were occasional street lamps to light the way. My own journey from Maputo's cement core to my new home in KaTembe had taken only about an hour and a half. Others, I soon realized, had much longer routes to take to reach their homes in what was ostensibly Maputo's largest and most rural district. These long journey times were often offered up by authorities I began speaking to as a major rationale for a planned bridge connecting KaTembe to mainland Maputo. I soon learned, however, that the plan for a bridge connecting Maputo to its own territory across the bay had a much longer history. Those studying the Portuguese colonial period offered the view that the Portuguese actually intended to build the bridge in the mid-twentieth century. Other accounts positioned the bridge as a central aim of the newly independent state of Mozambique, as part of the unification plan advanced by Samora Machel, the first Mozambican president—ensuring that the country's people from its northernmost provinces would be connected physically but also socially and politically with those in its most southern, dominated by the capital.

Despite the multiple rationales and histories I learned about plans for the bridge during my first few years of returning to fieldwork in KaTembe and riding boats zigzagging across Maputo Bay, like many others I met in KaTembe and elsewhere in Maputo, I did not think its realization was imminent.[16] The dock at KaTembe's port showed persistent signs of damage and was often in reconstruction. A second large ferry boat had been added to the normally scheduled rounds of the first, and it seemed unlikely that the bridge—an infrastructure project with what was presumably a large price tag—would be prioritized before the city's other basic needs. That perspective changed dramatically in 2012 when news accounts began reporting that the China Exim

---

[16] Some of the information and analysis presented here on the KaTembe bridge project was first published in Carolini (2017).

Bank—China's key state-owned policy bank funding many of the country's cooperation projects—had agreed to finance the project as part of its growing portfolio of infrastructure cooperation in Mozambique. Soon, work sites in KaTembe were being scouted for the CRBC—one of four major state-owned engineering and development enterprises (with origins in China's Foreign Aid Office of the Ministry of Communication) that won the contract to build the road and bridge to KaTembe. By 2013, I was excited but anxious about what the bridge would mean for KaTembe's future. I had met with the engineer charged with overseeing KaTembe's water and sanitation infrastructures, Manuel Nhone, several times over the course of my visits to KaTembe, but it was only in 2013 that he explained to me that the long-anticipated bridge was really being built and why it would be good news for KaTembe. He told me that it would carry much needed utilities and services to the district, including—I thought strangely—greater volumes of water.[17]

Water had preoccupied my concerns in Maputo early on due to the simple fact that I had taken up residence in KaTembe, where access to it was rather limited and relatively expensive compared with other neighborhoods in Maputo's mainland region. In a household survey I led in KaTembe's Guachene neighborhood, for example, respondents reported paying twice the rate that was charged in the rest of the city.[18] Household-level water connections were also among the main benefits they hoped new infrastructure would bring to their neighborhood. I was skeptical, however, about a water-carrying bridge. I knew from Nhone and engineers I spoke with at the *Aguas de Região de Maputo*,[19] the city's water provider, that while this was one of the central propositions of the bridge, it would also translate into less water and less water pressure for Maputo's business core and central neighborhoods, which seemed an unlikely proposition.

My skepticism in retrospect seems well founded, but for different reasons than I initially imagined. Maputo Sul, a state-owned development enterprise created in 2010 by the government of Mozambique, was charged with steering the building and management of the KaTembe bridge and the roads from Maputo to KaTembe, Boa Vista, and Ponta do Ouro, a beach town in the

---

[17] Interview with Engineer Nhone in the Municipal District Headquarters of KaTembe, August 9, 2013.

[18] More specifically, households in KaTembe paid 2–3 Mozambican meticais (MZN) for a 20- or 25-liter jerry can, whereas residents in other low-income neighborhoods in Maputo's mainland paid 1 MZN per jerry can.

[19] At the water utility, I spoke with the engineer Gonçalves Elias, Armindo João, and Arvone Tivane on multiple occasions in 2013 and 2014, during which time questions about the implementation of plans for the KaTembe–Maputo bridge were still ongoing.

southernmost tip of Mozambique, bordering with South Africa. Maputo Sul was the linchpin organization in developing the bridge project, overseeing its design and managing its planning and execution. It hired the Portuguese engineering consultancy Betar, which contracted the creation of a master plan for KaTembe from another Portuguese design firm, Promontorio. The new vision of KaTembe in these plans, endorsed by Maputo Sul, the national government, and CMM, anticipates a new residential population reaching over 400,000 people—compared with the just over 20,000 that currently occupied the district (Macauhub, 2012). What became clearer as plans for the district's development were made public was that while the bridge would indeed foster the extension of infrastructures and services to KaTembe, these improvements would also generate a rush to secure land. By the middle of 2011, because of the flood of new requests for land rights in KaTembe, the local office temporarily suspended the issuance of new land rights or *Direito do Uso e Aproveitamento de Terra* (DUATs). Further, much as Eduful and Hooper (2015) write about gentrification in the aftermath of a resource boom in Ghana, Maputo's KaTembe district is—for the first time since Mozambican independence—experiencing development-induced displacement and gentrification.

In community meetings I attended in 2013 and 2014, residents in KaTembe's Guachene neighborhood complained when they began learning about how the bridge project would affect them. These residents accounted for roughly 20 percent of KaTembe's overall population, and lived in some of KaTembe's most densely built-up, but also unplanned, environments. As a result of the bridge project, and their ideal location in proximity to KaTembe's dock, these residents' homes were targeted for displacement, which also meant the loss of their prized *machambas* (or small plots of agricultural land) upon which livelihoods depended. When construction on the bridge began in earnest in 2014, households there, as well as in Maputo's city-center side of the bridge, were forced to start moving. They were offered roughly 170 USD for every 300 square meters of land they occupied. By March 2015, already thirty households in KaTembe's Guachene neighborhood had been moved to KaTembe's Chamissava neighborhood—deep in the district's more rural landscape (Selemane, 2015). Overall, as the bridge's construction was completed in 2018, over 200 households were resettled, but many more were still facing problems with ensuring their secure tenure in KaTembe. As many long-term residents in KaTembe never secured the formal right, or DUAT, to occupy their land, they were now forced to compete with others newly interested in the district and requesting DUATs from the government. For those who had already lived in KaTembe for decades, working *machambas* and cultivating produce, this predicament was especially insidious (Emidio, 2018). The KaTembe district representative in CMM, António Tovela, insisted that residents' complaints did not have legal standing. He explained at a public meeting that while the legal right to land is afforded to those who occupy it for more than ten years, the law does not preclude the right of the government to remove residents from land for the public good (Emidio, 2018).

On the Maputo city-center side of the bridge project, residents in the Malanga neighborhood faced similar difficulties. Of the over 800 families displaced in the course of bridge and on-ramp road construction, the first group of residents who agreed to move were compensated roughly 3,600 USD and given land in the towns of Tenga or Mahubo, both in the district of Boane, west of the capital but still in Maputo province (da Silva, 2016). However, later groups noted they were not as well paid. Echoing the complaints often heard about such resettlement schemes, 400 of the households that moved from Malanga to Boane say that they were promised a school and a hospital in their new neighborhood of Mahocha but that these do not yet exist—forcing them to leave children with old neighbors in their former neighborhood of Malanga in order for them to attend school. Furthermore, they lacked basic necessities like water and electricity, and complained of the loss of livelihoods, as transportation costs into the capital ruled out commuting to work. Others in Malanga faced difficulties in the wake of the bridge's construction as well. Those who worked as vendors in the neighborhood's market space, *Mercado Nwakakana*, were harassed by city police and Maputo Sul, which removed their stalls only to find vendors again trying to rebuild them on sites within the construction area up until the bridge opened. After its inauguration in November of 2018, vendors have continued to try selling their wares on the bridge and its ramps, but have been repeatedly chased out by police.

The rationale for the bridge project, originally conceived of as enhancing opportunities for growth and development, is thus becoming clearer in practice. Despite the hopes that it would carry amenities like more water to KaTembe, its implementation has endangered water rights more than accommodating them for households who lived with vulnerabilities on either side of the bridge. In Chamissava, KaTembe's district that houses newly resettled households from Guachene, access to piped water for households and for agricultural work remains a major obstacle (Noticias, 2017). And in Boane, where residents from Malanga were moved, residents noted that water provided by Maputo Sul to their new residences was not potable. Instead, they have paid as much as 1000 *meticais novos* (MZN) to secure 500 liters of

potable water, whereas they used to pay 1 MZN for 20 liters in the city of Maputo (International Research & Exchanges Board, 2016). Meanwhile, the plan
for KaTembe's development into a "modern" new city continues, envision-
ing three phases of development to execute the introduction of new housing
developments, tourism, and leisure activities—including a water-hungry golf
course and a light industrial area. With the bridge now complete, these development phases are beginning in earnest. The repeat, incumbent mayor, Eneas
Comiche, made clear in November 2019 that, "Katembe is the municipality's
big bet, responding to the demographic explosion and the promotion of private initiatives, whether in terms of housing, urban agriculture, industry or
commercial activity; [it] will allow for an increase in investment" (Pila, 2019).
Indeed, by August of 2019, the city had already issued 6,000 new DUATs for
KaTembe, an unprecedented number. Long-time residents of KaTembe are
taking note. Already bitten by poor compensation for homes and land that
were cleared for the bridge project, residents are now balking at the toll costs.
In May 2019, residents of KaTembe took the unusual step of issuing a direct
petition to the National Assembly against the high costs of the bridge toll, complaining that they are paying for the bridge's construction but that it benefits
tourists more than residents who cannot afford the fee for light vehicles to
cross (Redação, 2019). However, no concessions have yet been made toward
long-term residents.

Although the financing of the project and its implementation have been
the source of much anxiety over the years of government planning and then
construction of the bridge, very little public engagement has come from the
two entities directly implicated in these areas. China Exim Bank stepped into
the KaTembe project after the Portuguese government rescinded its promise
of a loan for the bridge, as it faced its own fiscal crisis. Despite its role in
saving the KaTembe bridge project from its historical state in purgatory,
little information was forthcoming about why China Exim Bank provided the
loans in a context where their repayment potential has been repeatedly questioned in public discourses. Maputo Sul too was never precise about what data
were used to calculate how the 725 million USD project's loans from the Exim
Bank will be repaid in twenty to twenty-five years. The only indications of
how funds would be raised for debt service reflect the national government's
intention to create public–private partnerships with concession contracts for
the bridge and road network's management (Macauhub, 2018). However, just
months after the bridge was inaugurated, the national government was forced
to liquidate Maputo Sul, which was meant to manage this work (Macauhub,
2019). And while the National Roads Administration, which has taken over the

bridge's management since the closing of Maputo Sul, shows no indication of changing its tolls upward or downward to accommodate residents' complaints or debt service, the tolls as they stand are insufficient to cover the debt as well as the maintenance costs. Already, the first year of projected use of the bridge has generated insufficient revenues (Alfredo, 2019). At best, toll revenues help cover maintenance costs, which are already accumulating (Alfredo, 2019).

Despite the volume of funds on the line, neither China Exim Bank nor the CRBC engaged in the local processes of implementation, communication, or management required for the bridge's realization. Instead, Chinese partners acted in a way that private-equity firms might have, rather than engaging in the type of damage-control measures that other international cooperation partners pursued at length through participatory processes and planning in neighborhoods they worked in. That is to say, China Exim and CRBC have mostly outsourced potential local entanglements to local stakeholders themselves. For example, before the bridge's construction was completed in 2018, over 4000 Mozambican workers that the CRBC contracted went on strike (O País, 2018). Despite CRBC's stated "commitment to the host countries' government and people to do a good job in employee training and technology transfer,"[20] CRBC could not effectively adjudicate the demands of the striking Mozambican workers, and had Maputo Sul intervene with workers on its behalf to end the strike and move forward with the final weeks of construction. Interestingly, perhaps to allay the fears often incited by media reports about the quality of Chinese construction, CRBC also outsourced quality control and management, engaging a German firm, Gauff Engineering, as a consultant on CRBC's bridge work.

This distancing from local politics in its SSC project in Maputo is typical of the type of SSC in which China engages across Africa and elsewhere, but it is atypical compared with other international cooperation partners from both the North and South who have made direct efforts to engage in local processes of implementation and engagement with communities. Unlike the latter, China's cooperation in Maputo comes solely in the form of loans or infrastructure contracts with Chinese state-owned corporations or banks. Much as China's bilateral loans surpass those of any other country in Mozambique— for six years in a row (Caldeira, 2019b)—the scale of the Exim Bank's loans represented almost three times the funding involved in the next largest project I studied (namely with Brazil). This largely financial and materialist approach

---

[20] The quote comes from CRBC's explanation of its commitment to protecting employees' interests, accessed at https://www.crbc.com/site/crbcEN/ResponsibilityManagement/index.html?id=629efe42-9861-45ae-ac93-11951d80ae22.

employed by Chinese SSC on the ground in Maputo meant that China made no project-level claims regarding things such as capacity building, technological advancement, and learning in the KaTembe bridge project, although such objectives are typical of the other partnerships in international cooperation projects I studied in the city. Perhaps, then, it is not surprising that of the projects considered here, the material results of China's SSC project in KaTembe were the most readily apparent (i.e., a bridge has been built, with roads adjoining), while the procedural and cognitive goals centered on aspects such as learning, equity, and solidarity often claimed in development projects were entirely lacking with respect to how vulnerable residents and workers were engaged or simply ignored. Here, with the exception of labor relations with the CRBC, the rationales between Chinese stakeholders and the Mozambican public sector were not so much conflicting as complementary and capitalist. In line with China's fairly unique approach to international cooperation (and foreign policy), it did not get involved in what it would call the internal conflicts that arose between affected residents and Maputo Sul and CMM, even though its financing and work on the ground were critical to the bridge project and accompanying roadways development.

3.5 Multi-level Discord in Cooperation with Spanish Partners

> *Epa! Aqui na minha casa parece que tem que ter uma rua.*
> Whoa! Here where my house is, it looks like there is to be a street.
> (Alvaro Garcia, Engineers without Borders project coordinator,
> paraphrasing residents in Maxaquene A)

Maxaquene A sits just beyond the northern boundary of Maputo's cement core and just southeast of Maputo's international airport. Like the other neighborhoods which hosted international cooperation projects, its population sits at around 23,000. And much like other international cooperation projects I studied on the ground, the cooperation project in Maxaquene A involved a portfolio of upgrading efforts, such as the introduction of drainage and road improvements. Unlike other projects, however, this one was largely funded at the subnational level with support of the City Council of Barcelona. Barcelona's relationship with the CMM was one of the few that authorities in Maputo identified as ideal. Head of International Relations, Natacha Morais, praised Barcelona's steadfastness as a partner, noting that like other levels of government in Spain, Barcelona apportioned 0.7 percent of its annual budget for international assistance programs.[21] This financial predictability made Barcelona, in Morais's view, the ideal international partner. Felip Roca Blasco, director of Barcelona's Department of International Relations and Co-operation, further explained to me that Barcelona's approach to international cooperation was to identify its particular added value, vis-à-vis other levels of international cooperation led by the state or by regions.[22] In this respect, it pursued work in urban planning and its approach centered on building city-to-city, as opposed to government-to-government, partnerships. Blasco was reflecting upon that fact that Barcelona's partnerships in other cities often invoked work with civil society as well as governments. This approach was reflected in the work it supported in Maxaquene A through the Catalan chapter of EWB. Previously, it had supported the Catalan chapter of EWB in Yaoundé, the capital city of Cameroon, where EWB had worked to upgrade fifteen neighborhoods. In pursuit of expanding its work in Africa, and particularly in Maputo, where Barcelona was a welcomed financial partner, in 2007 EWB approached AMDEC (or Associação Moçambicana para o Desenvolvimento Concertado), a community-based organization working on development in various neighborhoods in Maputo, to help it identify a neighborhood in Maputo where it could stage an intervention.

Maxaquene A emerged as the chosen neighborhood in part because of AMDEC's existing work there, and because it was known as a neighborhood that suffered especially from flooding. In partnership, AMDEC and EWB organized a diagnostic survey in Maxaquene A to confirm that residents' priorities included water-and-sanitation-oriented projects for which EWB could provide technical assistance. In that effort, AMDEC reached out to ASCHA (or Associação Sócio-Cultural Horizonte Azula), a community-based organization in Maxaquene A, to help run the survey. The CMM and the physical planning department of the University of Eduardo Mondlane also eventually provided some technical assistance and logistical support, but it was not involved in the early phases of the project, nor did it provide any financing to implement the upgrading work envisioned. As Cesar Cunguara, a planner in Maputo's Directorate of Urban Planning and the Environment, explained, the CMM's attention—and budget—at the time was more focused on upgrading Chamanculo C.[23] For these reasons, the objectives within the upgrading project in Maxaquene A at first largely centered on making improvements to smaller side streets where, for example, EWB could introduce drainage canals

---

[21] Interview in Maputo, July 14, 2014.
[22] Interview in Maputo, July 15, 2014.
[23] I interviewed Cunguara several times during fieldwork between 2009 and 2015.

that could be managed locally, avoiding the larger road arteries where the CMM would be expected to complete and maintain work. In addition, the project envisioned building improved pit latrines across the neighborhood and launching an educational campaign on individual and community-level best hygiene practices.

Over the course of two years, between 2007 and 2009, the project built fifty pit latrines and introduced small-scale drainage channels. However, from 2009 onward, much of the work and relationship between partners began to hit obstacles and deteriorate. In 2010, AMDEC approached the CMM's planning department, and in particular Cesar Cunguara, who was charged with overseeing upgrading work in the city, with a proposal to form a committee comprised of the different organizations all working in Maxaquene A. Gilda Jossais, head of AMDEC, put forth the initiative, asking why two, three, or four actors were intervening in the same territory and not communicating with each other.[24] The city agreed to the idea of a neighborhood committee, including AMDEC, EWB, and ASCHA, as well as Water and Sanitation for the Urban Poor, the University of Eduardo Mondlane's physical planning department, and of course the city government. Together, these stakeholders held regular biweekly and monthly meetings and began working on a redevelopment plan to upgrade Maxaquene A. Though initially the CMM had largely overlooked work in Maxaquene A in favor of prioritizing the upgrading of Chamanculo C, some of the city's *vereadores*, or political councilors leading district-level decision-making and sectoral work, began to take interest in redeveloping Maxaquene. Cunguara explained the discord:

> From time to time we involved other technicians from infrastructure, from economic activities, but when the plan arrived at the CMM, the CMM had a different view. The councilors had another vision of what the future of that neighborhood might be. We had been working on the logic of the municipal strategy for the improvement of informal settlements that was developed in 2009–2010, which sought to improve basic conditions, at least, from a gradual point of view, so that the population's [situation] could improve. You can gradually improve the condition and gradually introduce infrastructure X, equipment Y, services Z. But because it [Maxaquene A] is a settlement that is in the first circular [zone of the city], more or less, just outside the city center, [it is] an area apparently desirable for real-estate development and income generation. The council [CMM], all the councilors, saw that area as a zone

[24] Interview in Maputo, July 16, 2014.

with a high potential to develop any type of real-estate project ... So for many, the improvement of the Maxaquene area was to remove people and negotiate with large investors [rather than the upgrading work that the city's planners, AMDEC, EWB, and others were working on].[25]

He went on to describe what he understood to be the different rationales underscoring the discord between the work that was being done to upgrade Maxaquene A, versus the aspirations that the city's leadership had for the area:

Many here today in Mozambique, particularly the decision-makers, think that the informal settlement is a temporary situation, a provisional situation that has its days numbered. One day it will leave; [it is] something that is apart, that is not part of the city or that is not part of the municipality. So the only solution [in their view] is to remove and build new things, new buildings ... but, fortunately, this mentality will change over time. As they say, let's all set foot on the ground. Because waiting for an investor to appear who can take everything, take everyone, build a building there, is complicated and it will not happen. At the very least, we have to face the problem head on, assume that it is a situation that exists, and work for people, gradually improving. I think this is probably one of the main weaknesses of this plan. But from the point of view of communication, the design of the plan, the communication in the elaboration, I think it had all the merit. The question is about the instrument for implementation.[26]

Coming from the city's own planning department, Cunguara's insights provide a rather remarkable window into the tensions that technical professionals and the international cooperation partnerships faced in upgrading work at the community level. Alvaro Garcia, the coordinator of EWB's work in Maputo at the time, concurred with Cunguara's narrative and recalled the local government leadership newly identifying Maxaquene as an ideal location for greater real-estate development in the city, and further how this aspiration collided with the cooperation project's and the neighborhood committee's work in upgrading the existing neighborhood for existing residents. After a year of putting together the redevelopment plan for Maxaquene A, the CMM approved the plan put forth by the neighborhood committee in 2011, but, according to EWB, that plan in its final form failed to reflect engagements and prioritization of the community's residents. As Garcia explained it, while their

---

[25] Interview in Maputo, January 28, 2015.
[26] Interview in Maputo, January 28, 2015.

original priority was to minimize the number of households that would need to be resettled, this did not appear to be a priority in the plan that the CMM ultimately approved. As such, EWB left the committee.

The rupture introduced when EWB left the city committee's redevelopment planning team was further materialized in EWB's break with AMDEC. A drainage channel which was nearing completion in 2011 was, to EWB's surprise, suddenly destroyed by the CMM. EWB team members looked to AMDEC as interlocutors with the CMM, and thus essentially saw the city government's destruction of the drainage channel they had almost completed as an affront to their work and as a poor reflection of AMDEC's capacity to coordinate their joint work in the partnership with the CMM. As one of the technical professionals working with EWB, Ana Carolina, explained, "AMDEC did not efficiently manage the project … EWB depends and believes in local partners, [but] in the end, with the channel destroyed, it was a great loss, a frustration of losing a year's worth of people's work, of a budget invested."[27] Indeed, she noted that when the CMM built its own drainage channel as part of its new redevelopment plan, the population made many complaints about it because it was oversized, and during the flood season, children who played there were hurt. AMDEC's director, Gilda Jossais, however, noted that EWB perhaps did not fully accept AMDEC's leadership on local contextual issues. For example, she related to me how EWB envisioned creating a community-based financial fee for the maintenance and upkeep of drainage channels that the cooperation project was building.[28] AMDEC noted that such fees would not work as the neighborhood's residents perceived drainage to be a basic service, the upkeep of which should be undertaken by the city government. However, EWB insisted that it could work because in its previous upgrading experience in Congo, such a program had succeeded. Jossais emphasized that AMDEC's local know-how on such socio-economic matters, and even its engineers' own experiences with the challenge of constructing channels in the neighborhood, were often overlooked or considered obstacles to the EWB's own vision of possibility. Ultimately, such conflicts between what were considered domains of expertise saw the relationship between EWB and AMDEC sour. While both groups continue to work in Maputo, EWB sought other community-based organizations to work with on other small-scale interventions, and identified as a new partner Kuwuka, another community-based organization working on development issues within Maxaquene A.

[27] Interview in Maputo, January 27, 2015.
[28] Interview in Maputo, July 16, 2014.

3.6 Contrasting Cultures and Habits in Cooperation with Japan

Ainda temos muitos desafios por enfrentar, principalmente com a área de edu-
cação cívica. Nós estamos a precisar muito de uma boa conscientização pública.
E necessitamos muito de trabalhar para divulgação destes mesmos projetos que
estamos a implementar gradualmente em piloto … A mudança de atitude das
pessoas … leva o seu tempo, é gradual, é pouco a pouco, não são mudanças
bruscas que vão nos trazer sucesso.

We still have many challenges to face, especially in the area of civic education. We are in great need of good public awareness … And we really need to
work to publicize these projects that we are gradually implementing as pilots.
Changing people's attitudes … it takes time, it is gradual, it is little by little, it
is not sudden changes that will bring us success.

(Stela Meriamo, technical professional, Directorate for Urban Solid Waste
Management and Health, Maputo)

The one project on my radar that was not "neighborhood" based or oriented
was the JICA project with CMM's DUSWMH. In 2012, the CMM approached
the Japanese embassy to help the city update its 2008 master plan for solid
waste, decrease waste production, and increase recycling. For JICA, this meant
starting with trying to understand progress in the city since the original
solid-waste master plan. In November of 2012 they launched a detailed planning survey of solid-waste management in Maputo, and by March of 2013
the 3Rs project was introduced as a four-year cooperation partnership that
would update the solid-waste master plan and introduce pilot projects in four
neighborhoods throughout the city before those interventions were further
institutionalized. The envisioned outputs of the project, beyond the updated
plan, included improvements to capacity around the collection and transportation of solid waste, financial management, and waste reduction through
the introduction of "Sustainable 3R Activities"—namely, by reducing, reusing,
and recycling waste. Toward this end, pilot programs were introduced across
different themes in four neighborhoods: household-level waste separation in
the neighborhood of Chamanculo D (adjacent to the Chamanculo C upgrading project I also studied), composting organic waste in the neighborhoods
of Mahotas and Costa de Sol, and a 3R station to promote valuable recyclable
collection in Zimpeto. The JICA technical professionals involved in the project
rotated their time on the ground in Maputo, traveling three to four times per
year, spending one to two months per visit within the offices of the DUSWMH.
The team itself was composed of nine professionals—eight Japanese and one

Filipino—whom JICA contracted from a leading Japanese engineering consultancy, Nippon Koei, which had won JICA's call for bids. Each JICA technical professional was then paired with a Mozambican technical professional from the directorate—as well as a translator.[29]

To facilitate the work program, there were two training sessions held which involved visits to city sites in Japan and discussions centered on the process of master planning for solid waste, how to improve management within the directorate, the 3Rs and civic education, as well as determining a final disposal site. These training sessions were originally intended to take place only in Japan—one in October of 2013 and the other in October of 2015. However, after the first meeting in Japan in 2013, Mozambican staff requested that instead of returning to Japan, they instead visit another country to see how solid-waste management was run there—and for this, Brazil, another Lusophone country, was chosen. The request from Maputo's DUSWMH hinted at some of the difficulties of the project's first years—including the deep difference of context between Japan and Mozambique that staff in Maputo felt made it difficult to translate Japanese pilots into their city. Florência Francisco and Luisa Langa explained the contrast not in that professionals like themselves did not have the technical knowledge capacities that the Japanese have, but rather in that habits and cultures in Mozambique did not yet correspond with what the cooperation project was working to achieve.[30] For example, referring to the pilot on the separation of solid wastes at the source in Chamanculo D, Francisco explained that "we don't have that habit, or that culture. We don't have landfills; we have open-air dumps … so it is not worth separating waste at the source if it all goes to the same place in the end. And we also do not have recycling industries ready to transform filtered out waste."[31] These shifts in habits and new technologies for how to manage waste were critical ideas and new practices that JICA introduced, but for Mozambican staff these ideas could only slowly enter into the practice landscape of households in Maputo, depending on when all the supportive institutions and industries were in place. Indeed, the conflict between ideas of who is responsible for waste—and in particular its sorting—were made clear to the JICA team at a local meeting on waste source separation in the neighborhood. Shungo Soeda, the chief adviser on solid-waste management for the JICA team, affirmed this challenge, recounting the JICA team's experience at a community meeting in Chamanculo D:

---

[29] Translators worked with English as the intermediary language that was then translated into Portuguese and back.
[30] Interview in Maputo, July 16, 2014.
[31] Interview in Maputo, July 16, 2014.

We had a meeting with the local people to let them understand what the project is. At the time, the local people asked for some compensation, some money for participating in this project. And it was like a missile [exploding], everybody stand[ing] up and ... shouting, singing. We were so scared. So, at the time, I talked to the director and the director walked out to solve this matter together with his higher-up person and some political party's person to settle the things.[32]

My conversations with project staff at the directorate, however, also revealed that the habits of residents and the contextual landscape of waste were not the only habits and contexts that came under scrutiny in the duration of the project. Both Japanese and Mozambican counterparts recognized the difficulties of aligning their work rhythms. Francisco described the frustration of different work habits on the project, asserting that "they [JICA] arrived with a rhythm and we couldn't find a way to respond to that rhythm, and so they became demoralized. But we are not obliged to enter their work rhythm."[33] On the Japanese side, professionals were frustrated not only by what they perceived to be the abbreviated daily work schedules of their counterparts, but what seemed to them a lack of adherence and recognition of deadlines and objectives. In a review of the project cooperation, for example, it was noted that it is "Mozambican custom that [Mozambican] counterparts took a paid leave for about one month every year" and that this was one of the difficulties for the implementation of the project (JICA, 2017).

The issue of compensation for what Mozambican staff considered to be overtime work also emerged as a major point of tension. The Mozambican public sector, by law, works from 8am through 3pm, but Japanese counterparts viewed that schedule as a truncated day. With the expectation of longer workdays and the fact that the pilot projects also required the presence of Mozambican staff at events scheduled on weekends, they asked for an allowance of overtime work from JICA—beyond their normal compensation from the CMM government. The internal view of staff at the directorate was that the cooperation project was extra work, beyond their actual mandate. However, the JICA team viewed the issue of compensation as internal to the CMM, as opposed to a point of negotiation in the cooperation project. As such, at times this created a resistance to the initiative of reforms that JICA counterparts tried to introduce. One such reform was in the financial management

---

[32] Interview in Maptuo, January 15, 2015.
[33] Interview in Maputo, January 26, 2015.

database, which the directorate used to record and categorize businesses and institutions producing waste and to monitor waste-collection tax revenues. According to Grace Neptuno, the Filipino technical professional working on the JICA team as coordinator for the financial capacity-building aspect of the project, when all the directorate's staff were asked to contribute to updating the database and correcting errors in how institutions were categorized, there was pushback. "Everybody was complaining, 'no that is additional work! We are not going to do that.' And some people were speaking in Changana [a local Bantu language], which we could not understand, saying that 'this is not for us, that is for JICA."[34] Ryu Koide, the project coordinator for the 3R planning as well as for impact evaluation on the JICA team, also recognized how the mandate of Mozambican counterparts in the directorate affected work, explaining that it was difficult to force staff working for the directorate itself to join in activities on the ground.[35] One of the ways in which the JICA team managed this challenge was then to revert responsibilities to Mozambican nationals that JICA itself employs in its local headquarters to engage in projects.

Despite some of these difficulties, staff within the DUSWMH that took part in training sessions and project meetings with JICA counterparts revealed shifts in their own habits and their appreciation for the idea of what they referred to as "Japanese" time, planning, and evaluation. A recurrent theme of discussions over the course of project's implementation was the work-culture difference—but conversations about clashes in the first two years of the project differed from assessments about work-culture difficulties toward the end, when staff expressed more admiration and appreciation for Japanese dedication to the job. As Meriamo put it, the Japanese never work without targeted goals in mind.[36] The introduction of goal-oriented meetings and progress reporting therein were indeed central elements of administrative organization around the 3Rs project that JICA counterparts worked to instill within the directorate. Geraldo Rosário Saranga, a JICA-employed Mozambican professional, noted that previously, technical staff at the DUSWMH would not participate in planning meetings, which were instead only between department heads.[37] With the cooperation project, this shifted to creating meetings where staff were given the space, expectation, and the leadership opportunity of presenting and engaging in planning meetings. JICA's Neptuno related her particular

---

[34] Interview in Maputo, January 27, 2015.
[35] Interview in Maputo, January 27, 2015.
[36] *"Nunca trabalham sem meta"* or "they [Japanese] never work without a goal," explained Stela in an interview on January 20, 2015 in Maputo.
[37] Interview in Maputo, January 20, 2015.

satisfaction in seeing how her counterpart on the financial-management sector of the project began to take more initiative and show leadership on financial-management reforms in these meetings. Sergio Manhique, a technical professional working on monitoring projects within the DUSWMH, concurred, noting that "progress meetings" represented a major shift in organizational management that was inaugurated by JICA counterparts.[38] These meetings took place every other Wednesday over the course of the project's four years to evaluate the state of affairs in implementing the cooperation project and to identify where strengths and weaknesses in the rollout of work were located. Indeed, during the eighth Joint Coordination Committee meeting of the project's main partners, the chairperson of the committee—namely the *vereador* or city councilor Florentino Ferreira, who oversees DUSWMH for the CMM—went so far as to highlight how the directorate would "continue with the teachings left [by the JICA team], *especially* the Progress Meetings" [emphasis added] (CMM-JICA, 2017: 4).

By the end of the cooperation project on 3Rs in 2017, while some of the objectives envisioned in the project were achieved—namely the updating of the master plan, the creation of an Office of Civic Education and Environmental Promotion, and the capacity building of the team with regard to their administrative and financial management of the sector—the pilot projects themselves demonstrated that the wider supporting landscape in Maputo would also require change for the pilot ideas to work at scale. In JICA/Nippon's project completion report, the JICA professionals noted that "one of the comments on the draft of [the] revised Master Plan given in the City Councilor's meeting of the CMM held in April 2017, was that 3R was too early to introduce in Maputo. Efforts [to help] citizens understand the importance and appropriateness of ... the 3R concept at this stage must be patiently continued" (JICA, 2017: 165). However, Soeda, JICA's project coordinator, felt that the fact that the concept of the 3Rs has now entered into the vocabulary of discussions within the directorate was in itself an important accomplishment. He explained that the CMM was trying to review the city ordinance on solid-waste management and proposed including the concept of 3Rs therein. Yet Soeda also noted that more coordination across internationally supported projects, and internal CMM communication therein, would be important. He explained that while his counterparts would often seek JICA's advice on issues outside of the 3R project—because JICA staff were co-located within the directorate's

---

[38] Interview in Maputo, January 20, 2015.

own offices—staff in the directorate did not also share what they were discussing with other international counterparts on solid-waste management.[39]
This was clear to me as well, given the potential overlaps and room for coordination between what the directorate was pursuing in its cooperation work
with Guarulhos and that which was occurring with Japan.

3.7 From Material toward Cognitive Equities on the Ground

The potential for what Watson has described as "conflicting rationales" in the
implementation of even the most seemingly participatory and procedurally
just urban plans in the African context was fully evident across the cooperation
projects I followed in Maputo. However, in uncovering the roots and tracing
the evolution and implementation of cooperation on the ground in Maputo,
I found another important characteristic of cooperation projects as practiced
on the ground. More often than not, projects I studied could not be purely categorized as bilateral, trilateral, SSC, or traditional (i.e., with Northern donors).
Nor had the partners involved in originating or carrying out cooperation
projects consistently been national or municipal actors—nor seemingly always
public sector agents. More typically, different scales and multiple actors—
both governmental and non-governmental, non-profit and for-profit—were
involved in the conceptualization and implementation of projects I reviewed.
These overlaps—what I call "turbidity" in international development cooperation on the ground—call to question the categorial claims tied to notions
like partners' hemispheric geographies or the number of stakeholder organizations or groups involved, though the branding thereof persists in macro-level
discourses on international development cooperation.

   A more forgiving read of what I found in Maputo might presume that the
overlaps of involved actors represent a win for coordination among international partners on the ground. However, I read the reality of overlapping actors
in projects and areas of concern between international players active in Maputo very differently, having witnessed how the priorities of locally affected
residents were often subsumed and how infrequently such overlapping between actors translated into coordination. At most, when coordination was
pursued, it was often pursued by Mozambican authorities to enable continuation of work started by previous projects. We see this in the case of the
national government of Mozambique pursuing a continuation of Maputo's

---

[39] Interview in Maputo, January 15, 2015.

cooperation programming in sanitation with Japan, picking up in the Hulene dump site where it left off with Guarulhos. Given the entanglements of co-operation in practice, the claim-making among international development actors—bilateral and multilateral, Northern and Southern—as well as the references to and support for the "Southern-ness" of cooperation projects appear misguided and more relevant for national discourses than for local realities.

From the standpoint of beneficiaries, namely residents and workers in Hulene, Chamanculo C, KaTembe, or Maxaquene A, there did not appear to be any more "solidarity" or "equity" delivered if a project partnership was with China or Brazil as opposed to Italy, Japan, or Spain. For example, while the project sponsored by Barcelona with EWB achieved its material goals, interviews with both local and external managerial staff made clear there was a sense of unease and dissatisfaction with the relationship. China's cooperation—operationalized by two companies long playing the part of cooperation partner—also achieved its objective of delivering a bridge and road network, but the basic amenities originally sold to local technical pro-fessionals like KaTembe's water engineer Nhone—and KaTembe's residents—were nowhere to be seen in the rollout of the physical infrastructure plan. Further, technical capacity-building was scarcely referenced as an actual de-liverable, unlike so many of the other projects I studied. The project with Guarulhos, on the other hand, failed to see the emergence of waste-picker cooperatives thrive in Maputo, and yet both local and external staff seemed intent on continuing their collaboration and working with one another. Simi-larly, while the project with Japanese partners has not seen the full adoption of the 3Rs in Maputo, Mozambican staff were most explicit about the benefits of working and learning new ways of working with their Japanese counterparts. In short, the material outcomes and attention to the distribution of benefits did not appear to arise or suffer from the particular macro or geo-hemispheric identities of international partners alone. However, in studying these inter-national partnerships on the ground—their constitution, rationales, values, practices, and their evolution—I realized that the specific architectures of re-lationships formed actually *did* matter to the kinds of capacity or knowledge they fostered (for all involved).

Southern donors, noted for macro-level claims on solidarity-building and equity in their international partnerships, expressed their cooperation strate-gies in different forms in practice in Maputo. For China, this meant non-interference in local decision-making and the politically tense local aspects of project management, while for Brazil, this meant leveraging the similarities of contexts and experiences as markers of solidarity in relationships. Yet it was the managerial make-up of teams (and inclinations toward hierarchy or heterarchy therein), their commitment (or lack thereof) to local embedded-ness in local organizations, and their attention to relationship building at the everyday level that revealed how macro-level claims really translated into solidarity on the ground—regardless of the geo-hemispheric origins of part-ners. While all international partners claimed that "relationships" mattered and that technical capacity-building was key to their partnerships, not all of them saw "relationship" equity manifested in their work. I wondered, then, to what extent this aspect of international cooperation was taken as a serious feature of project work. For this inquiry, I reexamined these projects to un-derstand how development partners conceived of and valued learning in their joint work.

4

Looking for Learning in Cooperation Projects

4.1 Learning and Epistemic Equity at the Project Level

Material benefits are, of course, not the only type of benefit to arise within cooperation projects, nor the only type of benefit that is worth assessing and evaluating. Projects—and a professional's experience therein—form the basis of epistemic communities within urban (and more generally, national) development. As Arden McHugh notes, epistemic communities "set the conditions so that particular types of knowledge and particular interpretations are accepted" (2017: 271). For example, within the international development industry, building up technical expertise and capacity—historically defined by donors—through "learning by doing" has been at the heart of practices and theories of development over several decades.[1] However, while learning and capacity-building are today long-standing subjects and objects of development studies, tracking learning is a very recent addition to existing institutionalized frameworks for monitoring and evaluation in development work. With the twenty-first century, we have witnessed monitoring and evaluation efforts within development banks and non-governmental organizations converted to monitoring, evaluation, and learning frameworks. However, as Kogen (2018) notes, in their drive toward evidence-based evaluations, major donor organizations' interpretation of learning is often confounded with accountability, and they continue to pay little attention to foundational questions about what precisely should be learned and how lessons will improve how aid works for beneficiaries.

Learning's late and incomplete blooming in twenty-first-century development evaluations is surprising given influential research on the importance of

---

[1] Within development economics, for example, Sanjaya Lall's *Learning to Industrialize: The Acquisition of Technological Capability by India* (1987) was one of the earlier accounts of this now basic development principle.

Equity, Evaluation, and International Cooperation. Gabriella Y. Carolini, Oxford University Press.
© Gabriella Y. Carolini (2022). DOI: 10.1093/oso/9780192865489.003.0005

professional maturity, bureaucracy, and organizational learning in the work of scholars such as Albert Hirschman, Judith Tendler, Donald Schön, and Timothy Mitchell, all of whom looked deeply at the role of professional agency (and learning) in how projects evolve and why, with an ultimate interest in for whom. For example, in *Good Government in the Tropics*, Tendler (1997) writes about how contrary to the assumptions about wholesale corruption and rent-seeking behavior within public bureaucracies in developing countries, evidence shows that there is a diversity of good behaviors among public servants. Just as in any organization, public servants can and do make choices, independent of donor-driven performance incentives, that merit their autonomy, greater discretion, and trust. In a book provoked by Hirschman's writings on development, Schön (1994: 71), whose work on reflective practice among urban planners remains the reference text for municipal practitioners interested in learning, explains that one could read development itself, as explained in Hirschman's *Strategy of Economic Development*, as a heuristic learning process where "the very difficulties ordinarily seen as obstacles to development now become its energizers." Mitchell's *Rule of Experts* (2002: 10) also notes that in studying development, one comes to realize that "human agency appears less as a calculating intelligence directing social outcomes and more as the product of a series of alliances in which the human element is never wholly in control." In other words, learning is not necessarily an efficient exercise for professionals or organizations. It is, nonetheless, a worthy one.

After a lull of almost twenty years, a recent wave of scholarly work again began pointing to the value of promoting learning in a wide range of policy and project arenas, as well as challenging the modes of knowledge production therein. Within the urban development sphere, authors such as Colin McFarlane, Hazel Johnson, and Gordon Wilson have discussed the centrality of reflective practice for learning among municipal project stakeholders. McFarlane (2010) suggests that "indirect" learning, or reflective knowledge, is required to question "cultures of knowledge production [that] preclude translation or allow for only particular kinds of translation." Johnson and Wilson (2009) also emphasize the critical role that reflection plays in municipal authorities' learning within development interventions. Planning scholars like Vanessa Watson (2003), Fana Sihlongonyane (2015b), and Tanja Winkler (2018), working from African cities, extend the discussion of learning in urban development to encompass the conflicting rationales and embedded politics of knowledge production through a postcolonial lens that challenges the presumptions of what is to be learned and valued in project work. Yet orthodox project evaluations ignore or underemphasize reflective or adaptive knowledge as legitimate development targets. Instead, they focus on promoting evidence-based prescriptions that implicitly or explicitly claim an optimized method of how best to achieve project objectives and show results. In this way, there is a double dilemma in the promotion of best practices via "hard evidence-based" or output-based evaluations. First, in determining what to call a best practice, deep learning is subjugated relative to accountability or causality. Second, the learning that is ultimately promoted as relevant is that which the evaluator, as opposed to the local practitioner, decides is relevant.

The presumption of universality in the promotion of best practices is a central critique of postcolonial theorists who question not only the Western-based knowledge regime embedded in the development industry, but also the myth-making it promotes about the origins of such knowledge. Jean and John Comaroff (2012), for example, both decry the narrative of a universal history and modernity, but also remind us how some of the tenets of industrialization and economic development in Western history—for example, mass production—actually found inspiration in the colonial encounters of Britain with India and China, where such techniques were already at work. Arguably, the evidence-based policy movement pushing best practices is an effort to leapfrog time lags in a learning trajectory. Yet policies that promote the generalizability of best practices remove an important premium on place-based learning and the experimental application of ideas as objectives in and of themselves. As Joseph Stiglitz and Bruce Greenwald (2014) argue in their book *Creating a Learning Society*, development strategies (and ostensibly how they are evaluated) should actively promote learning cultures as an objective in order to close global knowledge gaps. Learning-focused policies and learning-enabled environments acknowledge and emphasize the continuity of knowledge aggregation, the multiple learning moments—from both successful and failed project implementation. This differs dramatically from an emphasis on learning objectives and outcome indicators, which prioritize achievements over reflections. The question that then remains unclear in even the recent renaissance of learning in evaluation is not only how learning best happens, but precisely what types of learning experience and knowledge are important and to whom. However, there is much overlap and some consensus across varied scholarly disciplines about basic theorized typologies of knowledge and about pedagogical processes for learning them, even if recognizing and evaluating the presence of these types or process remains without standard.

Pedagogists, organizational learning scholars, and postcolonial theorists have long been concerned with how learning happens and how knowledge is created and recognized (or not). Within the educational and organizational-learning literatures, for example, there have been several attempts at classifying knowledge types in order to understand or forward methods for learning, and assessment therein. Table 4.1 consolidates some of the varied typologies of knowledge cited in these fields and relates them to learning processes. For example, at the most basic level, knowledge is factual, explicit, and declarative. There is a single-loop, learning aspect to factual/explicit or encoded/declarative knowledge as well, in that it is knowledge which is not questioned but accepted, with attempts made to correct experiences so as to align with the established, explicit knowledge. Other knowledge typologies reflect higher-level cognition and are generally more tacit and procedural, or difficult to articulate. Such knowledge can be conceptual (i.e., knowledge of interrelationships), procedural (knowledge of different methods and of which situations to use them in), or even metacognitive (knowledge of cognition and self-reflection) (Anderson & Krathwohl, 2001). Learning processes which reflect such knowledge types involve double-loop learning (where general assumptions about explicit or factual knowledge are questioned) and, ultimately, triple-loop learning (which includes reflection about one's own learning methods and cognition about what methods work best).[2]

Context also matters for learning different knowledge types. Organizational-learning scholar Linda Argote argues that whether organizations learn by doing or learn instead by simply planning depends heavily on the type of knowledge that is sought and whether or not context is important to that knowledge. She summarizes that "planning is effective

Table 4.1 Knowledge Taxonomies and Learning Processes

Knowledge Taxonomies			Learning Processes
Bloom et al (1956); Anderson & Krathwohl (2001)	*Polanyi (1962, 1967); Nonaka (1994)*	*Singley & Anderson (1989)*	*Nielsen (1993); Argyris & Schön (1996); Tosey et al (2011)*
Factual	Explicit	Declarative	Single-loop
Conceptual	Tacit	Procedural	Double-loop
Procedural			
Metacognitive			Triple-loop

[2] Triple-loop learning—or learning about how one learns best—is a concept inspired by Argyris and Schön's work on single- and double-loop learning, but also more recently forwarded by a number of organizational learning scholars (Nielsen, 1993; Argyris & Schön, 1996; Tosey et al, 2011).

when the knowledge base is understood well, when the knowledge is not dependent on the context, and when the task is certain. Conversely, learning by doing is preferred when the knowledge is uncertain, not understood well, and highly dependent on the organizational context" (Argote, 2013). In other words, when knowledge is factual or well understood, context is not particularly important and that knowledge is generalizable, but when knowledge is tacit, context is important and that knowledge may not be generalizable. A stylized representation in Figure 4.1 of one of the aforementioned knowledge taxonomies helps us also place them over what is generalizable and what is more contextually-based. Moving across the knowledge gradients of factual to metacognitive, both complexity and the relevance of contexts become stronger. Here, metacognitive knowledge represents the deepest or highest-level of cognition, or what Ash Amin and Patrick Cohendet describe, in reference to firms, as the cognitive architecture of knowledge. They explain this architecture as "the way knowledge is produced, stored, exchanged, transmitted, retrieved," which also "strongly influences the process of organizational learning, and in turn, the nature of the organization itself" (Amin & Cohendet, 2004).

Applying such insights into the sphere of a development cooperation project, if we accept that know-how becomes more tacit as contextual issues weigh more heavily, then we might also consider that during phases of development projects most dependent on conceptual, procedural, and even metacognitive knowledge, that contextually-based knowledge matters most

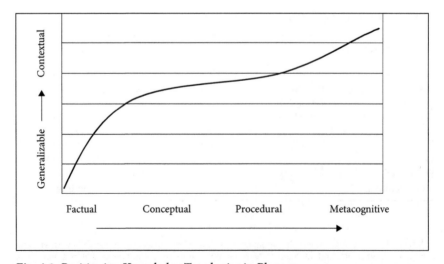

Fig. 4.1 Positioning Knowledge Typologies in Place
Source: Author's visualization.

and learning would best arise when project partners have shared contextual knowledge. In other words, while the basic technical or factual knowledge in a water or sanitation project can be supported and conveyed by any project partners, regardless of the context of their experiences with such knowledge types, for more discretionary aspects of project work, like decision-making and project management, we might expect that partners who have shared contextual experiences would understand and foster the kind of tacit knowledge and learning experiences that are highly relevant for effective project implementation. In her evaluation of knowledge partnerships for institutional development within the international development industry, Marra (2004: 152) argues, "partnering is not a contract that binds rational, utility-maximizing individuals, but a complex organization that draws upon the organizational structure of partners, their institutional opportunities, constraints, and history, their expectations for the future, and interaction in the present." The relative nearness of partners' own experiences and expectations, then, is arguably central to conceptual, procedural, and ultimately metacognitive knowledge accumulation, or the types of knowledge required for effective discretionary decision-making key to development projects.[3]

Of course, the major caveat here lies with which "nearnesses" or proximities of context matter, and who the precise partners are, since partners may clash and hegemonies may influence the production of knowledge even when there are shared contextual experiences. Postcolonial scholars have written extensively about how inequalities between actors shape assumptions of who has or can legitimately produce expert knowledge, particularly as it relates to development (de Sousa Santos, 2015; Mignolo, 2000, 2010; de Sousa Santos et al, 2008). Writing about different epistemologies, or what he calls "ecologies of knowledge," Boaventura de Sousa Santos argues that "rather than subscribing to a single, universal and abstract hierarchy among knowledges, the ecology of knowledges favors context-dependent hierarchies, in light of the concrete outcomes intended or achieved by different knowledge practices" (de Sousa Santos, 2015). Here it is important to clarify that he is not referring to knowledge typologies such as those outlined in Figure 4.1, but knowledge systems across geographies. Critically, he discusses what should happen when, in an intervention, different knowledge systems clash. His message seems pertinent for a discussion of international cooperation partnerships, where knowledge systems clash almost by design. Santos calls for precaution, urging that preference or *power* be given to the form of knowledge that can guarantee

---

[3] Pritchett & Woolcock (2004) argue that within the public sector, development project-level practices (as opposed to higher-level programming or policy-making) are the most transaction-intensive and require the most discretionary decision-making.

the greatest participation to social groups impacted by the intervention.[4] Santos's "ecologies of knowledge" further forwards the idea that in a learning environment, the teacher and the student need not be static or determined roles in every context. Just as Spivak (1996) insisted that speaking is "a transaction between speaker and listener," learning is a transaction between "teacher" and "student" and that transaction is constantly shifting. However, as recognized early on by John Dewey and later Paulo Freire, a learning transaction's quality depends on the relations and the openness of counterparties to one another's knowledge systems, an openness often explicitly or implicitly missing in development cooperation interventions. This is the longstanding central dilemma and critique of the idea of "development" as modernization and improvement writ large by the West. Epistemic injustice is essentially institutionalized in development projects when higher-income donor groups define modernization and evaluate improvements as objective standards, according to their own countries' experiences and knowledge systems, but accessible to all. As Haslanger (2017) notes, when the idea of objectivity in a knowledge system is normalized, it marginalizes and subordinates other ways of defining and knowing, deepening epistemic harm and injustice. For Dewey (1916) and Freire (1968), the resolution to this wrought power dynamic in learning and knowledge creation is to conceptualize knowledge and learning as "a mode of participation" or consciously active engagement and co-production. Applying such integrative thinking to the field of development would then position and value learning not just by doing, but also by teaching.

SSC in theory promises precisely this type of exchange in development cooperation, where teaching and learning happen for both cooperation partners, challenging the orthodox mentor–mentee knowledge model. But SSC partners in practice can still harbor a sense of mentor–mentee mentalities, fostering epistemic inequities in the learning-by-doing and by-teaching experience. In other words, if epistemic equity is about having one's credibility acknowledged and one's social experience collectively understood and valued, as Miranda Fricker (2007) suggests, then cooperation project partners would not position one partner's experience and expertise as more valuable or relevant than another's. Instead both partners would be open to learning and would, upon examination, reveal what I position here as high-level learning, or tacit learning that is contextually rich and highly relevant for discretionary decision-making within projects. With this in mind, I began to reexamine the cooperation projects I followed in Maputo for two types

---

[4] Santos's precise words include social groups participating in an intervention's "design, execution, and control and in the benefits of the intervention" (2014: 205), but here I emphasize the benefits of intervention.

of evidence: first, of learning and the room afforded to it within cooperation projects, and second, of proximities that appeared to matter to project professionals in their determination of what did and did not work on the ground. I concentrated primarily on engaging Mozambican professionals and their counterparts who were most implicated in the everyday work of cooperation—that is, those who were on the ground within Maputo, as opposed to those who were not. By design, I prioritized their voices to understand what types of knowledge and room for learning—by failing *or* succeeding, by doing *or* teaching—they revealed or highlighted in discussions and statements about their projects. Second, I analyzed whether these same professionals referenced any other proximities—beyond just the geopolitical labels offered in constructs like SSC—in discussions about what mattered to them and their learning in cooperation project work.

4.2 Looking for Learning on the Ground

Organizational cultures were not only legible but also critical influences on workflows in Maputo's cooperation ecosystem. Mozambican professionals'—and their international counterparts'—descriptions of work cultures sometimes veered toward gross stereotypes—be it of Japanese solemnity and order, or Brazilian openness and easy-goingness in the workplace. Such generalized depictions appeared especially grounded in my study of the KaTembe bridge, where staff with both Maputo Sul (which oversaw the project) and the CRBC (which built it) were particularly immune to my efforts at gaining their professional insights on learning in cooperation work. Perhaps this was not surprising as the project resembled an investment project more than the other cooperation projects I studied. Nonetheless, in the other four projects I studied, it was clear that cultures of work mattered in everyday cooperation practices, as well as the space that teams felt they had to adapt and learn. Interestingly, despite the anticipated added-value of SSC as a special medium for advancing grounded *high-level* learning, I found that partnerships with higher-income countries too could advance the more contextually influenced know-how (e.g., conceptual, procedural, and metacognitive knowledge).

4.2.1 Learning as Adaptation

Temos sempre espaço para ter a palavra e o que for necessário que vemos, [ou]que não é adequado a nossa realidade, nós não negamos a pedir a se retificar.

We always have space to speak, and whatever is necessary, [or whenever] we see that [some aspect of a project] is not matched or appropriate for our reality, we do not shy away from asking that the project be rectified.

(Stela Meriamo, technical professional, Directorate for Urban Solid Waste Management and Health [DUSWMH])

Discussions with professionals involved in JICA's 3Rs project with Maputo's DUSWMH illustrate why and how my own expectations of the nature of learning in international cooperation projects evolved away from the hypothesized notion of SSC bearing the most relevant fruits of practical and relevant knowledge. While there was little tolerance for flexibility around adhering to administrative and technical aspects of the project partnership, according to professionals involved in the project from both JICA and DUSWMH, the work advanced conceptual and procedural strategies for improving project implementation and sectoral work in expected and unexpected ways. One JICA consultant, for example, described JICA's work culture as (almost predictably) highly templated and systematic, noting that "if you try to deviate a little bit, it is very difficult for them [JICA] to make adjustments. For example, with the ADB [Asian Development Bank] or World Bank, they can let small things slip. It is easier for them to let things slip."[5] The consultant recounted an example of losing a boarding pass, and how for JICA, where operational efficiency is prized, this was a big deal. The prioritization of administrative efficiencies, or administrative inflexibility (depending on perspectives) also showed up in negotiations between JICA and Mozambique on compensation for Mozambicans' participation in the 3Rs project. As JICA's project was a technical cooperation project, there was no budget for Mozambican municipal professionals' salaries when they had to work overtime to contribute to the 3Rs project as well as their other work. Another JICA consultant, Grace Neptuno, noted that some Mozambican counterparts on the 3Rs project did not attend project meetings "because there is no financial incentive in this project.... no one is paying them overtime so it is additional work for them. So many of our counterparts are losing the fire to be in the project."[6]

Such administrative strictures of JICA around technical points, however, were less reflected in its substantive programming and room for learning in the 3Rs project. Staff on both the Mozambican and JICA teams related several accounts of how they had grown professionally from working with one another, and that there was critical space afforded to discussion and debate in

---

[5] Interview, January 27, 2015, Maputo.
[6] Interview, January 27, 2015, Maputo.

their project. Stela Meriamo, a technical professional working in DUSWMH, candidly described working with JICA colleagues:

> [They are] very hardworking; they are also very attentive, but also demanding. The rhythm of work, between us and them, was, I mean, it wasn't so equal. But from a certain point onwards, we started to adapt, to get used to the rhythm of work that has to be this. There was a time when ... I think we got a little lazy. We had a plan and activities, [and] maybe you have to answer [questions] at the next meeting, [but] we usually would forget or we ha[d] a lot of work and maybe even thought "No, it shouldn't be important," but at a certain point we started to realize that it was important.[7]

Sergio Manhique, who worked as head of Monitoring and Quality Control for the CMM and joined staff at DUSWMH on the 3Rs project, concurred, noting how working with JICA helped the Mozambican team also see the importance of knowledge-sharing and transparency about progress on individual tasks. "Every time we complete work, the idea is to always share it with the group, so that others may also realize what is being done."[8] Before the 3Rs project, Geraldo Rosário Saranga, a Mozambican project technical assistant hired by JICA to work with DUSWMH, noted that the idea of technical professionals speaking up in meetings was more foreign:

> They didn't have this habit of holding meetings to present [their work]; they just have a management meeting, a leadership collective that is held every Monday. But the technicians do not participate in this meeting, [instead] there were only department heads. And in one way or another, department heads may not bring what the decisions of this meeting are to reach the technicians—the employees who are the people who must implement the daily activities. Now we are trying to create a mechanism in which there can be direct communication from the boss, from the top, to the person who will implement the activity on the ground.[9]

Shungo Soeda, JICA's project lead for the 3Rs work, concurred, noting how DUSWMH technical staff began to embrace more fully the work of the project and the importance in solid-waste management of the concept of reducing, reusing, and recycling:

---

[7] Interview, January 20, 2015, Maputo. Translated from the Portuguese by the author.
[8] Interview, January 20, 2015, Maputo. Translated from the Portuguese by the author.
[9] Interview, January 20, 2015, Maputo. Translated from the Portuguese by the author.

Since we started this project, I feel they really keep in their mind the master plan. Some of them are always carrying the master plan by their hand. And also our project target is promotion of 3R (reduce, reuse, recycle). At the beginning of the project not all the counterparts understood what 3R is. They knew only the word 3R, but not its meaning, they didn't understand. Now, they really understand the meaning of 3R and always they are talking about 3R. Now the municipality is trying to revise the city ordinance of the solid-waste management and they proposed that the concept of 3R should be included in this new ordinance. This kind of understanding is one of the results [of the project].[10]

Here, DUSWMH staff grew with the JICA partnership and learned not only to assert leadership internally within the CMM's own hierarchy but to take ownership of the project's objectives.

While not formally captured, there was also a clearly a practice of self-evaluation among the professionals involved in cooperation projects on the ground. Meriamo shared that she and her colleagues often had the habit of scrambling to put together end-of-year or progress reports.[11] She described how DUSWMH's JICA counterparts, on the other hand, always worked with plans and objectives, and had frequent check-ins that enabled them to understand and report on progress more systematically and with greater ease. Meriamo felt that working with goals and clear parameters was a procedural aspect of project practice she was learning from her JICA counterparts.

Another procedural (and technical) example came in the management of the DUSWMH's financial recording database, where businesses and institutions were classified according to their waste production. According to JICA staff, the database was, at the start of the 3Rs project, entirely erroneous. While the average waste production of an individual is 0.6 kilograms, the database in Maputo had listed a restaurant as producing only 1 kilogram a day, which professionals like Neptuno questioned as very unlikely. At first, Mozambican counterparts were reluctant when JICA proposed fixing errors in the database. In particular, supervisors who were meant to inspect garbage collection on the street were not keen to also update the estimated volumes of waste production in the database to reflect the amounts that various businesses and institutions actually made. However, the Mozambican team decided that without updating the system to reflect how much waste was actually produced

---

[10] Interview, January 15, 2015, Maputo.
[11] Interview, January 20, 2015, Maputo.

and collected at different locations, they would not be able to also improve their waste-collection revenue. JICA staff, and Neptuno in particular, saw this kind of procedural learning as a major success of the project—DUSWMH's recognition that updating the categorization of businesses and institutions according to their waste production would also enable the team to make other improvements, in this case, in revenue collection.

DUSWMH staff extended critically thinking about reform procedures through to other areas identified as obstacles to revenue generation in the DUSWMH's reforms as well. Saranga, the Mozambican technical assistant hired by JICA to work with DUSWMH, noted that a questioning framework in review of DUSWMH's work allowed the directorate to negotiate for better contracts with other local organizations:

> For example, we had ... negotiations ... with *Electricidade de Moçambique* [Electricity of Mozambique, or EDM]. We were analyzing what the expenses and revenues were for the Municipal Council, [and] we saw that [in] the city's contract with EDM was also the collection of the garbage fee. EDM had a considerable margin [or revenue share] in the process of collecting that [garbage] fee [on electricity bills] ... [Our] conversation began with EDM, also involving all the staff [of the DUSWMH], in order to see if EDM could reduce the percentage they retain for providing the [revenue-collection] service. And after several negotiations, this rate was reduced. This represented an increase in the Municipal Council's revenue [from DUSWMH's solid-waste collection]. It's a success story.[12]

Not all of the critical learning involved in the 3Rs project, however, bore fruit in terms of improved project implementation. Some experiences led to the realization of fundamental challenges to the implementation of the 3Rs project. For example, Meriamo referenced the necessity of introducing a legal framework that would support the project's efforts to encourage households to separate their waste. She noted that:

> We only control solid-waste management. It is difficult, when raising awareness, to force [waste separation] ... as we did in the pilot project of Chamanculo D, [saying] "You have to separate" and then having to explain.... we [would] have to base it on a law. So if I don't have this law to defend me, I cannot force people to separate, to recycle. This [idea of a law] is fundamentally

---

[12] Interview, January 20, 2015, Maputo.

[about the] sustainability of recycling; we have to have a legal basis that will defend this request.[13]

Perhaps most critically to the idea of solidarity within international cooperation, the team at DUSWMH felt that JICA counterparts were open to learning from them as well. In the 3Rs project's effort at introducing composting in a low-income neighborhood, DUSWMH's staff related how they had to explain why certain elements of the composting practice initially envisioned by JICA—namely using the presence of worms—would not be locally picked up or accepted. Meriamo related how JICA staff accepted their rationales and shifted away from using worms in the composting aspect of the proposed work.[14] Saranga also explained that "Despite being normal, there are families or people who are not used to it; [using] worms is something out of the ordinary. So we had to try to inform them [i.e., JICA staff] that no, this methodology will probably not work. When people see maggots and worms, they have a different kind of thinking about them. So ... [JICA] also began to understand that there really are legal and customs issues, and thus we reformulated the project, in order to be in tune [with local realities]."[15]

JICA's project lead, Soeda, also described how he and his team recognized their work with counterparts in Maputo as a learning experience for them as well. When at times they reverted to a kind of mentor–mentee mentality, Soeda explained that their DUSWMH counterparts took the time to reflect on this and ask them to shift their approach, which was respected:

Really we learn, it's a very normal thing. But sometimes, it's not good of us, but sometimes each counterpart, including me, sometimes speaks with our [Mozambican] counterpart from [a] one-way side, like we are teaching to you. You are like a student. So I don't like those things we are saying. But sometimes [when] one of our team members asks [questions] very strongly to our counterparts ... the people come to me [afterward] to adjust those relationships. They always like keeping a balance of the relationships in this directorate. These kinds of things we also learn. Of course this is normal for other people but sometimes it's difficult.[16]

The other type of learning most referenced in discussion with JICA staff themselves centered on the metacognitive, with self-reflections about international

---

[13] Interview, January 20, 2015, Maputo. Translated from the Portuguese by the author.
[14] Interview, January 20, 2015, Maputo.
[15] Interview January 20, 2015, Maputo.
[16] Interview, January 15, 2015, Maputo.

cooperation work and being a transient figure on the ground. For example, Grace Neptuno expressed, "I have learned a lot but one is, I think, there is a need for us to be more patient, to be more tolerant, to give more time, to provide more effort. It is not because you want to teach them anything new but … because they have their own local knowledge they just cannot express, so you want to tell them that, 'Hey what you know is good! Let's improve on that. I don't have anything really new to offer you, what you have is [good] … let's just think of other ways that we can improve what you know.'"[17] Ryu Koide, JICA's project coordinator on the 3Rs project for planning and impact evaluation, concurred with Neptuno's perspective, sharing that he too felt that how well and openly counterparts discuss a project mattered: "Communication is important, language barriers are also important. I think that asking their opinions, their comments, is the most important thing. I mean, I think we shouldn't just suggest an idea by Japanese and decide things."[18]

4.2.2 Learning as Reconceptualization

É um desafio trabalhar com catadores. Principalmente com catadores, eles têm uma outra visão. Tu vais falar com um catador, a primeira coisa que ele olha pra ti, ele diz que tu vais gozar com ele, porque ele não trabalha, que ele vive de lixo para poder sustentar sua família. Então nós vimos que era um desafio que nós tínhamos que ter, mas que o município não podia ou não deveria trabalhar só isoladamente. Porque para conseguir pessoas sensíveis, nesse caso temos que ter psicólogos para falar primeiro com eles e temos que ter o estado envolvido todo, em vez de só o município.

It's a challenge to work with waste pickers. Mainly with scavengers, they have a different view. You're going to talk to a scavenger, the first thing he looks at you, he says you're going to make fun of him, because he doesn't work, that he lives on garbage to be able to support his family. So we saw that it was a challenge that we had to face, but that the municipality could not or should not work alone. Because to get to sensitive people, in this case we have to have psychologists to talk to them first and we have to have the whole state involved, instead of just the municipality.

(Florência Francisco Martins, technical professional, Directorate for
Urban Solid Waste Management and Health, Maputo)

---

[17] Interview, January 27, 2015, Maputo.
[18] Interview, January 27, 2015, Maputo.

The DUSWMH team visited Guarulhos, Brazil to get a sense of how *catadores*, or waste pickers, are integrated into the city's waste-management system, but left with a broader conceptualization of how such integration is made possible. Most specifically, DUSWMH staff understood from the experience the importance of enabling legislation for the enhancement of sustainable solid-waste management. As DUSWMH technical professional Martins related, a national legal mandate would be required to empower directorates like the one in Maputo or its neighboring cities to really make an impact on how waste is treated and whose responsibility it is to do so sustainably. In comparing the situation in Maputo and neighboring Matola with that witnessed in Guarulhos, she explained that:

> They [in Brazil] can even sanction the companies that produce [waste]. For example, here we have the large companies, Coca-Cola, GM ... they produce, but they are not obliged to collect the material itself to recycle. So the municipality sees this issue as a problem that really needs an urgent solution with the creation of a law that really obliges those institutions that produce this type of product [to] then collect or treat their waste. I think it would be a way to alleviate the waste we have here in Maputo and Matola.[19]

Beyond her emphasis on the understanding she and others developed of the enabling legal environment in Guarulhos for successful waste management, across the years I studied the Guarulhos project, Martins also related her reconceptualization of the processes—as opposed to just the technical knowledge—required to set up a successful solid-waste-management system that could incorporate waste pickers and recycling as core components. She explained how, through the cooperation project with Guarulhos, she and her colleagues saw consensus-building and participation in action, noting that:

> We saw that they [in Guarulhos] really have help from the government, they have help from everyone. There were meetings before, of the government, of the population in general, of the municipalities in general, they had meetings with the waste collectors, they had meetings with many separate groups, then they had a joint forum. So it was a process [as opposed to a technical waste-management issue]. [That] was really the most interesting thing that we saw that they did.[20]

---

[19] Interview, January 26, 2015, Maputo. Translated from the Portuguese by the author.
[20] Interview, January 26, 2015, Maputo. Translated from the Portuguese by the author.

However, Martins was also clear that the different circumstances of waste pickers in Maputo would really require special care in approaching them as city partners of the sort witnessed in Brazil. She indicated that DUSWMH "needs psychologists to work with us on the issue of waste pickers, because they are very sensitive people. You are going to say today that you want to help, then they start throwing stones, saying that you are going to take advantage of them, while the person really is not going to take advantage of them. They really want to help the person. So you have to have ways, you have to be able to talk to them, to pull them to your side." Martins's comments further reflected how conceptual learning about the nature of waste management would require a repositioning of the procedures of waste management in order to see what was successful in Brazil also be successful in Mozambique. She noted that in one of the seminars that DUSWMH staff had participated in during their visit to Guarulhos, waste pickers made a presentation, and then at the end said something that remained on Martins's mind. According to Martins, the waste picker said, "'What would the municipality or garbage be without the pickers?' Really, without the scavengers, I don't think the garbage would have any value. They see the waste picker as a profession there [in Brazil]."[21]

This broadening of the conceptualization of work that the DUSWMH staff at first perceived would be required to introduce recycling with waste-picker cooperatives in Maputo came directly from Maputo staff's firsthand account of what had been done in Brazil during exchange visits for the project. Elizabeth Affonso, the former International Projects Adviser for the city of Guarulhos, related how her team took visiting staff from Mozambique to the municipality of Embu das Artes, which is 100 kilometers from Guarulhos, because in that city waste pickers were included in the process of transforming the open dump to a landfill, akin to what was the ultimate hope in Maputo's plan for the Hulene dump site. Affonso noted the importance of DUSWMH's visit to Embu in broadening their conceptualization of waste work:

The professional collectors or *catadores* themselves were able to give their testimony [to the Mozambican staff]. [And] the municipality is trying to integrate these people into social programs, so that they are not left alone, so that they can be trained and know how to work with this ... it was cool because [the visiting staff from Mozambique] were able to get to know the complexity of the work, because it didn't only involve public services, it involved social assistance, it involved social funds, it involved other sectors of the city hall

[21] Interview, January 26, 2015, Maputo. Translated from the Portuguese by the author.

and other sectors of the federal government, which pass financial resources to the municipality.[22]

In many ways, Martins and others involved in the Guarulhos project were relating precisely the promise of what I had initially anticipated in my study of cooperation projects on the ground—in short, that Southern solidarity and the nearness of contextual experiences were important and mattered to high-level learning and solidarity among peers. Isabel Kinlim, who led the DUSWMH team when the Guarulhos project was first organized, provided further testament for this argument, noting that "there were people willing to teach and show the best, to train those who wanted to learn, but they [also] wanted to learn from what we knew, because there was passion in what we did and wanted."[23] Martins also felt her Guarulhos partners learned, and that working with DUSWMH in Maputo provided them with the opportunity to recognize different ways of achieving similar objectives:

> I think they learned a lot, although they're a little more developed, but there's a lot I don't think they had either. For example, we already have the master plan, they also have the master plan. But the way we conceived our master plan and the way they conceived their master plan is a little different. In the end, it's the same guidance tool, but ... they have everybody's involvement there, and we don't have everybody's involvement here. We work, I might say, in isolation, while they have government support.[24]

Here Martins was referencing the broader, multiscalar support she witnessed that the project's partnering department within the city of Guarulhos received—from the municipality, from the state government, and from the federal government—whereas the DUSWMH was working more independently within the public sector.

The references to learning the DUSWMH team shared was also mirrored by Guarulhos partners. Affonso from Guarulhos described how the cooperation project further allowed for the Guarulhos team to deeply reflect on their own recent experiences and lessons learned about how to better integrate waste pickers and improve the overall solid-waste-management system in the Brazilian city. Her reflections recalled the higher-level metacognitive thinking about how and why we work as we do. She recalled:

---

[22] Interview, February 11, 2015, online. Translated from the Portuguese by the author.

[23] Personal correspondence by email, February 1, 2015. Translated from the Portuguese by the author.

[24] Interview January 26, 2015, Maputo. Translated from the Portuguese by the author.

I worked in Guarulhos for twelve years and managed to get through a transition phase in Guarulhos [when there were] administrative reforms. I managed to remember a lot of Guarulhos as it was before the administrative reform. And that impacted me and [is part of] what moved me to this project. I felt like this project could make some contribution. Because when you see a lot of problems, you get there [to Maputo] and you see people eating in the garbage. We went to visit the garbage dump there. When I was sixteen, my school took me to the garbage dump in Guarulhos and it was the same situation that I saw there [in Maputo], years ago. That still happens in Brazil, in some areas. You see a person there, the feeling you have is that the world is not good, you think: "Wow, it's not possible, just with two hundred thousand euros for a project, you're not going to fix it." But then [that thinking] calms down and you can see ... try to think of what you can do to [help make things] better. And this project, the opportunity to go there, was to see that not so long ago, Brazil [was there]. Brazil is also still in transition, but [you can see that] it is possible to change, little by little.[25]

These descriptions that staff involved in the Maputo–Guarulhos *catadores* project shared with me would have had me contributing to the song of solidarity repeated in so much political propaganda around SSC, if materially it had not also been made clear to me that the project's actual objectives remained unrealized. As such, I came to question whether the Guarulhos–Maputo experience was a standard one for SSC, or more specifically standard for Brazilian SSC, by also studying the upgrading project that Brazilian and Italian cooperation teams were involved with in the historic neighborhood of Chamanculo C.

4.2.3 Learning as Imagination

Brasil, por exemplo, tem uma coisa que eu admiro muito ... é a técnica de comunicação, a técnica é muito boa. Eu admirei isso. Não só eu, os meus, talvez não a maioria, mas os meus colegas com quem eu converso, é muito boa. Eu acho que de alguma maneira tem muita semelhança com a natureza do próprio moçambicano, a maneira de ser, de se comportar. Ainda não vi um projeto europeu ou americano que seja social, ainda não vi. Ainda não tive uma ... já em algum momento participei em técnicas outras ocidentais, não so a brasileira. Mas o

---

[25] Interview, February 11, 2015, online. Translated from the Portuguese by the author.

brasileiro, a técnica foi … Eles não tiveram muitos problemas com adaptação. Agora, a Itália, talvez …

Brazil, for example, has something I really admire … the communication technique, the technique is very good. I admired that. Not only me, [and] maybe not the majority, but my colleagues I talked to. I think that somehow it has a lot of similarity with the nature of the Mozambican, the way of being, of behaving, I haven't seen yet a European or American project that is as social; I haven't seen it yet. I haven't had one yet … at some point I've participated in other Western technical [cooperation projects], not [only] the Brazilian one. But the Brazilian, the technique was … They didn't have many problems with adaptation. Now, Italy, maybe …

(Helio Manhisse, Mozambican social technician hired by AVSI, Italian NGO)

Chamanculo C's upgrading—from drainage and water connections to the improvement of roadways and public spaces—was envisioned as a strategic model for upgrading projects across Maputo's other vulnerable and substandard neighborhoods. As Cesar Cunguara, a planner with the city, related, the city's upgrading work in Chamanculo was a sort of pilot, where the city could learn and develop a procedural strategy for infrastructure interventions that could be replicated in other neighborhoods like Maxaquene.[26] It was also in Chamanculo C that Brazilian know-how—as well as an Italian NGO's experience in Brazil—in comprehensive slum upgrading practices, which encompassed both physical and social infrastructure investments and processes of engagement, was introduced and meant to shine. In other words, this was finally where the scaling-up of successes elsewhere—namely in Brazil—was meant to materialize. In reality, the material transformation of Chamanculo C through the cooperation project was stymied by the Brazilian national cooperation agency's own financial trouble and the staffing problems of the Brazilian physical planning team that ensued. However, despite even such challenges, the Brazilian reference remained prominent among Mozambican project staff on the ground who had either received training from Brazilian social-action professionals, or who had visited the country on exchange visits. Mozambican staff from both AVSI and the CMM related learning experiences that spoke to more than the technical aspects typically referenced as the aim of Southern partners' inclusion in trilateral cooperation contracts. They instead spoke of their own and Maputo's own growth potential as a realization emergent from

---

[26] Interview, January 28, 2015, Maputo.

the imagination provoked by project partners' experiences. In short, here were discussions revealing all the highest forms of knowledge—from the conceptual and procedural to the metacognitive—but *not* the technical know-how on physical planning that had been originally envisioned.

For example, the Mozambican AVSI staff's community-based presence lent itself to a deepening of contextual knowledge about Chamanculo residents' experiences, procedures for "getting things done" at higher levels, and a self-awareness and pride in the work they were doing. Flávia Nhassengo, a Mozambican social technician with AVSI shared that:

> Just the fact that we are here every day, every moment and we live the same way they do, entering their houses, stopping by and saying good morning, good afternoon, every day … [builds trust] … If I'm here eight hours a day, I feel like a resident of Chamanculo. I just go home to sleep. So the concern of a person from Chamanculo is my concern … Whenever I've seen a delay in solving some problems, or someone or some government institutions who should have been doing something … I would run over there, [and] slam the door. I went to the director of AVSI, because I felt and lived things inside Chamanculo C. And I already knew the right places [to make demands] … I already knew where to look. I would go directly, knock on the door, and say: "Why is so-and-so's problem not being solved?"[27]

The Mozambican social team also saw their work with AVSI in Chamanculo C as an opportunity to take on the role of teaching, sharing lessons, and refining strategies with others in the city. Nhassengo took deserved pride in this, noting:

> I went [around] to say in the first person what I really saw, what I lived, what was happening … There are other colleagues of mine who also directly and indirectly have already been giving lectures at UEM [i.e., the University of Eduardo Mondlane] and elsewhere … Their enthusiasm, it changes the mindset of other people [at these places] a lot. Because we had this space where we were invited, which was to talk about the project, to other people, to some students, to some organizations outside Chamanculo.[28]

Such reflections in practice also applied to the local AVSI staff's thinking about what could and perhaps could not yet work in their project. As in the case of the waste-picker cooperation project with Guarulhos, Mozambican staff

[27] Interview, January 13, 2015, Maputo. Translated from the Portuguese by the author.
[28] Interview, January 13, 2015, Maputo. Translated from the Portuguese by the author.

working in Chamanculo C again related clear metacognitive thinking about the challenges of how they might translate successes from Brazil to Mozambique. The AVSI social coordinator from Mozambique, Felisbela Materrula, noted that the lack of a community participation tradition in Maputo meant that the experience that AVSI had in Brazil would not easily be replicated in Mozambique:

> There aren't many [community] associations. So this makes it difficult, somehow, for anyone who wants to help to have a place to start, because there are associations, yes, but [only a] very few. People are not in the habit of participating in organizations in order to resolve community issues. There is indeed an administrative organization that has always been characteristic of governments here in Mozambique, which is to organize the community into quarters. There are the chiefs of quarters, chiefs of ten houses. OK, this helps a little. But it's not enough, because there is no free aggregation of people in associations to be able to discuss, even problematize certain issues that help people to solve their own problems without always waiting for the state. Not waiting for a project, but for them to take the initiative to do things, so that they become, as we say, protagonists of their own development.[29]

Similarly, Martins Navingo, another Mozambican social-action professional working with AVSI, indicated that learning, albeit briefly, with Brazilian partners on the ground was the best aspect of the work, but also required adjustments to plans. "What we did was to make our plan, adapting to the local reality, to the reality of Mozambique. Because some things from Brazil were not suited to our reality here in Mozambique."[30] For the Italian leadership within AVSI in Maputo, Alessandro Galimberti and Davide Valentino, adaptation was the point of AVSI's work. Galimberti described the key idea as reproduction, not replication. Indeed, he emphasized the importance of AVSI professionals in Maputo being different to those who had worked on the original project in Alagados, Brazil. Galimberti explained that this meant AVSI professionals in Maputo could access documentation and training from Brazil, but that they would not be overly biased by previous personal experiences in Brazil.

---

[29] Interview, January 28, 2015, Maputo. Translated from the Portuguese by the author.
[30] Interview, January 19, 2015, Maputo. Translated from the Portuguese by the author.

The emphasis on adaptation and inspiration held even for the Mozambican city planner Cunguara, who had at first described the Chamanculo cooperation project to me as an international bottleneck. He recalled the Brazilian experiences he witnessed in exchange visits as ones that expanded the possibility of what he felt could happen in Maputo:

> I think that one of the great positive aspects that I see in this type of cooperation … [was captured] in an experience that I enjoyed a lot in Brazil. I think it's Porto Maravilha. It is a very large operation to revitalize the port part of Rio de Janeiro. A whole set of operations took place there, public–private partnerships, etc. The municipality or the state or the government did not have to disburse large amounts of money … It was enough to define regulatory instruments to implement the plans. In this case, [for the upgrading of] informal settlements, [this] can be of great value. [One hears] "There is no money—There is no money!", but I think it is possible to improve gradually, without the municipality having to withdraw large amounts [of funds]. I think that in a period of two more years, we can have this [regulatory] instrument, an instrument or regulation that can guide this type of urban transformation. The land is well located, we have X, Y, Z conditions, [and] in return, an investor in this case can implement works and would benefit. I think it's possible to do that, especially when we go out and see things happen. "Why can't we do it too?" We can, I think we can. The experience for me, particularly, started to make me see that it is possible to do this, that it is possible for this to happen.[31]

Still, neither Cunguara or others like Materrula were blind to the difficulties still plaguing the trilateral cooperation work and its engagement with Brazil. Cunguara joked that he was tired of participating in exchange visits to Brazil, having visited the country already six times during his tenure as a city planner. Further, Cunguara's colleague in Maputo's Directorate of Urban Planning and the Environment, Rogerio Nuvunga, related that, contrary to the original intention, there was not much in the way of an actual technical learning exchange with Brazil on the physical planning side, where, instead of Brazil, Maputo's own city-planning team had to pick up the slack of work left still to be done.

---

[31] Interview, January 28, 2015, Maputo. Translated from the Portuguese by the author.

4.2.4 Learning as Navigation

Tem que ser uma parceria negociada em que ambos sentem-se que vão sair a ganhar. Agora quando falamos de ganho, não estamos a falar de materiais, nem monetário, mas um ganho institucional, em que cada um sente-se que "eu fazendo parte dessa parceria sinto-me bem, sinto que a minha instituição vai também ganhar e a outra também vai ganhar." Então, eu penso que uma parceria é melhor nesse sentido, que seja negociada e que cada um dos componentes se sinta dono, e não se sinta a perder e nem como servidor do outro.

It has to be a negotiated partnership in which both feel they will win. Now when we talk about gain, we are not talking about materials or money, but an institutional gain, in which each one feels that "me being part of this partnership, I feel good, I feel that my institution will also gain and another will also win." So, I think that a partnership is better in this sense, that it is negotiated and that each component feels the owner, and does not feel like a loser or a servant of the other.

(Ramos Nhachuchane, Assistant Coordinator of AMDEC, Maxaquene A,
Maputo)

Of all the cooperation projects I studied, the one in Maxaquene A perhaps emerges as the most differentiated in my examination of the types of and room for learning. Interestingly, my reading of learning in the Maxaquene A work revealed a bifurcation of knowledge produced and shared that aligned with different project roles and responsibilities. More specifically, both local and international staff emerged with clear reflections about their role, the value of their own experiences, and the weight of their own voices and approaches to project work. Whether those reflections were positive or negative, however, essentially correlated with a staff member's positionality within the project. When in 2014 I first met Gilda Jossais, the coordinator of AMDEC in Maxaquene A, for example, she was already troubled by the unevenness of experiences within the Maxaquene A upgrading project and hierarchies between the EWB and her team on the ground. Jossais gave the example of her engineering team often having to correct Spanish EWB partners and explain that, in Maputo, their conceptualization of a drainage system would not work. She also discussed how AMDEC most valued their international partners' scientific or technical knowledge, but that some staffing shifts among partners meant that this did not always materialize:

The last expatriate who came, I think, was the biggest failure of our partner, because he was a person who was at the management level ... he wasn't very technical like the first one. The first one had [studied] civil engineering. So [he knew how] to draw, to discuss these things, [which] was something that was perhaps very good for my team to see.[32]

Ramos Nhachuchane, the Assistant Coordinator of AMDEC on the project, concurred. He admired the on-the-ground and autonomous presence that EWB technical staff had in Maxaquene. Instead of having to engage with a decision-making authority located elsewhere, Nhachuchane emphasized that EWB's grounded and discretionary independence in the physical work in Maxaquene A enabled a requisite flexibility in project implementation. Critically, he felt it also allowed for a real exchange of technical knowledge between the two teams:

> It was important because for the transfer of knowledge and experiences with the Mozambican technicians, it [made it] very easy. The sharing of difficulties that were encountered; they were not issues that were just reported but that were experienced by someone who was representing the organization. So I think it was very good. It allowed them to also learn from Mozambican technicians and we also learned from them. The written reports we did were just a complement to having someone to always talk to, someone who was watching the work.[33]

This prioritization of grounded, technical learning as the center of cooperation did not, however, translate into the easy acceptance of a sometimes hierarchical relationship.

When I asked Jossais about her own experience with international partners, she expressed a clear preference for equivalent staff positions between international partners and her organization, with, for example, a director from the former engaged with a director from the latter. When international partners with which AMDEC was working in Maxaquene A diverged from this ideal, she felt that this put strains on building trust between the two:

> If the partner here is saying that there is this, that it's not working, and there's [a partner] on the other side, this person can take arrogant positions, positions that I [feel are] threatening positions. But you don't have anyone to talk

---

[32] Interview, July 16, 2014, Maputo. Translated from the Portuguese by the author.
[33] Interview, January 13, 2015, Maputo. Translated from the Portuguese by the author.

to outside of this person … [and] what I see recently [is that] there are partners with a tendency to want to interfere in the [internal] management of
human resources…. . I have partners at all levels, right? The ones who come
in and start screaming and I say "Can I talk? I can speak?" *Screaming?*—
[Partners] who aren't even my age? So then he says, "Speak up, speak up. OK,
if you don't do this, I won't do this," so I have to always do a psychological
exercise to keep calm.[34]

Where instead project governance worked well and created opportunities for
mutual learning and capacity development was at the most grounded level
of work, where not only technical knowledge was exchanged but also reflective thinking about the nature of the project's work and its worth for
professional development. This was especially true where community-based
partner organizations working under AMDEC with EWB were concerned.
For example, Emidio Mondlane, a social-action professional with ASCHA in
Maxaquene A, remarked on EWB technical partners' openness to ASCHA and
AMDEC's opinions about implementing upgrading interventions. He recalled
that "nothing was taken for granted without first interacting with us. They
came to us, 'we think this can be like that, and so, what do you think?' And
we also had our opinion, we put our idea [out]. Only after an interaction [with
us] was a final plan made. They were always open to suggestions, criticisms,
everything."[35] Mondlane was especially impacted by the voluntary nature of
EWB technicians' work in Maxaquene A, and reflected on that model of engagement as a representation of higher values and work incentives beyond the
remunerative:

> What strikes me is that not everything in life is done for money. I worked with
> them, who were practically volunteers, who came and [even] when facing
> a critical situation … they were there in the cause and without any benefit.
> Interacting with people like them [in EWB] was a very positive thing that has
> stayed with me. The work itself, for example, drawing up plans, I'm talking
> about technical terms, drawing up plans, how to make a small map, I learned
> from them too because I was always close by.[36]

EWB professionals in Maxaquene A shared both Jossais's and Mondlane's sen-
sibilities about what different hierarchies of staff understood about what did

---

[34] Interview, July 16, 2014, Maputo. Translated from the Portuguese by the author.
[35] Interview, January 22, 2015, Maputo. Translated from the Portuguese by the author.
[36] Interview, January 22, 2015, Maputo. Translated from the Portuguese by the author.

and what did not work on the ground. Alvaro Garcia, a Spanish engineer coordinating EWB's work in Maputo, shared that the technical work on the ground was an opportunity for both Mozambican partners based within Maxaquene A and EWB staff to learn outside their own areas of expertise:

> I, for example, learned a lot from working with social technicians … [As] engineers, sometimes we are very engineering [oriented] but we are not just working in engineering, we are working on social projects. So Kuwuka [a local community partner in Maxaquene A] has some good strategies [we] always learned from. [For example, they would explain] "Hey, you could not say that like that [to a resident] … OK, thank you!" Then, designing projects together enriches both EWB and Kuwuka. Kuwuka's technicians have also learned things from us, when we are writing the general objective, result, indicator. The more formal part [is where] the EWB has a consolidated experience … so our growth, it's [also] Kuwuka's growth.

However, challenges of trust and staff approaches to work in Maxaquene A loomed heavily over management-level partners from EWB and from AMDEC and the CMM. Another EWB coordinator originally from Colombia was frank in relating this point. She noted that EWB had proposed that their staff work embedded with AMDEC in the latter's offices, but that AMDEC leadership rejected this idea. When the CMM ultimately tore up the drainage ditch that EWB had worked to install in the neighborhood, EWB wanted to avoid continued negative interactions with managers at AMDEC:

> I will be very honest, the partnership changed because of the relationship with AMDEC. The management in many aspects was not good on the part of AMDEC. Many partnerships have complaints about leadership, about the management … [There were] a lot of difficulties with AMDEC staff. So EWB questioned whether it was worth continuing or giving up working in Maxaquene A with this partner. EWB decided not to continue with this partner [i.e., AMDEC] because it was not working … They had many difficulties, many constraints with the municipality … We wanted to avoid a direct confrontation. So the project also changed its strategy. It was no longer going to be a drainage project. So we continued with another counterpart, in another thematic area.[37]

---

[37] Interview, January 27, 2015, Maputo. Translated from the Portuguese by the author.

EWB felt AMDEC's inability to intervene effectively on behalf of the project with the CMM was a major constraint on its work in the neighborhood. As such, EWB lost faith in AMDEC's capacity as a local partner that knew how to navigate the local environment. After an internal discussion and evaluation of its work with AMDEC, leadership at EWB decided to close the partnership with AMDEC, and instead pursued one with other community-based organizations that could help with other upgrading work in Maxaquene A.

The abruptness of the end of AMDEC's work with EWB, and the perceived silence which followed it from AMDEC's perspective, remained a source of dismay and confusion. Nhachuchane, the Assistant Coordinator of AMDEC noted that perhaps EWB was experiencing internal challenges or organizational issues that they were not willing to explain in full. However, he suggested that if they had done so, their partnership would have ended on a better note. Instead, he said, "people only saw changes in attitudes, the disappearance of some people who had been doing work without a clear explanation of what was happening."[38] EWB management's choice—its very capacity to choose—relays their perception of a hierarchical relationship. It is thus perhaps not surprising that there were limitations for high-level learning among the managerial staff of the partners involved in the project. Instead, it was only the most grounded of team members from EWB and its local partners who relayed the opportunities for learning, from the technical to the metacognitive.

4.3 Parsing out Proximities that Matter

Neither the material benefits nor the learning potentialities advertised in the cooperation projects I studied were always delivered. However, discussions with the diverse group of project professionals on the ground in cooperation projects across Maputo did reveal that who teaches and who learns were far from delimited or singularly held roles, despite the continued persistence of hierarchical labels in international cooperation work. Further, these conversations also provided insights into what did matter, particularly for higher-level conceptual, procedural, and metacognitive learning, in partnerships. In reexamining practitioners' accounts, three proximities emerged as central levers shaping how they assessed and related learning experiences across cooperation projects: project governance, local embeddedness, and professional theories of practice.

---

[38] Interview, January 13, 2015, Maputo. Translated from the Portuguese by the author

4.3.1 Project Governance: Peer Relationships and Heterarchies over Hierarchies

When I arrived in Maputo to study cooperation projects on the ground, I had not anticipated the full extent to which different aspects of staff architecture and organizational governance would influence project outcomes. One clear reason for this influence was simply the level of turnover in staff and reconfigurations of partnerships in cooperation projects, shifting dynamics of project relationships and the learning context for all professional stakeholders involved. Other influences were more implicit—such as in how perceived differences in age shaped interactions and opportunities for high-level, reflective learning. And still other aspects were explicit, as in the balance of hierarchical positions between international and Mozambican staff and how that hierarchy encouraged or impinged on capacity development for both. Indeed, from the perspective of someone interested in studying SSC, what was most striking for me to hear from Mozambican staff involved in projects I studied was this last aspect, or their distinct sense of hierarchies involved in the design and the implementation of international cooperation projects in their own city.

Domingos Chivambo, head of solid-waste management in the DUSWMH, revealed early on that while he participated in trips to Guarulhos, Brazil as part of the project on waste-picker cooperatives, when he joined the project he was not initially informed why exactly the Maputo team was going to Brazil. Luisa Langa additionally offered that their office simply implements that which has already been decided. To a certain degree, these sentiments support what was revealed in a survey run by the OECD about the lack of engagement of bilateral donors with local governments in designing programs.[39] However, they also reflect the governance hierarchies within the CMM itself, and the place of street-level bureaucrats and local technical professionals in international negotiations. For international cooperation projects to work, Chivambo advised that local professionals within the city's bureaucracies needed to be more at the lead of project initiation and design, as opposed to what typically happens:

> First, we have to be the ones who need the project, to say what we want, and under the conditions, the one who offers us a project will have to evaluate [our request] and say "OK, yes I think I can do this [up to here and] do that,

---

[39] Interview, July 16, 2014, Maputo.

the rest you start doing," but projects often appear. We join many times without thinking what it is that we really want…. [Instead] projects appear, we are informed that there is a project in the area, for example, of solid-waste management. There is a project, so we have to try to choose one of the projects that we think belongs to our area, which can develop our area, and [we] often have no time to carry out an analysis, what is within that project, what can we develop to achieve what we want. That, perhaps, is also one of the problems that we encounter, in terms of projects.[40]

Chivambo implied that this was why the DUSWMH "stopped delivering the [waste-picker] project, [and instead] the project's protagonist became LVIA [the Italian NGO]."[41] Further, in the waste-picker project with Guarulhos, Chivambo noted that there were no person-to-person equivalent meetings, with instead all meetings conducted at a group level.

What did appear to work well was when there was more equivalency between staff from both partnerships. Elizabeth Affonso, from Guarulhos, noted this aspect was most pronounced during exchange visits in Brazil, highlighting how individual municipal staff from the Brazilian city were able to speak concretely about strategies they used when the municipal staff from Maputo visited:

Most of them had already been in Guarulhos for over ten years. And most of them followed the transformation [of the city's waste-management system], as it was done. So many of the doubts that arose [among Mozambican partners], many of the questions, the comments, the Guarulhos team saw themselves in that situation or had already gone through that or were still going through it … For example, [Mozambicans asked] "How does the inspector inspect if the garbage was placed outside at the wrong time?" The person in charge of this sector [from Guarulhos] would raise their hand and could respond. This [experience] was very new. There is no way to prepare for all the questions, but … we knew how to answer. This project was cool for that.[42]

In the 3Rs cooperation project with Japan, staff members of the JICA team and Maputo's DUSWMH team were also paired according to the themes of responsibility that the two cooperating partners shared. The JICA architecture

---

[40] Interview, July 16, 2014, Maputo. Translated from the Portuguese by the author.
[41] Interview, July 16, 2014, Maputo. Translated from the Portuguese by the author.
[42] Interview, February 11, 2015, virtual. Translated from the Portuguese by the author.

in effect afforded more specific capacity-building across team partners, in addition to organizational-management capacity at the group level. For example, all the staff at DUSWMH and JICA spoke about their specific "counterparts," as opposed to the general partner, in describing their day-to-day work, which was unlike the way local professionals in Maputo spoke about, for example, cooperation partnerships with Brazil's ABC (national cooperation agency). In projects for which there were no specified counterparts for each team member, hierarchies of management were often contested, as in the case between AMDEC and the EWB in Maxaquene A, where only local-level or ground technical staff felt they had counterparts. The presence of an equivalent mattered too, however, at higher levels, as very pointedly related by the Director of International Relations for Maputo—Natacha Morais—and her Barcelona counterpart, Felip Roca Blasco, the Director of International Relations and Cooperation. In retrospect, it is not surprising to me that during discussions about international cooperation with Morais and her team in Maputo, Barcelona was held up as the gold standard. In her telling, this was because of the consistency of Barcelona's budgetary support, built into Spanish law on funding international cooperation. However, she—and her counterpart—both made a point of letting me know that their partnership was also a friendship, based on their mutual respect and shared knowledge of the specific responsibilities each held.[43]

This individual pairing of counterparts had very specific implications for capacity development and learning. Grace Neptuno, a Filipino national working as a financial adviser on the JICA team, spoke at length about her interaction with her Mozambican counterpart, emphasizing that in international development projects, "everything is relationship; it is all about relationships.... if you are not friends ... they will not give you the correct data, they will not give you the complete information you need." From Neptuno's perspective, this element of the personal in the professional was critical for learning on the job and emerged from the pairing of equivalent staff members. She described how her Mozambican counterpart was initially very shy about presenting in group meetings and never spoke, but that has since changed and Neptuno related great pride in seeing her counterpart now act as a more confident financial manager within the DUSWMH. "I have learned to make sure that the local people take the lead. It is very important to make them take the lead especially in finance." As a Filipino national, Neptuno described her work as a conduit and translator of sorts, with a capacity to engage what she described

---

[43] Interviews with Morais and with Roca Blasco in Maputo, July 14–15, 2014.

as the more formal interactions of international consultants from Japan, as well as to engage with peer professionals from lower-income economies like Mozambique.

4.3.2 Local Embeddedness

The physical presence of international partners in Maputo is rather dense, and can have negative externalities, as I've argued elsewhere (Carolini, 2021). However, what was clear across several of the cooperation projects I studied was the difference between having partners in places where work actually gets done as opposed to partners in their own "local" headquarters. Here, then, it seemed that local embeddedness was not simply about having an address in Maputo, but *sharing* one. Alvaro Garcia, the Spanish EWB coordinator emphasized this distinction between independent local headquarters and a more embedded approach:

> I think this is one of the important things. We live together. Gilda [from Kuwuka] is at the table, I am, Tânia is. So I think that makes it no longer EWB and Kuwuka. I think this is an important thing for me; we live together. At lunchtime, we had lunch together. So that makes us united. Then Kuwuka is an organization that works well, that meets deadlines. Sometimes it's a bit boring, you ask for funding, you need the documents signed ... We always fulfilled those deadlines; those important things were always fulfilled ... What I learned, what Kuwuka learned, this learning, if I'm in Barcelona and call on Skype, I don't get it. And then, if I'm not close to you, I can't ask you for anything. I don't know *how* to ask. So I believe that presence is good, minimal too, in terms of costs. I'm a little more critical about macro organizations, which have a lot of presence, big offices, big cars. That, I don't care for at all.[44]

Garcia explained that larger organizations carry large budgets, but that those budgets are not necessarily also geared toward actual material improvements in a locale. "What percentage of money ultimately stays in the organization, and what percentage of money goes to building a society or a neighborhood? There are many costs that for me are avoidable."[45] Similarly, the depth of embeddedness pursued in the office integration of JICA staff with Maputo's DUSWMH staff was a specific cooperation strategy, according to JICA

---

[44] Interview, January 26, 2015, Maputo. Translated from the Portuguese by the author.
[45] Interview, January 26, 2015, Maputo. Translated from the Portuguese by the author.

coordinator, Ryu Koide. He explained that he felt that "it's much better to split our team into their offices. I got that idea when I came initially, [and] our management said: 'OK, this is better.' So, for example, we have an expert on financial management, and we could put her inside their financial-management office. And … we could put another expert of 3R into maybe, you know, their offices in charge of 3R, and then have our daily conversations."[46]

The idea of embeddedness here was not to ensure international partners became experts on the local context, but rather simply that it allowed for the development of professional relationships and removed the potential of transaction costs that typically delay discretionary decision-making. Indeed, as Sergio Manhique, Head of Monitoring and Quality Control for the CMM, asserted, local knowledge and contextual familiarity in an international cooperation partner was not as important as SSC advocates suggest. "We already have a command of the local situation. So it's not relevant that the partner has a lot of expertise on the situation here."[47] Instead, what was important was a partner's capacity to engage effectively and efficiently in daily interactions. An element that mattered to such integration was language. On this score, Shungo Soeda, the project head from JICA, was clear about the impact his own team's language limitations brought to the table:

> If I were to say that there is still some problem I would say it is the time, because the translator takes time. So I expected to finish this meeting within two hours, though all the time [it finishes in] three hours, sometimes three hours and a half … After lunch time everybody loses their motivation [and] concentration to meeting. So that is one issue we still have, but we are trying to improve with that. Also, we are trying to study Portuguese, but it takes time. These younger guys, most of them can speak Portuguese a little but [for] the older guys, it's hard.[48]

Indeed, Mozambican professionals felt that the capacity to communicate easily with partners, in their own language, was paramount to effective partnerships. Luisa Langa, the head of monitoring at Maputo's DUSWMH, explained that very few of her own team at the directorate spoke English, but that, for example, partners from JICA used English as the basic communication language for their work in Maputo, thereby requiring the presence of translators at every project meeting. Langa expressed frustration with this and

---

[46] Interview, January 27, 2015, Maputo.
[47] Interview, January 20, 2015, Maputo. Translated from the Portuguese by the author.
[48] Interview, January 15, 2015, Maputo.

pinned language as the greatest challenge in international cooperation work, as the implications for efficiencies in meetings, documentation, and basic daily communications were materially substantial.[49]

4.3.3 Theories of Practice: Professionals and their Work Rationales

What is nominally termed a bilateral cooperation project between two countries in reality can involve a much more complex and diverse set of international stakeholders. JICA's 3Rs project was actually implemented by a Japanese consultancy that won the JICA bid for work in Mozambique. That consultancy, Nissan, comprised international "experts," as they were referred to internally by staff interviewed, from Japan and the Philippines, as well as national counterparts from Mozambique who were directly hired by Nissan for the project's implementation. The EWB team from Spain working in Maxaquene A actually involved a Colombian national. Similarly, staff from the CMM working in Chamanculo C were led by a Portuguese national, while the Italian NGO partner AVSI was largely staffed by Mozambicans. In short, the global nature of the international cooperation workforce in practice betrays efforts to flatten the nature of partnership with staid geographic labels. Instead, what did matter were practitioners' own professional theories of practice, or the rationales they brought to the table in their work.

At times, it was clear that epistemological legacies and biases professionals carried prohibited their abilities to openly engage their partners. For example, Helio Manhisse, a Mozambican social technician working for AVSI in Chamanculo C, noted the different attitudes that his Italian and Brazilian colleagues brought to meetings:

> Italy had a focus, a goal to be achieved, a focus. And I've witnessed several times that it's normal for Brazilians to be doing something, talking, conversing, but the Italians, they don't allow that … I always heard my [Italian] colleagues say either "You can't talk" or "You can't laugh." You could see that when we had our Brazilian colleague [in contrast], he would give examples, talk about realities, at some point he laughed, at some point he made a joke. So I relaxed my mind a little. Perhaps because Mozambicans are not yet used to a level, I don't know how to say … the right way to do things.[50]

---

[49] Interview, August 14, 2014, Maputo.
[50] Interview, January 20, 2015, Maputo. Translated from the Portuguese by the author.

The Coordinator of AMDEC in Maxaquene A, Gilda Jossais, emphasized that when Mozambicans in such situations assert themselves, as did she, this also creates a vulnerability for them and their inclusion in a project with an international partner. She clarified that "maybe also because I'm a person with a very strong personality, I say 'It's like this or nothing' ... so AMDEC is also under the risk of becoming even more fragile, but I think at some point we have [to] have the ability to—it's like the revolutionaries, isn't it?—to lose but to demonstrate consistency on a given subject."[51]

In a city like Maputo, where so much of urban development is intertwined with international cooperation, these attitudes toward work matter a great deal beyond the limits of a specific project. In part, this is because of what one might call an ecosystem of internal recycling and mobility across international cooperation projects within the city. As Jossais's colleague within AMDEC, Ramos Nhachuchane, noted, there is an African expression of relevance to the international development industry in Maputo: "We're not going to cross paths just once."[52] For this reason, both local professionals from Maxaquene A and EWB staff highlighted the importance that individual professionals' own work rationales carry to a project's success and failure. Emidio Mondlane, one of the Mozambican social-action professionals from Maxaquene, was blunt:

> Personality is key. It's not enough to all be together [working toward] a single cause ... personality is indispensable, the approach of the person, the person's heart. We have had situations in which people are involved in an intervention, but they don't give themselves. But ... behavior, the way of being, was fundamental for a relationship between us, a good relationship. Because even after work, our relationship didn't just end at work. Even after work was finished, we continued, we exchanged experiences.[53]

Garcia, the coordinator from EWB concurred, noting that much in their own project depended on how professional staff interacted, which created welcome or unwelcome perceptions of partners and their contributions to work.

4.4 Learning in the Aggregate

While most of my research and conversations with professionals spoke to the nature of learning across staff involved in separate cooperation projects and

---

[51] Interview, July 16, 2014, Maputo. Translated from the Portuguese by the author.
[52] Interview, January 13, 2015, Maputo. Translated from the Portuguese by the author.
[53] Interview, January 22, 2015, Maputo. Translated from the Portuguese by the author.

their understanding of what works in development, an additional aspect that came out across the portfolio of projects was the high-level learning among Mozambican municipal staff from the aggregation of their experiences across projects. In other words, there was not simply learning at the individual project level, but also in managing the group of different cooperation projects. Despite the fact that very little time is afforded to internal reflections and meetings, Mozambican leaders at DUSWMH and in the CMM were thinking strategically about how to leverage the various cooperation projects they were engaged with on the ground to improve city services overall.

For example, Chivambo explained that given the overlap on the topic of recycling between Maputo's partnership with Guarulhos and its partnership with JICA, the DUSWMH hoped to leverage and connect the work of each. This meant, for example, that they were aiming to organize waste pickers into collectives in the style of Brazil, which could then help Maputo also forward a program of recycling being introduced with JICA's assistance on the 3Rs projects.[54] However, the staff at DUSWMH did not necessarily relate this thinking to their international partners consistently. JICA's 3Rs project lead, Soeda, for example, noted that "sometimes our counterparts don't tell us what they are discussing about [their work with other consultants]. So it is not good for us. We should understand what is going on under this directorate."[55]

Personally, while I understood Soeda's point in terms of work coordination, I also saw Chivambo's example as a positive one of local professionals from the city of Maputo asserting the city and its development as their own project, as opposed to the project of one of the myriad of international partners dotting its landscape, partnerships which were often negotiated at levels above that of the city staff itself. It gave me some hope that perhaps the primacy of geopolitical and technical proximities in the labeling of cooperation relationships might also be challenged and that partnerships might one day be redesigned according to other ideas—such as project governance, local embeddedness, and theories of practice—which appeared to provide greater opportunity for high-level learning. For this to happen, however, I knew that there was still a remaining question to answer about whether the combination of proximities that mattered in Maputo, also mattered outside Maputo and Mozambique.

---

[54] Interview, July 16, 2014, Maputo. Translated from the Portuguese by the author.
[55] Interview, January 15, 2015, Maputo.

5

Recognizing Potentials

Moving from Mentorship to Proximate Peers

5.1 If Solidarity and Equity were Real

Southern cooperation, with its distinct normative priorities of commonality and equity, gestures toward a transformation of power relations in international cooperation, as Julius Nyerere recognized in his contribution to *Dialogue for a New Order*. In this edited volume, Nyerere and other leaders from the South called for unified action to resolve the political impasse in creating a new international economic order in 1980. The Tanzanian president explicitly suggests that countries in the global South needed their own international organization—outside the auspices of the UN—to facilitate Southern cooperation, as paying members of the UN system outside the G77 would otherwise divert the organization's objectives toward their own, higher-income ends. He wrote:

> But it may be that the Group of 77 should be looking again at this question of whether it needs its own full-time economists and other professional people as a technical aid to the policymakers and negotiators. I would only add that, if we decide this to be the case, then we must pay for that technical office ourselves. He who pays the piper calls the tune.[1]

This point hints at why the politics of labels in international aid cooperation persists.

SSC and trilateral cooperation programming in the UN appears to materialize the kind of vulnerabilities that Nyerere foresaw. Embracing SSC and trilateral cooperation has been preferred to making fundamental challenges to the Western mode of development, peculiarly by the South's own

---

[1] Nyerere, 1980: 9–10.

Equity, Evaluation, and International Cooperation. Gabriella Y. Carolini, Oxford University Press.
© Gabriella Y. Carolini (2022). DOI: 10.1093/oso/9780192865489.003.0006

leading economies as well as Northern partners. Rather than advancing and mobilizing around complementary Southern-born concepts or frameworks of development—what scholars like Arturo Escobar have called "transition discourses"—that eschew capital accumulation and growth in favor of capital distribution, solidarity economies, and/or ecological accountability,[2] the largest economies in Asia, Latin America, and Africa are pursuing models of economic growth and hierarchical development partnerships with lower-income countries of the sort long supported by orthodox international financial institutions and high-income countries in the North. International-relations scholars such as Marco Vieira (Vieira, 2012) insist that the emergence of Southern regional leaders and their collective development-assistance initiatives—such as the India, Brazil, and South Africa partnership (IBSA)—constitute an important countervailing power and alternative "standard" for development that contests the West's dominance therein by its mere being. However, the push to materialize distributive justice within international political fora like the UN Security Council, for example, is perhaps a necessary but insufficient turn toward building out a more equitable international governance system, as first aspired to at Bandung. The realpolitik of regional leaders engaged in SSC hints at the fact that the primary concern of technical cooperation has not been so much technical as financial and political. Even when and where development "alternatives" from Southern countries have gained some institutional ground, there are contradictions in how governing regimes balance domestic demands for new equitable futures with regional or even global aspirations for a different distributive system.[3]

Examples of this tension between the rhetorical promotion of equity and its translation within regions are especially revealing among some of the leading Southern economies. The South African constitution, for instance, highlights the importance of *ubuntu*, the African social philosophy emphasizing reciprocity and collectiveness—or an understanding that "I am because we are" (Eze, 2018; Gade, 2012; Metz & Gaie, 2010). However, evidence of *ubuntu* as

---

[2] Such discourses—like that of the Zapatistas and La Via Campesina within Latin America—contest the equation of progress with economic growth and materialism, and often arose from the struggles of marginalized communities in the global South (Beling et al, 2018; Escobar, 2011), though of course such groups also exist and have forwarded alternative modes of "economy" in the global North (Gibson-Graham, 2006).

[3] See, for example, Sarah Radcliffe's work on the ways that alternative development thought has been incorporated by mainstream development actors and governments in Latin America; Patrick Bond and Carmen Martinez Novo's works on the contradictions of post-neoliberal experiments in South Africa and Ecuador; or David Barkin and Blanca Lemus's (2014) work on how social movements' efforts to promote social and environmental justice are challenged by national initiatives that threaten ecosystems in Mexico (Elwood et al, 2016; Radcliffe, 2015).

the philosophical purveyor of South Africa's foreign-policy interventions on the continent and efforts to build a regional economic bloc are hardly consistent. This is manifest in the contradiction of an explicit claim of *ubuntu* as a guiding value of South Africa's Department of International Relations and Cooperation (DIRCO) at the same time as DIRCO prioritizes an economic diplomacy centered on building South Africa's regional authority and its lead in regional market shares of trade.[4] This inconsistency between the realities of a neoliberal nationalist race to the top, and the hoped-for countervailing approaches to enhanced quality of life through an *ubuntu*-inspired regional cooperation, is also reflected in the relative weakness of the country's African Renaissance and International Cooperation Fund and its envisioned replacement in the SADPA.[5] In the latest annual report from DIRCO, South Africa's contributions to SSC and continental cooperation have both declined and are lower than its North–South cooperation expenditures, as shown in Table 5.1.

Furthermore, despite its diplomatic efforts, South Africa's regional economic policies and political leadership on issues like trade are often viewed by its neighbors as rather mercenary as opposed to inspired by ideals of reciprocity. While leading African international-relations scholar Ian Taylor (2011) argues that the actual "imperial" potentiality of South Africa within the Southern African region is delimited by what he calls the neo-patrimonial modes of governance in the region, other scholars of SSC and Africa, like Chris Alden and Maxi Schoeman (2015), still contend that South Africa's push for an "African Renaissance," anchored by its dominance in growing African commerce and trade, positioned South Africa as international organizations' preferred African representative. This status and South Africa's global market aspirations complicate its claims of a diplomacy centered on equity with its neighbors.

Similarly, it is not Brazil, but Ecuador, Bolivia, and Venezuela that provided the more vociferous (if equivocal) promotion of alternative frameworks of development based on solidarity and equity, such as the indigenous South American concept of *buen vivir* (or "good living"), or the Bolivarian aspiration of regional solidarity and integration in the *Alternativa Bolivariana para*

---

[4] The inconsistency of South Africa' foreign policy is addressed by authors elsewhere (Qobo & Nyathi, 2016); here, I seek to emphasize the political embrace and use of, if not practice in, the *ubuntu* reference in South Africa's foreign policy. The extensive reference to *ubuntu* in South African politics— used in everything from DIRCO's own monthly publication, which is entitled "Ubuntu Magazine," to the constitution—as Sihlongonyane argues about other rhetorical devices in the country—has made it a rather empty signifier (Sihlongonyane, 2015a).

[5] Patrick Bond discusses the rise of "neoliberal nationalism" in South Africa as counterintuitive given the anti-imperialist post-apartheid leadership and strength of social movements in the country (Elwood et al, 2016).

Table 5.1 South Africa's DIRCO Programmatic Spending (2016–2018) in R'000

Program Expenditure	2016–2017			2017–2018		
	Final appropriation	Actual expenditure	Under-expenditure	Final appropriation	Actual expenditure	Under-expenditure
Global System of Governance	289,912	282,300	7,612	285,438	283,110	2,328
Continental Cooperation	101,834	91,503	10,331	77,808	74,593	3,215
South–South Cooperation	4,405	3,341	1,064	1,375	820	555
North–South Dialogue	85,799	85,799	–	88,535	86,785	1,750
Total	481,950	462,943	19,007	453,156	445,308	7,848

Source: South Africa Department of International Relations and Cooperation—Annual Financial Report 2018.

las Américas y el Tratado de Comercio de los Pueblos (ALBA-TCP).[6] *Buen vivir,* however problematic in practice, nominally advances a balance among social, environmental, and spiritual "development" goals, as opposed to the more consumption-based environmental degradation of the Western, capital-driven development tradition (Campodónico et al, 2017; Gudynas, 2016; Muhr, 2016; Villalba, 2013). *Sumac kawsay*—as it is called in the Kichwa language in Ecuador—was incorporated into a new Ecuadorean constitution in 2008, forwarding the idea that state interventions across economic, social, political, and ecological policies should all work to ensure *sumac kawsay* (Gudynas, 2011). In Bolivia, *suma qamaña*, the Aymaran word for *buen vivir*, was adopted constitutionally in 2009.[7] At the regional level of international cooperation, *buen*

---

[6] ALBA-TCP stands for the "Bolivarian Alliance for the Peoples of Our America–Peoples' Trade Treaty."

[7] However, much as in the South African case, there is little evidence that the constitutional promotion of alternative concepts effectively applies in regional or foreign affairs even in countries where *buen vivir* has been nominally advanced at the national level (Gudynas, 2016). One of the most cited examples of this contradiction between the internal and external promotion of alternative development frameworks is the experience of the former Ecuadorean president, Rafael Correa, who dropped an oil moratorium he had introduced on drilling in the Amazonian Yasuní region—well known for its

vivir principles are incorporated into what former Venezuelan president Hugo Chavez promoted with the 2004 creation of ALBA in an agreement with Cuba, which later grew to include eleven member states from Latin America and the Caribbean.[8] ALBA-TCP's central premise is one of an anticapitalist and endogenous development, nurturing a regional socialism by supporting solidarity economies in the concept of regional networks of production, or what are termed "grand-national" projects like ALBA-Food, ALBA-Energy, and ALBA-Forestry (Aponte-Garcia, 2017; Lubbock, 2019; Muhr, 2011; Riggirozzi, 2014; Riggirozzi & Tussie, 2012).[9,10] Brazil, however, contrasted ALBA's leftist ideology for regional cooperation with its own leadership behind the creation of the Union of South American Nations (UNASUR) in 2008. As with ALBA, several early signatories to this organization of regional integration have since backed away. Nonetheless, its creation with Brazil's leadership reflects the country's more orthodox approach to regional cooperation—modeled after the European Union and intended to advance infrastructure projects that address common political, social, economic, and environmental concerns under current—not alternative—economic norms and trade rules.[11] Indeed, some scholars argue that Brazil's push toward cooperation is not directed at its own

biodiversity and importance to indigenous communities in the region. Indeed, much hope had been placed on the potentiality of the moratorium—approved in 2007—to mark the dawn of implementable alternatives to extractive forms of capital accumulation and neoliberal development. For example, de Sousa Santos references the case of the Yasuní drilling moratorium and the turn toward *buen vivir* at the international scale as hope in the concept's potential to bolster alternatives to Western-centric modes of development as extraction (de Sousa Santos, 2015). The central tenet of the moratorium was that the international community at large would be responsible for its maintenance through the establishment of a trust fund, managed by the UN and paid into by other countries, that would be used to compensate Ecuador for the opportunity cost of not drilling for oil in specific segments of the Yasuní. When in 2013 Correa declared that international contributions to the fund failed to meet the USD 3.6 billion needed, he ended the moratorium, and along with it much of the excitement about *buen vivir's* capacity to move to scale at the regional level (Associated Press, 2013).

[8] The ALBA member states are now down to ten, with the withdrawal of Ecuador in 2018 (Lubbock, 2019). The TCP was added to ALBA in 2009 to provide guidance for trade and investment agreements between ALBA members to foster cooperation along the lines of complementarity as opposed to comparative advantage (Cusack, 2019).

[9,] While much scholarship has explored the conceptual bases of ALBA-TCP, only a few studies have actually provided empirically-based assessments of how ALBA principles function at the ground level, most of which reveal contradictions between principles and practices (Lubbock, 2019; Riggirozzi, 2014).

[10] While political leaders behind the scaled application of *buen vivir* or the Bolivarian aspiration of regional solidarity have left much to be desired in practice, recent developments offer yet another glimpse of the promise of Southern cooperation. For example, after former Ecuadorean president Rafael Correa left office, the new president, Lenín Moreno, called for a referendum on drilling in designated blocks of the Yasuní. On February 4, 2018, over six million Ecuadoreans voted to reduce the oil-extraction area in the Yasuní from 1,030 to 300 hectares (Tegel, 2018). While activists remained vigilant with regard to where precisely the expansion of protected lands would be (Aguilar, 2018), the public referendum was a clear victory—boasting the support of over 65 percent of the population.

[11] The organization's efforts to form a regional bloc are detailed by the Council of the Americas (see https://www.as-coa.org/articles/explainer-what-unasur).

neighbors but instead at other higher-income countries outside of the region. For example, Brazil negotiated its own bilateral agreement with the European Union, and UNASUR, under Brazil's tutelage, is seen as a regional organization that *competes* rather coordinates with the Common Market of South America (or MERCOSUR), a regional economic governance organization established in 1991 (Gratius, 2018; Hoffmann, 2019; Krapohl, 2019).

China too—particularly within cooperation projects on the African continent—is seemingly mired in contradictions regarding solidarity and power imbalances in its work with lower-income countries in the South. Chinese rhetoric on solidarity within the global South is longstanding, able to be traced at the very least to Chairman Mao Zedong and the socialist legacy upheld by subsequent leaders. During the Cold War in particular, China positioned itself as a non-imperialist ally to new African leadership, offering its help and expertise for infrastructure and construction projects. Both Chinese and African authorities at the time "lauded the non-hierarchical, intensely collaborative nature of [cooperation] projects in contrast to what they considered to be the imperialist and 'revisionist' imbalances between foreign and local expertise on display in American- and Soviet-funded work, respectively" (Roskam, 2015). As the architectural historian Roskam argues, however, an examination of those projects reveals that China was adept at reproducing power imbalances between itself and various other lower-income countries for half a century before its major cooperation push with the BRI.

The BRI for infrastructure development across Southeast and Central Asia, the Middle East, and East Africa is perhaps the most iconic of recent efforts by Southern economies to lead and underwrite development initiatives in the service of economic growth. Whereas earlier engagements between China and countries in Africa such as Ghana and Guinea espoused an ideology of opposition to the economic order cemented during the Cold War, a statement authorized in 2015 on the BRI's principles and strategies embraced that same order, now that China's role therein had strengthened. That statement referenced China's work in the BRI as a move "toward a multipolar world, economic globalization, cultural diversity and greater IT application ... designed to uphold the global free trade regime and the open world economy in the spirit of open regional cooperation."[12] Of course, the reality of the BRI's operationalization depends heavily on competing domestic interests in China, weakening

---

[12] See the full text on the BRI issued by the National Development and Reform Commission, Ministry of Foreign Affairs, and Ministry of Commerce of the People's Republic of China, with State Council authorization, on March 28, 2015 at http://english.gov.cn/news/top_news/2015/03/28/content_281475079055789.htm.

Chinese leadership's claims around the BRI as a grand, cohesive strategy (Jones & Zeng, 2019). Nonetheless, President Xi continues to emphasize the BRI's wide support for multiple nations' economic development, emphasizing that "the programs of development will be open and inclusive, not exclusive. They will be a real chorus comprising all countries along the routes, not a solo for China itself."[13] The timing of these statements at the end of March 2015 also strategically reminded other economies of a looming deadline to enter China's other serious foray into infrastructure development at the global scale, namely the Asian Infrastructure Investment Bank (AIIB), for which membership applications were due at the time. The launch of the AIIB speaks to the competition—real or exaggerated—between China's development-assistance (and coalition-building) approach and that of traditional multilaterals and the OECD's DAC member countries. However, that competition does not displace hierarchical relationships between "donor and recipient" countries established earlier with Northern donors—it simply challenges who is at the helm. A senior economist with the China Exim Bank, Zhao Changhui, was critically pointed in explaining to *The Guardian* that the "founding of AIIB is a challenge to the US's economical [*sic*] and political dominance. It's also a challenge to the establishments controlled by the US, such as the World Bank" (Branigan, 2015).

In only their first years of operation, new multilaterals like the AIIB as well as the New Development Bank (NDB) were living up to Changhui's promise and already each authorized capital lending up to USD 100 billion. In comparison, in 2018 the World Bank had access to USD 274.7 billion in subscribed capital (i.e., funding that is paid in, as well as callable capital), while the Inter-American Development Bank's authorized capital sat at USD 170.9 billion, the Asian Development Bank's at USD 151.2 billion, and the African Development Bank's at USD 91.2 million (African Development Bank, 2019; Asian Development Bank, 2018; Inter-American Development Bank, 2019; World Bank, 2018). Furthermore, in Africa alone, China's Exim Bank already surpassed the World Bank for loans to countries on the continent (Müller, 2014), giving some indication of why China–Africa relations are the center of so much scholarly and media attention.[14] These new lending windows from Southern players and alliances therein are further testament to the rising economic narrative of

---

[13] As quoted in a statement on the BRI issued by the National Development and Reform Commission, Ministry of Foreign Affairs, and Ministry of Commerce of the People's Republic of China, with State Council authorization, on March 28, 2015 at http://english.gov.cn/news/top_news/2015/03/28/content_281475079055789.htm

[14] For more reflective accounts of this attention and questions about its drivers, see Brautigam, 2009; Mohan et al, 2014; Lee, 2017.

power among countries at their helm.[15] Unlike the World Bank (whose largest shareholder is the United States), the NDB's founding countries, Brazil, Russia, India, China, and South Africa, all hold equal shares in the bank. China holds almost 30 percent of the AIIB's voting power, the largest percentage by far, with India next at just over 8 percent.

This combined growth, however, does not go so far as to mark the arrival of the long-hoped-for NIEO. In other words, today's international celebration and advocacy for SSC—much promoted by Southern economies themselves, as depicted in Table 5.2—does not distinguish who wins and who loses in this expanded economic and political playing field. This is no accident. The fuzziness is part and parcel of a longstanding prescription for SSC over the past several decades. The rhetoric of solidarity is now just enhanced by the stronger

Table 5.2 Major Alliances among Southern Leaders since 2000

Alliance	Description
Forum on China–Africa Cooperation	Starting in 2000, a summit on cooperation for leaders from China with all but two African states.
IBSA Dialogue Forum	India, Brazil, and South Africa (IBSA) Dialogue Forum was established in 2003 and hosts summits as well as a dedicated project fund for cooperation.
BRIC Summit	Leaders from Brazil, Russia, India, and China (BRIC) began holding informal gatherings during UN meetings in 2006, but launched a formal annual summit starting in 2009 to foster cooperation (including for the New Development Bank).
One Belt, One Road Initiative	In 2013, China launched a strategy to address the infrastructure gap across six global corridors connecting Asia, Europe, Russia, and parts of Africa.
New Development Bank	At the Brazil, Russia, India, China, and South Africa (BRICS) Summit in Fortaleza, Brazil in 2014, leaders agreed to launch a new multilateral bank, formerly referred to as the BRICS Development Bank.
Asian Infrastructure Investment Bank	A new multilateral bank aiming at building up infrastructure investments across Asia and the Pacific was spearheaded by China and opened for business in 2016.
Asia–Africa Growth Corridor	While Japan helped launch this 2016 initiative (along with India), its focus is on establishing SSC connectivity and cooperation across the Indo-Pacific region in development projects on health and pharmaceuticals, agriculture, disaster management, and capacity-building.

---

[15] The inclusion of private-sector funding for infrastructure has also considerably grown in leading economies within the global South, especially in India, China, and Brazil (Carolini & Cruxên, 2020).

economic base of the largest Southern economies. Instead of a generalist (and essentially unattached-to-government) call for cooperation and consensus in the South as emblazoned in the report of the diversely populated South Commission in 1990,[16] we now have Premier Li of China explaining in 2019 that "no country can stay immune or resolve all the problems on its own. It's imperative to seek an inclusive path of mutually beneficial cooperation. We need to embrace the vision of a community with a shared future for mankind" (The State Council of the People's Republic of China, 2019). Despite Li's reference to the need for a community approach to development, it is China's own work and leadership—with the BRI and AIIB, among its several other projects—that is especially generative and informative for a new configuration of power in international development agendas. As the geographer Emma Mawdsley (2018) suggests, in contrast to earlier assumptions that Northern donors and organizations would help to socialize emergent Southern development agents, Southern development partners are influencing their Northern counterparts. China especially fits this profile, making efforts like those of the UN and the World Bank to forge SSC seem almost polite in their punch.

Upgraded from a 1970s "special unit" for SSC within the UN Development Programme to a dedicated UN Office for South–South Cooperation (UNOSCC) in 2012, UNOSCC most excels at supporting small SSC projects and producing promotional videos detailing the virtues of SSC and triangular cooperation.[17] In addition to coordinating SSC across the UN system, UNOSCC independently manages two targeted SSC funds, namely the Pérez-Guerrero Trust Fund (PGTF) for South–South Cooperation and the United Nations Fund for South–South Cooperation, originally started as the Voluntary Trust Fund for the Promotion of South–South Cooperation in 1995. Both are decidedly small trust or endowment funds, though the draft outcome statement for the Second High-level United Nations Conference on South–South Cooperation, held in Buenos Aires in late March 2019 to commemorate the *Buenos Aires Plan of Action for Promoting and Implementing Technical Cooperation among Developing Countries* adopted in 1978, is explicit about the need to change this and to better capitalize these funding windows so as to prevent further SSC funding fragmentation. For example, the PGTF, established by the

---

[16] The Commission comprised intellectual and political leaders from Tanzania, India, Egypt, Kuwait, Brazil, Philippines, Mozambique, Sri Lanka, Ivory Coast, Argentina, Uruguay, Zimbabwe, Jamaica, Mexico, Nigeria, what was then Yugoslavia, Venezuela, China, Guyana, Cuba, Pakistan, Senegal, Malaysia, Samoa (then Western Samoa), Indonesia, and Algeria. Interestingly, only Brazil and India had two nationals on the Commission—the rest were singular voices from their countries.

[17] See the 2011 promotional video made for UNOSCC entitled, "South–South Cooperation: Delivering Solutions, Initiatives, and Success:" http://ssc.undp.org/content/ssc/library/videos.html.

UN General Assembly in 1983, provides at maximum only USD 35,000 toward seeding project work at the subnational, regional, or local level between at least three "developing" countries, eschewing national-level proposals. Presumably this is in part because of the nature of its funding, as it only distributes funds from the interest it makes on its endowment. PGTF's priority areas include food and agriculture, technical consulting, trade, technology, knowledge sharing, industrialization, energy, raw materials, and finance, and as of 2016 it had funded only 278 small-scale projects in over thirty years (Deen, 2016).

The World Bank is similarly engaged in smaller SSC projects. After decades of positioning itself as the "knowledge bank"[18] with robust claims to its superior art of knowledge production, the World Bank now sustains a rather perky if ironic perspective of the relevance of SSC writ large. In 2008 it established a just-in-time, flexible, funding mechanism, the South–South Experience Exchange Trust Fund (now referred to as the South South Facility or SSF). The fund is the brainchild of the former Nigerian minister of finance, Ngozi Okonjo-Iweala, who originally approached the World Bank to help identify successful pension-system reforms in other developing countries. Okonjo-Iweala ended up using her own professional network to secure a connection to information about Chile's pension-reform experience. Later, when she joined the World Bank as a managing director in 2007, she formalized the SSF funding mechanism precisely to facilitate such knowledge exchange (World Bank, 2010). Relative to the World Bank's subscribed capital, however, SSF grants between 2008 and 2015 were rather unsubstantial—averaging roughly USD 56,000 for a pool of 217 projects—much like the PGTF funding.[19]

Okonjo-Iweala's experience forging SSC at the World Bank is telling. While the World Bank publishes step-by-step guidelines on how to run knowledge exchanges,[20] the choice of which partners to pair on which projects and for what reasons remains rather ad hoc and reminiscent of Okonjo-Iweala's original reliance on an existing personal connection or network. In other words, which countries are connected depends on the World Bank staff's own experiences and familiarity with countries' experiences, through previous missions or project work, for example, as opposed to having more nuanced strategies

---

[18] Professionals in the World Bank have often referred to it as the "Knowledge Bank" (Wagstaff, 2012).

[19] Calculations by author, referencing the World Bank's available list of SSF grants: https://www.knowledgesharingfordev.org/funding/portfolio

[20] *The Art of Knowledge Exchange* (Kumar et al, 2018) provides step-by-step guidelines on essentially how to do SSC.

or criteria for identifying whom to pair—*and* an informed theory for why.[21] The World Bank today appears instead to be following a logic of convenience in facilitating development.[22] It is not alone. SSC programs are proliferating in number, in sponsorship, across scales, and by sector—but often by national or international stakeholders pursuing a particular political economic strategy. To understand whether, despite such strategies, the nominal targets of *equitable development* and *solidarity* espoused by so many cooperators existed, I turned toward examining a promising effort led by the UN to promote peer cooperation between urban public utilities in the water and sanitation sector. Given what I had learned from professionals on the ground about how and what types of learning happened across international cooperation typologies in Maputo, I questioned whether the proximate peer cooperation characteristics that mattered to learning in subnational cooperation in Mozambique were also present in other international cooperation partnerships that were reaching scale through localized partnerships across global regions.

5.2 Hierarchical Orthodoxy by International Design in SSC

In 2009 UN-Habitat took over the leadership over the UN's Water Operators' Partnerships (WOPs), originally launched under UN Water and Sanitation Advisory Board's 2006 Hashimoto Action Plan. WOPs are peer-mentor groups of urban public water and sanitation operators aiming to support the spread of good practices. The reference to peer-mentoring was conceived as a "high-potential" approach to reduce the proportion of the world's population un-served by water and sanitation services, and, when UN-Habitat took its helm, it established the global WOP platform—GWOPA. GWOPA supports regional WOPs in Africa, Asia, Latin America, and Southeast Europe, and records over 200 WOPs at a national level throughout the globe. Of established partnerships, the majority at the time of this writing, or 114, are between Southern urban water operators, most of which are regionally bound (Beck, 2019). In addition, three Southern partnerships within GWOPA are promoted as trilateral WOPS.

---

[21] One of the authors of *The Art of Knowledge Exchange* described to me how, for example, Bank-supported work in Tanzania connected Tanzanian professionals with similar project implementers in India, because that is where the Bank itself had had experience in the specified project. August 30, 2017, Washington, D.C.

[22] The irony here is a reference to the low regard afforded to convenience sampling as a method of conducting research in the social sciences, particularly among economists, who dominate at the World Bank.

GWOPA is reflective of a trend toward building international *learning* networks within specific sectors, so I had high hopes for its relevance to my study. I knew that such professional learning or epistemic communities were seen as mechanisms that could evade engagement in esoteric development debates about whether the norms and practices emerging from the Washington Consensus help or hurt potential for improvements in environments of scarcity. Instead, partnerships among peers in the public sector have been heralded as providing highly relevant, more sensitive, and practical learning opportunities in countries experiencing challenges in the provision of basic services and more (Bakker, 2007; Bontenbal & Lindert, 2009; Hall et al, 2009; Mayaki, 2010; Campbell, 2012; Bradlow, 2015; van Ewijk et al, 2015). In establishing its programmatic architecture, GWOPA began by positioning itself as an explicitly non-profit effort among urban water utilities with shared difficulties, ranging from the need to extend services to the poorest households to non-revenue water and water-quality management. The alliance's platform works by situating one utility as the "mentor" and the other as the "mentee," each with their own, plus shared, motivations for the partnership. The GWOPA model, much like SSC more broadly, presumes that both utilities are engaged in the WOP due to notions such as solidarity and learning, as highlighted in Figure 5.1.

While Mozambique was not active in an SSC-framed WOP during the time of my field research in Maputo, at least one of the other international bilateral partners I had studied in the capital was—namely Brazil. As such, I began

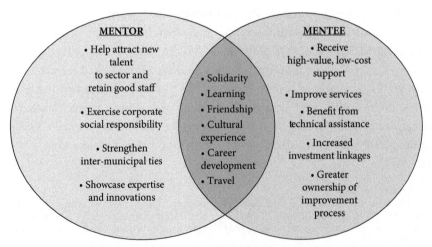

Fig. 5.1 GWOPA's Conceptualization of Motivations in WOPs
Source: GWOPA, 2013:12.

exploring Brazil's engagement with SSC-oriented WOPs and learned quickly that within the Latin American WOP platform, Brazilian water utilities were largely—indeed always—positioned as the "mentors" in partnerships. I was interested in the implications of this "mentorship" model for learning given that Dumontier et al (2016), who had examined work within GWOPA, noted the potentiality of WOPs to act as a mechanism for promoting equity.

Toward this end, I turned my attention toward studying one of the active WOPs hosted by a Brazilian utility. There were thirteen WOPs in which Brazilian public utilities were involved between 2008 and 2017 when I examined GWOPA's database, mirroring the period of my fieldwork in Maputo. These WOP agreements, much like the cooperation projects I studied in Maputo, lasted for the most part between one and three years. Given my interest in equitable learning and knowledge production, I chose to focus on one of the longest-lasting WOPs in which a Brazilian utility was engaged. Among such international partnerships, there were three WOPs lasting three years— namely with utilities in Argentina, Costa Rica, and Suriname.[23] I chose to focus on the Brazilian WOP with Argentina for two reasons: first, because it was renewed, potentially reflecting the participants' interest in maintaining the relationship; and second, because of the socio-economic proximity between the two countries.

The Brazil–Argentina WOP was centered on Brasília's water utility— *Companhia de Saneamento Ambiental do Distrito Federal* (Caesb) and the water utility in the Argentine city of Salta, *Compañía Salteña de Agua y Saneamiento S.A.* (Aguas del Norte).[24] The cooperation between the two utilities was stylized under the narrative of SSC, with the Brazilian utility entering as a mentor and the Argentinian as a mentee. In this case, however, the "mentee" had specifically chosen the "mentor." Professionals at Aguas del Norte had participated in a WOP workshop for Latin America and the Caribbean held in Medellín, Colombia in 2009, where they engaged in exercises meant to help them identify specific technical gaps in their work. A year later, the regional GWOPA secretariat offered the Argentine utility the opportunity to partner with either a Dutch firm, or the Brazilian Caesb. Initially concerned with the transaction costs of travel and the potential language barriers with the Dutch, Aguas del Norte began meeting in the region

---

[23] I was also especially interested in the WOP between Belo Horizonte and Addis Ababa's utilities listed on the GWOPA website, but learned that the WOP contact listed on the site for Addis Ababa's utility had passed away and others were not able to share information about the relationship. Interview, July 20, 2016.

[24] Parts of this section are adapted from my previously published work, "The Promise of Proximate Peers," in *Environment and Planning C* (Carolini et al, 2018).

with Caesb before making its decision. The Argentine water operators also related their perception of organizational asymmetries with the Dutch, as Aguas del Norte was a small organization and feared "becoming students of much larger operators that wouldn't understand our situation."[25] Critically, the utility's management also wanted to avoid what it termed a chasm in technological and organizational sophistication between the "North" and the "South."[26] GWOPA, in short, had sought to dispel the fear of working in asymmetrical cooperation partnerships, but managers expressed that the SSC playbook narrative was effectively widespread among smaller water operators. Ultimately, Caesb was deemed the best choice as a partner, and the two utilities formalized their cooperation partnership in April 2010. As in the projects I studied in Maputo, I knew that technical learning here was presumed to be critical to the material outcomes of the partnership, especially given its concern with physical infrastructures like water and sanitation. But I wondered to what extent other knowledge typologies and non-technical or geopolitical proximities would matter in the partnership. My questions thus centered on examining how the technical cooperation translated materially, and on understanding how project governance, local embeddedness, and professionals' theories of practice influenced the WOP between Aguas del Norte and Caesb more broadly.

5.3 Examining Materiality and Proximities in Place

On the technical front, the cooperation between Caesb and Aguas del Norte started to pay off dividends rather quickly. Caesb shared with Aguas del Norte strategies for conserving energy without significantly investing in a new industrial plant, which would have been prohibitively expensive for the latter at the time. Instead, the partners focused on improving Aguas del Norte's technical use of remote monitoring equipment and adjustments to its energy contracts, the latter of which reminded me of how JICA and Maputo's DUSWMH renegotiated the fee which the city's energy provider charged it for gathering the waste-collection fee with the electricity bill. In the Argentine case, this translated into a 50 percent reduction in fines from Aguas del Norte's energy supplier according to its logistics and operations manager.[27] Given

---

[25] Interview with the Logistics and Operations Manager, Aguas del Norte, Salta, June 23, 2016.
[26] Interviews with the Logistics and Operations Manager and General Manager, Aguas del Norte, Salta, June 22 and 23, 2016.
[27] Interview, Aguas del Norte, Salta, June 23, 2016.

that success, the Brazilian and Argentine utilities extended the focus of their technical cooperation to other areas, including flow measurement and metering, tariff structures, wastewater treatment, and information management and georeferencing. For example, Aguas del Norte devised a pilot program in consultation with Caesb's experts for ramping up its micrometer network and avoiding the kind of resistance to metering it had run into in previous efforts. Following Caesb's guidance on staggering the installation of micrometers over a longer time period—and first piloting it in a wealthy neighborhood—Aguas del Norte began to install new meters in 2014 and successfully expanded the metering system. This allowed the Argentine utility to detect leaks and led to 35 percent reductions in water wastage in some areas. The Argentine utility was also able to tap Caesb's expertise on improving its water tariff structure, using the Brazilian model to win the support of other Argentine utilities in order to gain approval from local regulators who had previously resisted changes therein. But how did the actual governance of staff on the WOP partnership, their embeddedness, and professional rationales or theories of practice matter to these changes?

5.3.1 Heterarchy over Hierarchy, Again

While the WOP between Aguas del Norte and Caesb was initially positioned as a partnership that would benefit the Argentine utility, the concept of a unidirectional flow of knowledge and learning dissolved in practice as the two utilities began to meet. Critical therein was the capacity of staff to see equivalencies in their counterparts. For example, Caesb's metering specialist explicitly observed this sentiment of parallels between the two utilities. He noted that the team at Aguas del Norte was facing a similar situation to the that one he and his team had worked through in Brasília. He recalled, "When I started working at Caesb, things were much less structured than they are nowadays. We have had many problems and still have several. When we looked at Salta's team, we saw ourselves in their shoes."[28] It was thus not surprising to learn from Caesb's staff that they too were gaining from the partnership—not simply at the individual level, but also technically.

A special projects manager at the Brazilian utility also pointedly noted the two-way learning process. He explained that "at first we were [seen] more like the company that would give away [or share] the technology, but as it [i.e.,

---

[28] Interview with Metering Specialist, Caesb, Brasília, July 14, 2016.

the partnership] started, we saw that it became an exchange. There are areas where they somehow helped us, and we also helped them in something."[29] For example, Caesb's geoprocessing department had been interested in moving from commercial software for computer-aided design to a Geographic Information Systems platform to improve its management and analysis of spatial data. IT and geoprocessing professionals at Caesb were still working to address the limitations of such a move when the partnership with Aguas del Norte began and they were exposed to the Argentine utility's information system. In September 2013, the team from Caesb traveled to Salta for a week to learn more about Aguas del Norte's information system and the ways in which data integration facilitated operational management. Ultimately, the Caesb team took inspiration from Salta and implemented its system in Brasília. In other words, staff participating in the cooperation work did not delimit the possibilities of the technical cooperation that had been defined for them in hierarchical terms. Instead, both utilities' professionals found opportunity to learn in the partnership, despite the mentee–mentor notions from which it was born. One manager at Caesb described their partnership as a "convergence of wills," noting that the fact that the utilities were very similar organizations in terms of technical staff and technical level strengthened the partnership's possibilities for learning on both sides.

While one cannot know if the Dutch partner would or would not have expressed similar sentiments, it was clear to Aguas del Norte's staff that uneven power dynamics between staff would have been a vulnerability to their ability to gain and learn in the partnership. As the Argentine utility's logistics manager noted:

What was our fear and that of other very small operators? That we become students of someone very important, who does not understand our problems. For example, micro-measurement. If you go, for example, to Germany or some very advanced countries, it is not understood that we do not install meters; it is not understood, because it is the solution to many problems. Then, you share with them, "Well, but we don't have money," and they say, "Well, get it because you save anyway." And that was a bit of our drama. It was a topic that was covered in the Barcelona [WOP] conference regarding the search for a way [to address] this problem, [but was] especially aimed

---

[29] Interview, Caesb, Brasília, July 8, 2016.

at, not so much Latin America but at Africa, which has many North–South exchanges which have paid off, so far.[30]

A caveat to the manager's comment, however, is required. Here the geopolitical is (again) offered as a proxy for the more specific description of needing partners who could identify with and recognize one another in an exchange. As my exploration of partnerships in Maputo made clear, other proxies of near equivalencies—outside the geopolitical—could also serve this purpose, making project staff feel they were heard and their knowledge valued by partners.

5.3.2 The Value of the Visit

The cooperation between Aguas del Norte and Caesb, unlike the cooperation projects I studied in Maputo, was not envisioned as one that would require Brazilian boots on the ground in Argentina for any significant period of time. As such, the types of local embeddedness central to project relationships in Maputo did not translate perfectly in the WOP. Nonetheless, site visits between Salta and Brasília were repeatedly identified by staff at the utilities as a means of gaining perspective and inspiration by seeing first-hand the day-to-day capacities with which the other operated—similar to the objectives professionals in Maputo had in pursuing shared work space or joint field engagements. As an operations manager in Brasília related, "It's no use just looking at theory, you have to see the practice happening and the difficulty in implementing these practices."[31]

The visits also created the impetus to broaden the scope of the original partnership beyond energy efficiency. For example, it was because of a visit to offices in Salta that the team at Caesb realized that they too could learn from how Aguas del Norte managed its information system. The Brazilians were impressed by their partners' ability to "do so much with so few resources." As an IT specialist at Caesb explained, their Argentine counterparts worked in an environment with fewer human and financial resources, yet were able to devise innovative technical solutions, leading Caesb professionals to ask themselves "How could we do more with less?"[32] Similarly, the team at Aguas del Norte found inspiration in witnessing in person how their neighbor to the North had

---

[30] Interview, Aguas del Norte, Salta, June 23, 2016.
[31] Interview, Caesb, Brasília, July 8, 2016.
[32] Interview with IT Project Leader, Caesb, Brasília, July 19, 2016.

achieved such operational strengths. The general manager at Aguas del Norte echoed this point, noting that:

> When we went to Brasília, seeing another successful company opened up new hopes. From around thirty years ago, we [in Argentina] had forgotten about excellence. To see that other countries with similar contexts can have an excellent service raises the bar. It's one thing for them to tell you that in Dresden, or London, the service is efficient ... but to see it in Latin America opens real possibilities.[33]

In short, it was his situated knowledge of Caesb's success and context in a city like Brasília that mattered to shaping the Argentine professional's vision and belief in the possibility of improvements in Salta's utility. The visit afforded him a critical opportunity to see in practice what the Vice Ambassador of Brazil to Mozambique had first described to me years earlier, namely a "harbinger of possibility." In the case of this partnership, however, the power of possibility from visits was unexpectedly but critically bidirectional. Caesb's geoprocessing specialist's visit to Salta provoked a very similar reaction as that of the Argentine general manager. He shared, "When you see an innovation, when you see something that the other company has done, you begin to imagine 'How can this be applied to our case? Is it possible to reach this level of maturity? Can we innovate as well?' So [the visit] provokes ideas."[34] This kind of dualistic exchange was not explicitly part of the UN's GWOPA platform which instead had situated Brazilian and Dutch water utilities as potential mentors for the Argentine utility, without entertaining that the latter could also help improve operations of the former. Yet this possibility arose from on-the-ground visits to see daily operations and contexts of work.

5.3.3 Theories of Professional Practice

Discussions with professionals in Aguas del Norte and in Caesb made clear that their cooperation not only bore technical fruit, but also spurred creative adaptation and professional growth at home. As one manager in Caesb explained, staff who participated in the technical cooperation partnership were importantly revealing their professional ambitions and motivations, the kind that ultimately might help the utility improve too:

---

[33] Interview, Aguas del Norte, Salta, June 22, 2016.
[34] Interview, Caesb, Brasília, July 21, 2016.

A program like this, a WOP, it's an interesting program from the staff's point of view. I think it's a motivating thing ... I don't think it's something that's decisive for the company, but I think it's a motivating thing, because people who get involved are usually more engaged with their own work, to be able to show, to share. So, like this, it is a perhaps indirect benefit for the company.[35]

Another Caesb colleague described that rationale or motivation for involvement in the partnership as being mirrored between the two utilities' staff. He explained that his own motivation and that of his partners at the Argentine utility went beyond remunerative—much as Mozambican social-action technicians described the motivations of EWB staff in Maputo. Instead, the interests of both Argentine and Brazilian staff centered on really expanding sustainable access to water and sanitation systems in their cities and countries:

Many people look at the work we do without seeing the importance it has ... Of course a company has to be financially sustainable, but it is more important that we manage to preserve this resource [i.e., water], [and] that sanitation reaches as many people as possible. That's our priority. And what I felt in the [Salta] team is that they were also very concerned about that.[36]

Further, it was clear that Aguas del Norte's staff had incorporated into their decision to work with Brasília's Caesb the potentiality of cultural biases and political economic influences on how well the two utilities' staff members would understand one another and the contexts of their work:

Geographically, it was much closer [than another international partnership]. They [at Caesb] speak [more or less] the same language and the political context is the same. So even if you lose the richness of other international perspectives, you have someone with whom you share political problems, and can work together to find solutions to them.[37]

For the professionals involved in the actual daily work of the partnership, this emphasis on proximities that mattered to how staff understood challenges was a nod to the kind of high-level metacognitive learning I had also come across among Mozambican professionals in Maputo's cooperation projects. They too shared an awareness of how professional viewpoints were shaped

---

[35] Interview with Special Projects Manager, Caesb, Brasília, July 8, 2016.
[36] Interview with Metering Specialist, Caesb, Brasília, July 14, 2016.
[37] Interview with General Manager, Aguas del Norte, Salta, June 22, 2016.

by partners' cultures and epistemic backgrounds, and critically, how this translated into the workplace environment for learning.

5.4 Questioning the Persistence of Hierarchies

While the Aguas del Norte–Caesb cooperation challenges the orthodox modalities of building peer partnerships, GWOPA continues to elevate power-reinforcing notions of "mentorship" through the partnership opportunities it promotes. Like other international cooperation efforts, peer relationships continue to be chosen largely through conceptualizations of "supply and demand," or "provider and beneficiary," as opposed to *reciprocity* and *equality*. This has implications for the kinds of learning and service improvements that are and can be fostered. Little nuance or strategy in the name of equity, for example, was evidenced in how the designation or process of partnering in WOPs rolled out in the Brazilian–Argentine case. Instead, the partnering possibilities proffered by GWOPA leaned heavily on the presumed value of either geographic proximities or what were requisite technical abilities. In practice, however, the partnership between utilities in Brasília and Salta provide further evidence for the other types of ingredients key to effective cooperation. Interestingly, it appears that outside the system of international development organizations and nation states, this type of heterarchical learning and exchange holds more sway.

For example, the national federations of slum dwellers and their international secretariat, Slum/Shack Dwellers International (SDI), represent one of the best-documented Southern-based urban advocacy networks working to change the balance of benefits afforded to the urban poor through networked exchanges among urban peers.[38] Working since the 1980s and across thirty-seven countries in Africa, Asia, and Latin America, SDI promotes strategic learning among organizations of the urban poor themselves to help address some of their commonly experienced adversities. Their learning strategies have centered on a wide set of needs, from savings schemes to organizing capacities, self-enumerations, and informal neighborhood mapping, and, perhaps most critically, counter-planning in the face of development-induced displacement or eviction.[39] Successful exchanges among SDI-affiliated federations in India and Kenya, for example, centered on how to resolve conflict

---

[38] For example, SDI members are "representatives" of civil society who are sought after by a number of international organizations working on urban development—including the UN and Cities Alliance, both of which have appointed SDI leadership to prominent task forces or advisory groups.

[39] Bolnick (2016); Bradlow (2015).

between urban communities settled on land owned by railway corporations. The Indian federation's strategy helped facilitate the successful voluntary relocation of similar communities in Nairobi, thereby avoiding evictions.[40]

These community-focused efforts share the same principle of learning by exchange among peers that is offered by international organizations such as UN-Habitat and United Cities and Local Governments, but they differ critically in the presumptions of hierarchy and in their prioritization of equity in processes and outcomes of their work (Albrechts, 2013; Bradlow, 2015; McGranahan & Mitlin, 2016). While not all subnational, networked community groups have the same success or similar heterarchical orientation,[41] SDI's focus on reciprocity not mentorship, and the importance of acknowledging diverse knowledge bases, holds lessons for larger-scaled efforts to counter development hegemonies. More pointedly, heterarchical organizing à la SDI arguably has done more to build solidarity and equity among stakeholders traditionally excluded from international and local economic and political affairs than much of the current SSC programming advanced through international organizations forged both in the North and the South. SDI's long-term success in forging equity among networked membership suggests that the organizational forms and presumptive roles of project partners may matter as much as other qualities typically assumed as key to SSC—namely geopolitical and technological similarities. Why then, do more hierarchical relationships and notions of mentorship in learning remain the norm in international development cooperation projects? This question brought me back to an examination of the roots of development practice as made legible in one of its most formidable narrative-setting tools, that of evaluation.

[40] Bradlow (2015).
[41] Not all networks of professionals working on urban concerns have brought positive results for cities. Smith (2002) cites the spread of gentrification across the globe as a result of neoliberal networks, while Rapoport and Hult (2017) and Sklair (2005) each note the emergence of professional networks of planners and architects whose work has facilitated a homogenization of urban forms and plans across diverse contexts.

6

The Governmentality of Evaluation

6.1 Lags in Evaluation

The self-interested politics of international cooperation has been widely doc-umented in examinations of donors' aid policies (Barthel et al, 2014; Findley et al, 2011; Fuchs et al, 2015; Fuchs & Vadlamannati, 2013; Mosse, 2013; Tierney et al, 2011). Anthropologists in particular have offered rich ethno-graphic accounts to expose donors' social construction of development in international aid work (Crewe & Harrison, 1998; Ferguson, 1994; Mosse, 2005). Evaluations too require such scrutiny, but receive less attention from critical constructivist social scientists concerned with development. Like aid policies, development evaluations tell us just as much about the evaluators as about the projects or policies they examine. As technologies of govern-ing, they serve to raise or suppress priorities in the daily work and vision of the development industry. In evaluating urban development, and particularly infrastructure projects, for example, one commonly asks how much a project costs, how long it took to implement or build, and how many stakehold-ers it has affected.[1] Unless projects or policies produce obvious, contestable inequalities, equity concerns are not integral in evaluations. Instead, the cen-tral concern is accountability, measured in terms of efficiencies—especially financial and temporal—of implementation.

An evaluation report concerning the Maputo Municipal Development Pro-gram, a World Bank-financed project, exemplifies this logic. Also known as *ProMaputo*, the program was designed to build municipal capacity to improve infrastructure development and delivery in Maputo. The programming was broken into two phases between 2007 and 2017, focusing on institutional

---

[1] For example, Bent Flyvbjerg, Nils Bruzelius, and Werner Rothengatter, in their 2003 publication, expose how planners often underestimate mega-project costs and time-for-completion estimations in order to get projects approved. Their work ultimately emphasizes the importance of cost and time management in urban development projects, but here I point to the relevance of other aspects of urban development projects—namely equity in the distribution of their benefits and in their power to produce expertise.

Equity, Evaluation, and International Cooperation. Gabriella Y. Carolini, Oxford University Press.
© Gabriella Y. Carolini (2022). DOI: 10.1093/oso/9780192865489.003.0007

development and governance, municipal finance, and improvements in the delivery of basic services and infrastructure planning. In a 2012 evaluation report of its first phase,[2] the assessment of outcomes included the World Bank's standard review of:

1. *Relevance* of the planned program (to Mozambique, to global priorities, and to the Bank's own assistance strategy);
2. *Achievement* of project development objectives (including raising the city's own revenues and the quantity of urban solid waste collected); and
3. *Efficiency* of work (e.g., net present value/economic rate of return; cost effectiveness; and financial rate of return).

While this report is only illustrative, it provides insights into the project-level treatment (or lack thereof) of the multidimensionality of development and priorities therein. Here, as in other evaluations, the consideration of equities—as well as of multiple stakeholders—of development projects at the local level is peripheral to the central evaluation template concerned with a project's relevance, achievements, and efficiencies. The report, for example, celebrates the increased collection of solid waste from 250 tons per day to over 650 tons per day, as well as the rise in the city's own-source revenues from USD 3.5 million in 2006 to USD 9.8 million in March 2010. The expansion of solid-waste services to underserviced, poor suburban neighborhoods of Maputo—where the majority of the urban poor live—is presented as an extra benefit of *ProMaputo*'s strategy to increase the quantity of urban solid waste collected in the report's telling. However, the report does not indicate whether the increased collection of fees and taxes represents an equitable distribution of the burden of raising local revenues. For example, where I worked and lived in the KaTembe district of Maputo, there is a 70 percent incidence of poverty, and neighbors often complained about suddenly having to pay for a waste-collection fee on their electricity bill, when in fact no one was collecting their waste.

Further, in the fifty-page evaluation report, only a summary of the CMM's own comments on *ProMaputo*'s objectives and outcomes is included in an annex (half of which was dedicated to an "evaluation of the borrower's own performance," or the CMM's Bank-requested self-assessment). Another annex in the report celebrated the introduction of Maputo's first "citizen report card" exercises, initiated in 2005 as an input into the design of *ProMaputo*'s

---

[2] As the second phase of *ProMaputo* had only recently ended at the time of writing, here I use the *Implementation Completion and Results Report* of its first phase. For more details, see World Bank (2012).

objectives. The annex indicates that the citizen report card survey acts as a substitute for the Bank's own beneficiary survey, and that the results are widely used by authorities and "broadly disseminated both at the time of their release, including a formal presentation to the municipal assembly, and subsequently in neighborhood meetings and as a basis for civil society consultations" (The World Bank, 2012). However, this assessment directly contradicts what the citizen report cards themselves indicate, namely that very little communication exists between the municipal government and residents.[3] My conversations with Luis Nhaca, head of urban planning for Maputo, corroborated this point. He complained that the city needed to do a better job of letting residents know about all that the city was doing to improve infrastructures and basic service delivery.[4] It seemed that the "broad dissemination" the Bank referred to in its evaluation was actually rather limited to municipal authorities themselves, as even Bank staff in private indicated the difficulty of gaining access to full survey results.[5] Indeed, municipal staff across international cooperation projects in my study reported little time for outreach or their own evaluative exercises. They were busy instead with requests from international cooperation partners seeking reports of activities or a log of productivity. Making time for reflection on their portfolio of project work, or accounting for the equity implications of projects, seemed a luxury or a burden in a city where inequalities seemed so obvious and so insurmountable. When so much of today's "development" epistemology has evolved toward a fuller prism of the concept and an explicit attention to participatory practices, how and why does an evaluative orthodoxy, underlined by a faith in efficiency and hierarchy, remain in place?[6]

[3] For example, results from the 2012 citizen report card, based on a survey of 2721 individuals, indicate that only 10 percent of reporting residents had any contact or received any information from municipal authorities (COWI Moçambique, 2013).

[4] Interview with Luis Nhaca in Maputo, July 15, 2014.

[5] I first learned of the existence of citizen report cards in Maputo in 2009 from Ali Alwahti, an urban specialist with the World Bank working on *ProMaputo*. At the time, Alwahti reported that he himself had never been able to access the survey results from the exercise, as the CMM had never shared them with the Bank—a complaint that other senior Bank staff informally shared with me in later years of *ProMaputo*'s implementation as well.

[6] At the national level, deeply influential development scholars drove a revisiting of precisely which development impacts matter, moving development's early conceptualization as a national modernization project aiming at efficiencies and growth toward a socio-economic and political concept rooted in human capabilities now famously translated into the Human Development Index. Dudley Seers, for example, was the first director of the Institute of Development Studies (IDS) at Sussex University, and questioned the objectives and meanings of development as practiced in the 1960s and 1970s (Seers, 1969). Amartya Sen's *Commodities and Capabilities* (1985), of course, also powerfully articulated an alternative conceptualization of development that is now the basis of the UN's Human Development Index. At the project level, however, practitioners are still admonished to design work that reflects efficiencies first and foremost—can a project be "scaled up" (read: more bang for your buck) or will it satisfy the falsely apolitical call for "evidence-based" results (read: if you cannot point to and touch it, you cannot value or claim it as your success).

6.2 Constructing a Rational Culture

In its infancy, the post-World-War-Two development industry was not overly concerned with its performance. At least, not performance in the strictly eval-uative sense we know today. It would be two decades before Hirschman's (2014 [1967]) *Development Projects Observed* marked a formal turn toward introspection and evaluation in the development industry. Today, however, an array of tools and methodologies vie for prominence in a professionalized discipline known as "development evaluation." Yet viewed in historical con-text, this discipline has veered only marginally from its roots in rationalization exercises within national military administrations.[7] Indeed, as I discuss here, the remarkably consistent concern over efficiencies in development evalua-tion has produced a strong evaluation culture driven by the prioritization of a universalist (as opposed to pluralist) rationality in the industry.[8]

6.2.1 The Domestic Frontier

Before moving to the World Bank, Robert McNamara served as Secretary of the US Department of Defense, where he initiated the Planning, Program-ming, and Budgeting System (PPBS) (Novick, 1968). PPBS was a centerpiece of *Project Prime*, which sought to reform military administration by shifting focus away from the means of achieving objectives toward the actual objec-tives to be achieved. PPBS was seen as a process through which programs could be evaluated and optimized using rational planning and systems anal-ysis, leaving military commanders free to consider broader strategic issues. At its heart, PPBS deployed a logic premised on inputs, outputs, products, programs, and alternatives to discretize administration into mission and sup-port units, to establish clear lines of command, and to obligate internal cost recovery between units that aimed to deliver efficient choice on the part of command and subservient units (Gruening, 2001). In terms of process, PPBS in the US Pentagon began with the Joint Strategic Objective Plans written by the Joint Chiefs of Staff and service chiefs. These were then broken down into broad programs and subprograms. Subsequently, programming comprised

---

[7] Kerr (2008) traces public management exercises in international development to the Manhattan Project to develop the atomic bomb, but here I focus on the emergence of project-level evaluations.

[8] Power's (1999) work on audit culture is useful here. He discusses the structured hierarchy of knowl-edge and practices in the auditing industry that, together, form a culture, though of course my focus here is on development evaluation.

the identification of project alternatives, considering cost-effectiveness, cost-utility, or cost-benefit, forecasting the consequences of alternatives, and deciding on the course of action to be executed. The PPBS exercise produced highly detailed five-year defense spending plans, with base and incremental financial commitments, inventories, and logistical capabilities.

Adopted more broadly by the US federal government in 1965, PPBS faced several implementation challenges outside the military sector (Poindexter, 1969). In the education sector, for example, difficulties included the quantification and incorporation of non-dollar costs and value-laden terms for analysis. Such challenges in implementing PPBS as a wide, federal reform of decision-making processes soon became apparent across other government departments as well, leading to skepticism that a system-wide, universal reform of government operations was viable or desirable in the US.

Similarly, the Conservative Party in Britain in the late 1960s, then in opposition, promised a "war on government waste" that would introduce the American systems-analysis techniques that McNamara was famous for to combat what was seen as an inefficient bureaucracy (Savoie, 1994). British treasury officials sent emissaries to the US to study PPBS in the late 1960s. Though Britain never adopted PPBS wholesale, under Conservative prime minister Ted Heath in the early 1970s, another "rational planning" system known as Programme Analysis and Review (PAR) was instituted. Heath promised his cabinet ministers that PAR would grant them unprecedented insights into "the particular activities of individual departments," rendering visible "what their department [was] up to" and arming them with a granular view into the procedures and processes followed by their subordinates (Savoie, 1994).

Despite the allure of control, by the 1970s both PAR and PPBS were on the rocks. PPBS was formally terminated in the US in 1972 (Schick, 1973). Its downfall stemmed from the vast quantities of systems-analysis and operations-research specialists the system needed, along with vast reams of paperwork and meetings. Indeed, PPBS and PAR had increased, not reduced, administrative costs in government. Their reach into the discretionary terrain of civil servants had been interpreted as an overreach and beaten back. In their aspirations to expand governmental rationalities into new areas of administration, PPBS and PAR had perversely led civil servants to suppress controversies, lest they be subject to scrutiny from above and the course correction to which such scrutiny would lead (Savoie, 1994). The rationality aspirations of national PPBS and PAR exercises, however, extended into the international arena with US leadership in international financial institutions like the World Bank.

6.2.2 Making the World a Better Place

Throughout the late 1960s and 1970s, evaluation began to take hold in bilateral and multilateral development organizations, including USAID and the World Bank. When McNamara left the US Defense Department and took up the World Bank presidency in 1968, his quest to rationalize operations—now to reduce global poverty—moved with him. The World Bank's Operations Evaluation Department—now the Independent Evaluation Group (IEG)—was created under McNamara in the 1970s to provide internal evaluations of Bank interventions and find out what worked, what did not, and why, and then to disseminate "lessons learned from experience" (IEG, 2016). McNamara's great faith in evaluative reporting as a management tool, however, was often translated into what later was criticized as the Bank's obsession with numbers and targets—a sort of "bean-counting," as described by Mervyn Weiner (2002), the Bank's Director-General of Operations Evaluation between 1975 and 1984. In an internal archival interview, Weiner admits that a widespread misperception existed about the role of numbers at the multilateral organization. He recalled how an evaluation report on a major municipal water project in an unnamed North African country elicited a great deal of concern from the project department's director, as the project's economic benefit was estimated at close to zero. In conversation, the director asked Weiner (2002), "How can we possibly proceed with a project with this low rate of return? They'll have our heads for it." Weiner himself offered to defend the project's merit for reapproval in front of the World Bank's board, one of whose members congratulated McNamara for finally presenting the board with a project whose economic value did not make sense, but whose social value under the human right to water was clear. It seemed then that a project's worth was more typically presented in terms relating to its efficiencies and scales achieved.

USAID was another early adopter of evaluation techniques. The agency commissioned Fry Consultants Inc., a private consulting firm, to support a "scientific" sorting of evidence in an effort to improve evaluation of USAID's non-capital projects (Rosenberg et al, 1970). The resulting 1970 Fry Report found that contrary to USAID staff's claims of evaluating continuously, there was no evidence of actual project evaluation, only monitoring and management on the ground across the forty-two projects studied. Project staff were wary of having to fill out evaluation forms to send back to headquarters, but were found to be generally amenable to the idea of introducing an evaluation process within their offices that would help them with their own work (Rosenberg et al, 1970). The report noted that "from the standpoint of what is truly important to the evaluation process—that is, whether or not our projects are truly having development impact—the [existing proposed] PAR [project appraisal report] is particularly deficient in not helping to clarify the relationship between project outputs and the higher goals" (Rosenberg et al, 1970). It was in response to these deficiencies that the logical framework approach, or "log frame" as it has come to be known, was presented. The log frame as conceived in the Fry Report called for explicitly indicating a project's activities, outputs, purpose, and goal, alongside information about assumptions, verifiable indicators, and means of verification. Critically, the report pushed for a shift in management's thinking toward USAID's responsibility for project outputs as opposed to only project inputs. In short, the log frame forwarded accountability as a major concern in evaluations.

Since the introduction of such evaluation exercises among development organizations in the 1970s, the motivational orthodoxy for evaluation has harmonized around accountability translated as efficient administration and implementation. Cost-benefit and cost-efficiency analyses are prime examples of the types of analysis that capture this ethos. This orientation also took hold at the national level across several high-income countries, forming part of the repertoire of neoliberal techniques in public administration that are today widely recognized as hallmarks of New Public Management (NPM).[9] In its nascent era, NPM was largely characterized by a rhetoric of modernization that rested on the conviction that private-sector business models merited universal application in public organizations because of the former's perceived relative efficiency.[10] However, NPM's launch in national liberalization policies of the late 1970s marked a break with earlier experiments of rational government planning captured by PPBS and PAR. NPM shifted emphasis from leveraging hierarchies and command lines in large government operations to promoting contestability, user choice, transparency, and incentives in a shrinking public sector (Hood, 1991). In an account of the rise of NPM, Gernod Gruening (2001) finds that NPM first emerged at the national scale in Britain and in municipal authorities in the US that had suffered economic recession and tax revolts, before spreading to New Zealand, Australia, and throughout the rest of the OECD. In such advanced capitalist countries, the major driver behind

---

[9] Kerr (2008) also situates his critique of the discursive governing technology of the log frame in British development agencies within a broader critical analysis of NPM's entrance into international development management practices.

[10] Of course, efforts to instill private-sector efficiencies in government at the national and local scales much predate NPM. For examples of early-twentieth-century efforts of the same in the United States, see Chase (1906) and McBain (1921).

the rise of NPM emphasizes a political-ideological reaction to "big government." However, in lower-income environments, the vectors of force behind the adoption of NPM were predominantly external and linked with aid incentives and coercion—from the World Bank, and more significantly from the OECD (Haque, 2004).

The rise of the use of the NPM portfolio in the OECD DAC's work in the 1980s can in part be traced to Margaret Thatcher's Conservative government. Under Thatcher, the UK's official development assistance (ODA) was cut from 0.51 percent of GDP in 1979 to 0.27 percent of GDP in 1990 (Booth, 2013). The adoption of austerity in budgets brought renewed attention to evaluation. In 1983, the UK's Overseas Development Administration, a wing of the Foreign and Commonwealth Office then responsible for development finance, convened a two-day international conference on evaluation (Cracknell, 2000). That conference compared evaluation approaches across global and national organizations. In line with emerging critical scholarship on user-oriented assessments in evaluation theory that advanced the idea that evaluations should serve those most affected by them,[11] discussions at the conference also marked a turn toward expanding aid recipients' role in evaluation work. Mervyn Weiner, the aforementioned Director General for Operations Evaluation from the World Bank, suggested to conference attendees that the Bank's project performance assessments could be based predominantly on evaluations by borrowers rather than Bank staff within a decade (Cracknell, 2000). The Overseas Development Administration's conference report concluded with a speech by Robert J. Berg, founding director of evaluation at USAID and founding chair of evaluation for the OECD-DAC. Berg chose to underline in his short closing speech the view of the World Bank Director General—namely that donors ought to be dependent on recipient countries for project evaluations—though he urged a shift much sooner than ten years thence.

The conference proceedings captured a mood of high-level introspection at a time in the early 1980s when the evaluation profession was expanding globally and growing increasingly standardized. Though evaluation was evolving on its own terms within national governments in Europe and North America, a clear transfer of knowledge was also occurring outward from a small group of influential thinkers at the OECD. According to Basil Cracknell (2000), an experienced development evaluation consultant, the

---

[11] See, for example, the early work of Michael Patton (1978) or Marvin Alkin (1990) on utilization-oriented evaluation, particularly in educational evaluations.

European evaluation community emerged from the OECD's active role in professionalizing evaluation in its early days across geographical boundaries. What remains less known, however, is the extent to which evaluations have been used politically across borders.

6.3 Evaluation's Governmentality

The use of evaluations, and indeed their findings, has never been immune to political manipulation, though much of the field's professionalization has positioned evaluation methods as efforts to remove the political and create a technical orthodoxy. As I detail in this section, when Berg (2014) advocated beneficiary involvement in development evaluations, he did so with personal knowledge of its explicit political misuse, as revealed in an interview he gave for the Foreign Affairs Oral History Collection in 2012. An implicit misuse has also evolved, however, since Berg first took the helm of evaluations for OECD-DAC. A major concern of his day was that evaluation work undertaken until then could not provide substantial evidence of the effectiveness of development assistance. With donor agencies under domestic pressures to justify the continued provision of aid, the DAC began to focus on demonstrating that supported development interventions caused specific outcomes.[12] An unintended result of this shift has been that funders have favored the types of project that can be subjected to impact evaluations.

6.3.1 The Explicit Politics of Evaluation

When the political stakes were high, Berg personally led USAID evaluations, as he did in the Israeli and Zimbabwean interventions he related in his Foreign Affairs interview. He described how following the 1978 signing of the Israeli-Egyptian Camp David Accords, the US ramped up development aid to Israel and Egypt. In 1980, Berg led an evaluation of a USAID-funded program in Israel to promote urban housing through mortgage guarantees. Through that guarantee scheme, the state of Israel welcomed USD 750 million in mortgage guarantees, which led to the construction of 15,000 housing units receiving the lowest market-rate mortgages. Impressed during the early phase of the

---

[12] Mawdsley (2012) further points to the turn from "aid effectiveness" to "development effectiveness" as the result of donors' underestimation of the implementation challenges of the Paris Agenda commitments as well as the diversification of the development agenda with the rise of the non-DAC emerging donor class.

evaluation by the physical infrastructure constructed, Berg's team began to examine the question of who benefited from the program. Their study revealed systemic discrimination against Israeli Arabs, who numbered a quarter of the target population, and yet did not feature among the beneficiaries. Having discussed the program extensively with the mayors of cities in the Galilee region, as well as key media and political stakeholders, Berg's team concluded that Arab cities had been systematically denied planning and zoning approval dating back decades, meaning they could not qualify for the mortgage guarantees provided through the aid program. Israeli Arabs, consequently, "*could not* benefit from any government housing program" owing to "a consistent pattern of discrimination" (Berg, 2014). In his final evaluation of the housing program, Berg noted that the USAID evaluation team reported controversially that the program had been "executed perfectly, except that it had set back the peace process rather than fostered it." The US State Department, on receiving the report, "went berserk," pressuring evaluation staff to change its assessment. Ultimately, they suppressed the report (Berg, 2014). When evidence generated through evaluation does not support prevailing geopolitical aims, stated or otherwise, that evidence can be silenced indefinitely. It can, as Berg also admitted, be used for strategic purposes.

Following a fifteen-year civil war that ended with its independence from the United Kingdom in 1980, Zimbabwe's political and economic direction was under close scrutiny from overseas as well. In his interview, Berg (2014) recalled that when Mugabe came to power, USAID quickly provided aid to Zimbabwe. He told USAID staff in the country that the political aim of the project was clear: to "demonstrate to South Africa that an integrated society could work" during the continuing period of apartheid (Berg, 2014). This instance reveals that where USAID's projects sought to influence governments in neighboring countries, evaluation knowledge played an important role in reinforcing that political aim. The nomination of Berg, as the most senior evaluation expert at USAID, to lead the evaluation and his role in ensuring its findings would be published, demonstrate the seriousness with which USAID took the power of evaluation to bolster political aims. It also suggests that evidence generated through evaluation, when it supports the social change that donors consider politically expedient, can be summoned to support change, rather than suppress it. In southern Africa, evidence was *summoned* to make a political point against the continuing apartheid. In Israel, in contrast, evidence was *suppressed* to stave off a challenge to the continuing Judaization of society.[13]

---

[13] See Yiftachel (1999) for further details about the Israeli use of planning to suppress an Arab state.

These instances, involving some of the most influential organizations and personalities in the evaluation profession, should urge us to question the OECD's recent suggestion that evidence produced through evaluation acts as a counterweight to political manipulation. In 2013, OECD-DAC released a glossy report entitled *Evaluating Development Activities, 12 Lessons from the OECD DAC*. Aimed at disseminating lessons for learning and decision-making in evaluation, the report opens in bold typeface, declaring "Lesson 1: Base development policy decisions on evidence." In a one-and-a-half-page drill, it extols the importance of "evidence, suggesting, among other claims, that decisions driven by "evidence" are "less likely to be dictated by political interest" (OECD, 2013). The claim, we can infer, is that evidence acts as a control on political interest. Evidence, the authors are clear, is to be desired, and more evidence is a good thing. Yet Berg, the OECD-DAC's own founding chair of evaluation, provides detailed insights into the complex relationship between evidence and politics in development projects, reporting on at least two instances where political interests instead controlled evidence. The British Department for International Development (DFID) also appears to acknowledge the relationship in its 2014–2019 Evaluation Strategy, noting that decisions on whether to evaluate a project or not should be undertaken by the "spending unit" (i.e., country office) using a proprietary Evaluation Decision Tool (DFID, 2014). The implication, of course, is that even local staff of bilateral organizations may be prone to present evaluations of their in-country development work with a positive bias.

In light of historical evidence, it seems appropriate to conclude that evaluation evidence can act *either* to subvert or to support political interests. The deployment of evidence for social, political, and economic change appears to depend less on the quality of that evidence, and more on the degree to which it concurs with the political aims of donors. Shepherding knowledge produced through evaluation should indeed renew our critical focus on contemporary rhetoric regarding objectivity and scientific rigor, now largely embodied in the advance of "evidence-based impact evaluations."

6.3.2 The Implicit Politics of Evaluation

At the urging of European representatives at the aforementioned 1983 Overseas Development Administration conference in Britain, a shift in evaluation focus was encouraged to justify aid budgets. Instead of seeking to address the question of whether aid did or did not promote development, evaluation was to shift to "what could be done to improve the impact of aid" on development

(OECD, 1993, 2013). Such a turn had important implications for project-level evaluations. Evaluation was thereafter increasingly seen as a tool to demand more results. The evaluation community turned its focus to "optimizing the benefit" of the development budgets that remained during a time of austerity in higher-income countries (Cracknell, 2000). However, as "before" and "after" project comparisons failed to account for the dynamic environments where complex social, political, or demographic shifts could account for observed outcomes, evaluators were concerned that impact could not be attributed to development interventions. It is in the growing desire to attribute change to development interventions through causal evidence that one can understand the twenty-first-century rise of impact evaluations, especially randomized-control trials (RCTs) and *randomistas*.[14]

Technically, the quest to establish a project's or a policy's causal link with a desired outcome in impact evaluations centers on the post-intervention measurement of predetermined indicators between a "treatment" group and a "control" or counterfactual group of eligible beneficiaries. The impact evaluation method's promise of rigorously determining what works has translated into its wide institutionalization in development organizations over the past two decades. Separately from the IEG McNamara established, the World Bank's Development Research group now also hosts the Development Impact Evaluation (DIME) program, an initiative that seeks to increase the use of impact evaluation throughout the Bank's portfolio. In 2014, DIME secured a major step forward for its mandate through the *Impact Evaluation to Development Impact* (i2i), a multi-donor trust-fund program launched with support from DFID to run impact evaluations. The i2i 2016 annual report boasts that 58 percent of development agencies undertake impact evaluations—with the World Bank at the top, rising from fewer than twenty impact evaluations in 2003 to 226 in 2016 (World Bank, 2016). The i2i report also quotes an internal study that found that World Bank projects approved between 2005 and 2011 with impact evaluations were better than those that had not used this evaluative technique. The more specific claim was that impact evaluation "increases average cumulative disbursements [a proxy for project implementation] by two-fifths (40.8 percent) and reduces the planned-to-actual disbursements gap by half (54 percent) ... suggest[ing] that [impact evaluation] is a powerful tool to move projects from design to implementation" (World Bank, 2016). In short, projects using impact evaluations were more efficient—financially and

---

[14] Economists who champion randomized-control trials as the gold standard for evaluating development work, including Esther Duflo, Michael Kremer, Abhijit Banerjee and their students, have taken on the moniker, "*randomistas*."

in terms of timeliness of implementation. And once again, accountability was diminished to efficiency (here in capital transfers).

Randomized-control trials add an experimental element to the basic impact evaluation function by assigning "treatment" and "control" populations randomly. Adherents and proponents of RCTs at research labs, including MIT's Poverty Action Lab (now the Abdul Lateef Jameel Poverty Action Lab) and its sister organization Innovations for Poverty Action in New Haven, have risen to prominence, effectively moving past the mid-1990s debates centered on whether randomization was suitable to evaluate economic and policy research (Burtless, 1995). Its suitability in the development context was cemented with the influence of a randomized evaluation of the PROGRESA program in Mexico, a conditional cash-transfer program launched in 1998 aiming to increase school enrollment and academic performance by paying grants to mothers.[15]

Since that early experience with PROGRESA, *randomistas* have successfully expanded RCT's evaluative punch through its wide integration among organizations running impact evaluations of projects and programs, including not only bilaterals and multilaterals but also philanthropies.[16] In a wide review of randomized evaluations in education programs in low-income countries, the Harvard economist Michael Kremer argued that randomized evaluations were not only feasible, but that an understanding of program effects were an "international public good" and thus, randomized evaluations should be financed internationally (Kremer, 2003). "Ideally," he wrote, "just as regulators require randomized trials before approving a new drug," the World Bank and other development funders should require randomized evaluations before undertaking development interventions at scale. As the movement for randomized trials has consolidated, however, so have debates about its claim of wide relevance for evaluating development interventions. Some skeptics express professional offense at the notion that project evaluations were not already sufficiently rigorous,[17] but most simply note that they are not a silver bullet.[18] As the Georgetown economist Martin Ravallion, formerly director of research

---

[15] PROGRESA was evaluated as a clear success, and since its implementation, conditional cash transfers have spread to countries around the globe (Schultz, 2004).

[16] For example, the Bill and Melinda Gates Foundation.

[17] On the advocacy side, see Savedoff et al (2006), while more critical views of RCTs are found in OECD (2013).

[18] Critical voices on RCTs include most prominently Angus Deaton, who urged evaluators to "take the halo off the RCT" at an NYU Development Research Institute debate in 2012 (https://wp.nyu.edu/dri/events/auto-draft/annual-conference-2012-debates-in-development/deaton-v-banerjee/) and MIT economist, Daron Acemoglu, who has also expressed reservation about RCT's exclusion of wider political-economy issues (Acemoglu 2010).

at the World Bank, noted, it is also sometimes simply unethical or unfeasible to run a RCT of a development intervention. He highlights that one cannot randomize, for example, the location of a key infrastructure project to determine where it would best serve (Ravallion, 2009).

The RCT's ethics and methodological rigor on determining causality, however, are not the concern here. Instead what gives pause is the effect of the near-ubiquity of RCT adoption among funders. While even impact evaluators acknowledge that not every project, policy, or program should be evaluated by established impact evaluation methods,[19] the allure of the RCT is the quantified justification it affords to funded projects and interventions. As with most public-sector projects or policies, development interventions are ultimately in competition with one another for funding. The rise of impact evaluations, and RCTs in particular, thus can be problematic for development as broadly defined for at least three reasons.[20] First, in political climates demanding evidence, those projects which are suitable to impact evaluations, or RCTs in particular, are advantaged in the budgeting process, with their renewed funding legitimized if it is found that the intervention causes the specific achievement of an objective. The concern thereafter is that those objectives are thereby prioritized over others that may be equally, if not more, critical but not amenable to the impact evaluation gold standard (H. Jones, 2009; N. Jones, Jones, & Datta, 2009). At the urban scale, taking the earlier noted example of the World Bank's *ProMaputo* programming in Mozambique, a randomized impact evaluation on how or where to best extend waste collection seems both nonsensical and unethical. If the Bank were in a position of having to choose which projects to support in Maputo moving forward, this would create a concern about funding for projects for which these types of evaluation simply do not work. This was apparently Ravallion's concern in his commentary at a 2016 World Bank Conference on the "State of Economics, State of the World." The economist expressed alarm about the World Bank's substantial adoption of RCTs for the majority of its impact evaluations, warning that the Bank's IEG's use of RCTs had grown from only 19 percent of its impact evaluations previous to 2005 to over 80 percent of its evaluations by 2010.[21]

---

[19] Practically, the financial costs and ethical concerns of running impact evaluations themselves may be too high to justify (Gertler et al, 2016).

[20] There are of course others. Jeffrey Hammer, a professor of economic development at Princeton, nominates three reasons why RCTs are problematic. See https://www.brookings.edu/blog/future-development/2017/05/11/randomized-control-trials-for-development-three-problems/.

[21] Ravallion's comments were repeated on a World Bank blog about the conference: https://blogs.worldbank.org/impactevaluations/have-rcts-taken-over-development-economics.

Second, while evaluations are typically presented as promoting both accountability *and* learning, RCTs excel at showing causal impacts, not at explaining the granular processes by which x is claimed to cause y. Instead, the policy relevance of RCTs—as well as other impact evaluations—seems weighted on the political call for accountability. This point is underlined in DFID's present evaluation policy, published in 2013 by the Conservative and Liberal Democrat coalition government. In it, DFID boasts its "major investment in new, high quality evaluations – including rigorous impact evaluations," which will ensure "greater transparency and scrutiny of aid spending" to deliver value for money for British taxpayers (DFID, 2013). Note that here what impact evaluations are providing accountability for is a project's financial worth, as viewed by the British taxpayers, not targeted beneficiaries.

Third, while impact evaluations are meant to foster dynamic learning for policymakers, along with increased accountability, who learns and what is learned seems to escape critical review. In the World Bank's i2i 2016 annual report, i2i claims to transfer "knowledge and tools needed to support evidence-informed policymaking to country institutions through a medium-term learning-by-doing approach" (World Bank, 2016). Here the learning-by-doing reference is to i2i's workshops for governments on how to run impact evaluations. Thus the claim to learning here is delimited to learning what donors think should be learned—evaluation methods. In a talk Mervyn Weiner gave about the origins of evaluation at the World Bank, the former Director General demurred in reaction to an audience member asking for examples of how lessons learned from evaluation were actually later used to make changes. Weiner noted that in his experience, change came from both internal and external pressures. He went on to assert that evaluations were primarily about accountability, and that learning comes afterward: "My own view is that accountability came first; hence the emphasis on 100 percent coverage completion reporting and annual reviews. Learning was a product of all this, but the foundation was accountability. The mechanisms for accountability generated the information for learning" (Weiner, 2002).

The secondary placing of learning through evaluations speaks to the enormous complexity of assessing the concept. However difficult it is to establish causality, there is consensus among researchers about the very foundation of needing to show an association, the directionality therein, and its non-spuriousness. There is not a universally accepted methodology, however, for establishing that "learning" has happened, nor that what has been learned is important or relevant. Likewise for equity. In describing his experience with evaluation in Israel, Berg explained that USAID's original evaluation intent was "not to ask those questions"—i.e., about inequities in who benefited from USAID programming—as "it was not in their brief" (Berg, 2014). What was in their brief was the question of efficiencies and causality.

6.4 Cultivating a Learning Culture and Equity through Evaluations

The contemporary fascination with impact evaluations, and RCTs in particular, reflects more than an interest in methods. International development stakeholders—not to mention so-called beneficiaries—remain frustrated with the same dilemmas that assaulted them years ago. RCTs and impact evaluations more widely hold out the promise that the future of interventions will be more precise and more effective. In short, these methods are valued for their prescriptive power.

It is precisely because of their prescriptive heft that impact evaluations also provide a rationalization for what we typically refer to as best practices and the promotion of a data-driven, objective, and universalized expectation of experiences—with a knowledge creator and a knowledge receiver.[22] The promulgation of best practices, however, can also delimit rather than distribute power over the learning experience and the production of knowledge among local stakeholders involved in the implementation of a "best practice." This has long been a grievance of Southern countries who question the relevance of "expert knowledge" from the North and the mandate to abide by that knowledge as a condition of international aid. "Best" practices, after all, must be identified, chosen, and championed by a demarcated and privileged group. Further, their distribution through international organizations belies the truth behind learning in development—namely that it happens from failures as much as from successes, and that in practice, within every project there are successes, failures, and mixed results, as I saw in the projects I studied in Maputo. That range of experience, however, is lost when impact evaluations like RCTs instead seek to identify and promote policies and projects with strong *average* treatment effects (Bardhan, 2013; Dehejia et al, 2015; V. Dehejia, 2016). The prioritization of a project or policy's average effect in RCTs comes at the cost of understanding the margins, as well as of valuing high-level, heuristic learning-by-doing—or learning that exceeds a textbook's "how-to" (on average) orientation.

---

[22] John Friedmann, an acclaimed theorist and urban planner who worked across the globe, wrote an early, extensive critique about the objectivity of knowledge, borrowing heavily from Paul Feyerabend's 1975 book, *Against Method* (Friedmann, 1978).

Like RCTs, cost-benefit analysis (CBA) also provides a robust evidence-based evaluative tool for decision-making in the public policy realm, but at the project level. However, unlike RCTs, CBA does not promote projects on the "policy mobility/best practice" international circuit given CBA's fundamental dependence on a project's contextual cost inputs and benefit outputs. Nonetheless, CBAs share a foundational interest in efficiencies with RCTs. As CBA advocate Cass Sunstein recounts in his recent book on the *Cost-Benefit Revolution*, CBAs have transformed the public sector's decision-making apparatus from one driven by political ideals and values into one that leverages technical expertise in deriving public interventions' costs and benefits quantitatively and qualitatively. However, Sunstein also acknowledges three major challenges to the reliance on CBA as currently devised as a public-sector instrument of evaluation. One is the lack of necessary data to determine the full costs and benefits expected. The other two—which also occupy a major concern in this book—are a project's distributive justice and well-being effects, questions about which CBA is inadequate to answer. Indeed, Sunstein points to (and concurs with) the work of philosopher Matthew Adler, a leading advocate of prioritarianism (or the philosophy of prioritizing changes that improve the well-being of the least well-off) as a strong if impractical argument for rejecting CBA as an evaluative public-sector management tool (Sunstein, 2018). Nonetheless, Sunstein's defense of CBA is in the arena of internal public-sector management—not within the industry of development aid partnerships and programming therein, much of which falls under the umbrella of poverty reduction within international development organizations.[23]

The reference to poverty alleviation and reduction as one of the major rationales for both social and economic programming and project interventions in the development industry in theory should give a special platform and preference to prioritarian thinking in development project evaluations. As the history discussed earlier here makes clear, that is not—yet—the case. However, if we are to operationalize a conceptualization of development as about efficiencies *and* equities gained through interventions, then practitioners must not only use evaluations to arrive at an understanding of why projects work where they do and how, but also most critically *for whom*.

---

[23] My colleague at MIT, Balakrishnan Rajagopal (Rajagopal, 2003), wrote a book in which he describes, for example, the turn in the World Bank's focus from development projects in the economic infrastructure realm toward poverty alleviation programming toward the end of the twentieth century. Today, these two objectives—of economic development and poverty alleviation—are more often than not explicitly intermingled in the development industry's rhetoric about itself. For example, the World Bank describes its work to "reduce poverty and build shared prosperity in developing countries" on the homepage of its website (www.worldbank.org).

6.4.1 Justice at the Project Level: Tracking Benefit Distribution and Procedural Fairness

Questions about "whom" a project benefits (or should) implies a person-centered assessment of the distribution of material impacts or well-being benefits emergent from a development project. John Rawls's *Theory of Justice* (1971), and his later work on *Justice as Fairness* (1985) were generative for several debates in political philosophy and for discussions of the application of distributive justice to policy and planning. While Rawls was initially criticized for his emphasis on the individual as a unit of analysis as opposed to the social group, his difference principle remains a helpful framework for thinking about distributive justice and inequalities within societies (Young, 1999). Rawls's difference principle maintains that the only justification for social and economic inequalities must be that they are to be of the greatest benefit to the least advantaged persons. This is also the basic distribution bias of the prioritarian viewpoint, namely that benefits to people who are worse off matter more than benefits to others.[24] In contrast, as political philosopher Nils Holtug describes, utilitarianism and egalitarianism have a "lack of distribution sensitivity" (Holtug, 2010). While prioritarianism is criticized by philosophers for several cognitive points, including its need for a measure of a person's well-being and the difficulty of arriving at such an equation,[25] the quantitative scale of an individual's well-being does not necessarily have to be surmised at the general level. It could conceivably be quantified or more generally analyzed within a delimited, theme-specific context—such as that of a particular project's parameters.

Inserting prioritarian thinking into project planning and evaluation to determine where and to whom immediate (or priority) material benefits should accrue would clearly require a discussion within the public sector and with implicated communities about how to define associated needs and how to rank them. Within international cooperation work, one might envision a process whereby project professionals or planners do not arrive in neighborhoods with plans, but leave with them. In short, project practitioners might consider project design and development that *begins* with co-design

---

[24] Prioritarianism is positioned as a moral framework within philosophical literatures and within discussions of the social-welfare function in behavioral economics. It encompasses a moral "ranking" of outcomes from decisions made.

[25] See, for example, John Broome's work on measuring equality versus priority in his book *Weighing Goods* (Broome, 1991) and related articles (Broome, 2015), or David McCarthy's (McCarthy, 2017) recent work on challenging prioritarianism's ethical and conceptual grounds.

or co-production. Participation parity—or the equal capacity to participate—in such co-productions, however, also requires attention to the distribution of material resources that could ensure that *all* participants have independence and voice, according to Nancy Fraser's influential work on distributive justice (Fraser, 2000; Fraser & Honneth, 2004). These are central concerns in and about theories of communicative action and consensus-building envisioned in participatory planning—namely to provide all stakeholders with the opportunities to participate freely, and to ensure that, regardless of status, all stakeholders' perspectives are recognized and valued in an effort to build an overlap in consensus around what actions the public sector should take.[26] In practice, such efforts often falter because planners or local authorities fail to recognize project resistance by those who feel marginalized, or they dismiss alternative competing project visions offered by stakeholders, especially within marginalized communities. Thus, planning scholars have recently considered the utility of what the political scientist Chantal Mouffe situates as agonistic politics, or struggles between adversaries which can be productive if legitimized in political institutions (Kühn, 2021; Legacy et al, 2019).

While here I do not adopt agonistic planning as a replacement for deliberative or participatory action, I do see a role for project practitioners in the discovery and articulation of contextual conflicts as key to their efforts at building toward consensus thereafter.[27] Here, one might situate a deliberative process to first look for conflict rather than consensus. Such discussions about a neighborhood's fault lines would attend to some of the major vulnerabilities identified in participatory processes which gloss over conflict and especially tacit power dynamics. Ultimately, however, the scale of process of deliberation is important. Within infrastructure development, the scale of the process would need to be sufficiently limited for conflicts to be well recognized, and sufficiently broad to attend to, for example, questions about production

---

[26] There has been much written about participatory planning, following from—among others—Rawls's and Jürgen Habermas's work on distributive justice and communicative rationality, respectively. Among the most widely cited planning scholars on participatory planning and communicative action are Patsy Healey (1992), John Forester (1988; 2013), and Judith Innes and David Booher (1999). Of course, the communicative turn in planning, and participatory discourses more broadly, has also received heavy criticism for understating enduring power dynamics and inequalities within consensus-building initiatives. In short, initial inequalities make the consensus-building experience biased toward those participating members who already have power. My concern here, however, is not with the validity of communicative theory, nor of its criticisms. Instead, it is with considering how principles of prioritarian thinking have a place within planning processes that, like participatory planning, aim to speak to inequalities.

[27] Outside of urban planning, this approach approximates what development scholar/practitioners like Matt Andrews, Lant Pritchett, and Michael Woolcock (2013) call problem-driven iterative adaptation, which focuses on iterative learning processes within public policy-making.

and distribution efficiencies of an infrastructure good. A negotiation of scale, then, might also emerge in the initial deliberative process of project co-design. With the scale determined, project practitioners and residents would need to consider the types of conflict that may matter to the ordering of interventions, i.e., how the initial project site and the first beneficiary group would be determined. This is where prioritarian principles may be most helpful.

For example, in a city like Maputo, where several different neighborhoods have substandard access to water, a place-based approach to an improvement project might at the outset involve discussions among municipal practitioners and development partners on outreach to and engagement with a site's residents, looking especially for traditionally marginalized community residents. To build trust and ensure that such residents' participation is respected and recognized is likely to prove time-consuming, yet critical as an initial step. Here is where a process of "conflict discovery" may be especially useful to project managers. With fault lines—or at least some of them—exposed, project stakeholders could work to refine the scale of intervention, asking whether the "neighborhood" is the appropriate scale or unit of analysis by which to study vulnerabilities, which vulnerabilities should be considered (e.g., across sectors like water, education, and health or within the water and sanitation sector alone), and finally, who are the "most" vulnerable households. After one or more specific groups and spaces are collectively determined as priorities, local practitioners with their development partners and community stakeholders might further debate what "access" would actually translate into (e.g., household connections, community standpipes, covered wells).[28] This list of questions and discussions is of course far from exhaustive; instead, it illustrates the sort of heuristic and necessarily situated discourse (i.e., contextually driven and evolving, as opposed to technically driven and set) required to fairly bring open considerations about equity and justice into the very early stages of a development project's planning—and later into its evaluation.

If the distributive justice principle behind prioritarianism were extended from project planning into project evaluations, the determination of how successfully a project met its objectives would incorporate both the logic of equity (in whether the project improved the well-being of the worst-off persons as initially defined) and the logic of efficiency (in how cost-effectively

---

[28] Here I suggest that a "place" as opposed to a "community" might be first determined as an approach to improving water and sanitation, though of course that place's identification would depend on the community of persons that resides in it. Further, my emphasis on place in this hypothetical case reflects the very physical characteristics of water and sanitation delivery—and thus the need for a place-based approach.

a project achieved its objective to improve the well-being of the worst off). Susan Fainstein, an urban planner whose book, *The Just City*, situated much of the justice discourse from political philosophy into the critical domain of urban scholars, argues as much in her critique of how cost-benefit analysis has been used as a utilitarian metric to choose between policy alternatives. She writes:

> The counter-argument to the advocacy of utilitarian metrics [as in CBA] is that justice as the yardstick for measuring public policy effectiveness does not negate efficiency as a goal but instead requires the policy-maker to ask to what end efficiency applies. If a policy serves the goal of assisting the most disadvantaged without wasting resources, in line with Rawls' difference principle, then the policy is efficient even if it does not maximize an aggregate benefit-cost ratio.
>
> (Fainstein, 2014)

While Fainstein's discussion of the just city is centered on experiences within high-income contexts, the application of the underlining bias toward prioritarianism in her application of Rawls's theory of distributive justice to urban policy decisions and planning is also highly relevant for decision-making processes in the international development industry at the project level. It is at the project level that the practicality objections to prioritarianism hold the most concrete promise of getting resolved. Material benefits from development projects are already typically measured in evaluations, as highlighted in earlier sections of this chapter. What remains unspecified is the discussion of beneficiaries and *their* "ranking" of need—namely the distributive justice of material benefits. At the project level, this is a challenge that is conceivably resolvable, and is, in fact, the very basis of attention to procedural equity or fairness in urban planning under the participation parity principles forwarded by scholars like Fraser, who bring attention to the need for efforts to equalize the status of participants in the advance of material distributive justice (Fraser & Honneth, 2004). Procedural equity's role in the achievement of distributive justice through participatory planning practice explicitly seeks to empower all stakeholders and to foster a dialectic conversation between them at the neighborhood or even city level in what scholars describe as a consensus-building project (Forester, 1988, 2013; Healey, 1992; Healey & Upton, 2010; Innes & Booher, 1999). Of course, as many scholars—including Fainstein—again note, conflict therein is also typical, or even necessary. However, the pursuit of procedural equity through the support of a co-design process could serve to carve out an explicit space for the consideration of conflicts and a plat-form for more explicit discussions of epistemic equity, or the fair treatment and credibility afforded to the diverse epistemologies of knowledge shaping different stakeholders' perspectives (Sandercock, 2003). In other words, project practitioners need to bring "situated" judgment to bear in projects, explicitly concerning themselves with context and learning about the diverse values and conflicts therein carried by those whom projects are meant to serve and themselves (Campbell, 2002). Within countries like Mozambique, such a process would also demand that local planners and authorities heed warnings about the conflicting rationales of stakeholders participating in a planning process, as expressed by South African planning scholars like Watson (2003), Winkler (2018), and Sihlongonyane (2015a). Their scholarship points to the importance of uncovering the diverse epistemologies and the specific values, ideologies, and meanings that households bring to negotiations about planning in their neighborhoods and cities. In other words, they draw attention to how distributive and procedural equity must still contend with epistemic equity in planning projects, particularly within marginalized communities, if projects are to successfully guide participatory processes for improving living conditions and opportunities for and with the urban poor.

6.4.2 Epistemic Equity: Valuing Learning and Different Ways of Knowing in Projects

A project's take-away or "deliverables" are perhaps the bluntest capture of intended project objectives and how managers perceive of a project's success. Nowhere is this clearer than in project evaluation reports. The history of project evaluations, however, demonstrates that discord remains between what the development industry aspires to do—namely to promote development as a multifaceted norm—and what it does in practice—too narrowly delimiting its performance standards and measures of success/accountability to economic, political, or social efficiencies. As a result, I argue that orthodox evaluation will inevitably boost and promote projects and programs pursued through orthodox development strategies.

For instance, a recent report by UNDP reflects on fifteen years of SSC and laments the lack of standardization across Southern partners in comparison with the OECD's approach to evaluation (UNDP, 2016). It further draws concern to the pluralistic way that SSC has been understood across Southern contexts, compared with the "homogeneous understanding" among traditional donors. Although the UNDP report does not explicitly express hostility to the difference in evaluation principles (among which it mentions horizontality, participation, and gender), it does speak of a disjuncture in Southern principles as posing "challenges for traditional [evaluation] processes," as if it were the processes themselves that ought to be upheld. The report cites as further challenges, for example, the refusal of Brazilian officials to monetize institutional investments in SSC, which "[makes] cost-effectiveness evaluations unfeasible" and makes it difficult to measure capacity enhancements.

The UNDP report's defaulting to universalistic evaluation processes is symptomatic of the orthodoxy of efficiency in the contemporary evaluation profession. That evaluative orthodoxy necessarily finds that the most fruitful cooperation partnerships are those characterized by efficiencies created by capital availability, predictability, and stability. Projects with traditional multilateral development partners, Northern donors, and most recently China are thus poised to secure most favorable evaluative reviews. SSC, at least in theory, however, gestures toward a transformation of power relations. Operationalizing such a shift in practice requires a heterodox, heterarchical framing of evaluation beyond the prism of efficiencies alone. Here then is where we could and should expect epistemic justice to be given a greater priority of place in the evaluation of projects and practices. Fricker's work on epistemic injustice provides a helpful framework for thinking about how and why such a consideration of power relations within epistemologies matters to practices like project evaluation. Within her discussion of epistemic injustice, Fricker (2007, 2017) offers a clear distinction between testimonial and hermeneutical injustices in relation to epistemologies. The former signifies how identity powers translate into prejudicial credibility deficits; in other words, when someone's identity in a certain context confers to them less credibility on a range of subjects. The latter, or hermeneutical injustice, instead refers to when someone's personal background renders their participation out of reach; for example, someone's lack of education or socio-economic background may marginalize them from being or feeling able to participate in a vote, or, as it may be, an evaluation report. The recognition and address of such potential injustices is key to creating a space for learning—both in the co-design of projects *and* their evaluation. However, as cooperation projects in Maputo and elsewhere demonstrate, such attention to notions of justice and equity is not yet the norm in international partnerships. Further, it should not be simply presumed as present in projects falling under the SSC rubric.

Conclusion

Anticipating Proximate Peer Partnerships

Looking for evidence of the particular value of SSC versus other typologies of international cooperation on the ground, what I instead found was that this very question obscured the complex and more critical realities of how international cooperation is constituted in place, particularly over time, and how knowledge production and learning-by-doing is fostered. Ultimately, my own fieldwork also led me to question how the object of my study—namely international cooperation at the project level—is and should be understood or evaluated. The aspiration toward equity that had first attracted me to the study of SSC did not translate into how the projects I found were formally evaluated, nor how I myself had been trained to evaluate them. As such, I found that I could not answer my own question as originally conceived. Instead, I came to realize that the convenient traditional proxy of geopolitical and hemispheric categories of cooperation predicted little about what drove a cooperation project's material outcomes. Nor did SSC in practice claim exclusive rights on fostering the types of learning that matter to the discretionary decision-making capacities long at the heart of international development initiatives.

While I acknowledge that the administrative and financial architecture of international cooperation is and will likely remain tied to the specific bilateral, trilateral, and multilateral organizations behind projects, the research presented here shows that cooperation projects in practice neither maintain such national-level or organizational clarity, nor have geo-hemispheric characteristics that in themselves ultimately determine the types of equity pursued and produced on the ground. Projects in Maputo showed that no one organization or stakeholder could absolutely claim the material effectiveness to which their projects aspired on the ground, even when they incorporated some efforts at procedural justice through participatory decision-making. Similarly, in studying the types of learning in evidence across projects, I found

Equity, Evaluation, and International Cooperation. Gabriella Y. Carolini, Oxford University Press.
© Gabriella Y. Carolini (2022). DOI: 10.1093/oso/9780192865489.003.0008

a mixture of evidence across international cooperation types. In other words, a project's Northern, Southern, or trilateral architecture was not an especially robust predictor of cooperation success in material and knowledge terms on the ground. Furthermore, the varieties of SSC—and for that matter other cooperation typologies—diminish the value of using geopolitical and hemispheric labels as a general proxy for the types of equity only some of them achieve.

Removing the developmentalist labels assigned to geopolitical regions of the North or South would allow and encourage cooperation partners—and those of us who study them—to instead see themselves simply as partners-in-place, to understand that despite differences in financial, technical, or other capacities, there may be administrative similarities, responsibilities shared, burdens carried, and more. Such heterarchical thinking speaks to what scholars like Jennifer Robinson (2006) call the study of "ordinary" cities, as opposed to the categorical hierarchies that dominate the way we write about and speak about urban landscapes. Here Robinson's call is applied not to cities, but to the cooperation partnerships that are increasingly present across so many of them. The densification of international bilateral actors—and, often, their private-sector partners—means that, increasingly, projects or cooperation on the ground has overlap and overturn. Further, the globalization of the international development labor force means that the geopolitical labels assigned to projects hold even less meaning. A Filipino can represent Japan, a Colombian Spain, a Mozambican Italy, and a Portuguese Mozambique, while the very same land can host an infrastructure project first funded by the Portuguese, and then Chinese interests. How then can we take North–South, South–South, or even trilateral labels as serious categories by which to understand aid or cooperation on the ground?

Fostering epistemic communities beyond and despite of convenient but lazy geopolitical aggregate categories allows project professionals to approach projects valuing and leveraging the proximities that actually matter on a day-to-day basis in any cooperation-driven and diverse project environment, proximities like a professional's rationale or theory of practice, or whether their work responsibilities and positionality within a project are mirrored in their partner organization. Such a heterarchical approach to conceiving of partnerships gives *all* stakeholders—"beneficiaries" and "foreigners"—the leeway needed to pursue different types of knowledge and learning at different phases in their work, from the technical to the metacognitive. But introducing heterarchical relationships still leaves us with the need to address how they might promote distributive, procedural, and epistemic equity. For this, not without some trepidation, I turn again toward project evaluation as a tool with potential.

The ideal of procedural justice is already widely accepted, if equivocally practiced, in development projects and their evaluations. So much has the ideal of, for example, participatory planning been incorporated and critiqued in the implementation and evaluation of urban development projects across the globe, that there are now tomes of scholarship (including my own) warning of the use of procedural justice proxies like community participation as a distraction and ruse that powerful actors use to pursue their objectives without interruption. As such, we already know that dependence on procedural efforts to foster epistemic equity cannot alone guarantee that all stakeholders' viewpoints will be equally valued and equally incorporated simply because they spent equal time in a participatory planning meeting. As Fraser (2000) argues, material inequities must be addressed if the inclusion of marginalized or less powerful stakeholders' voices is to achieve participatory parity. In short, we must start with prioritizing the distribution of material benefits to achieve epistemic justice and to institutionalize effective methods for arriving at procedural justice. Yet it is precisely this attention to distributive justice that lags behind in development planning designs and evaluations. Here I refer to an explicit attention to the intended and achieved distributive impacts of projects in terms of costs and benefits, as well as a project's spatial footprint.

Quantitatively accounting for the costs and—to a certain degree—benefits that arise in a project is widely considered more practical than efforts to also consider the distribution of both in an evaluation. In part, this is because the categories by which a distribution should be considered are not always straightforward nor without potential for conflict. For example, should the distribution of a project's costs and benefits be determined primarily according to gender, ethnicity, race, generation, political affiliation, income, or wealth? At the individual, household, or group scale? Complexity alone, however, should not be a deterrent. Scholars have spent over five hundred years expanding and refining systems of cost accounting. We need to start somewhere—literally. Here I suggest that place-based thinking and prioritarian principles can help. Particularly in the physical domains of resource-based infrastructures like water and sanitation systems, the materiality of benefits lends itself to a spatial distribution analysis by service providers, as I have argued elsewhere (Carolini & Raman, 2021). Similarly, the projects I presented in this book could have been assessed by their designers according to the physical dispersion of water and sanitation services rendered and whether that distribution reached those who might most benefit from improvements to existing water and sanitation in use. This latter assessment of course would still demand an effort at situated consensus-building in the design of the project, with a clear consideration of potential conflicts between groups (and groups and project managers) first before determining which individuals, households, or groups should be prioritized. While such an effort seems complex, I was interested to find that in Maputo, this kind of thinking was already at work within community-driven discussions, if not always in those of cooperation partners.

The Secretary of Chamanculo C, Zeferino Chioco, explained that when international partners like AVSI and WSUP first started working in the neighborhood, they did not understand that they needed to engage and get project approval from local leadership, like himself, as well as leaders serving at the sub-neighborhood level—in Mozambique called *chefes de quarteirões* (i.e., leaders of blocks, of which Chamanculo C had seventy-six), and beneath them, *chefes de dez famílias*, or leaders of groups of ten families within each *quarteirão* or block. That local hierarchy, complemented by a *conselho consultivo*, or advisory council, was overlooked by international partners at first because they had already secured approval for projects from the Municipal Council of Maputo or because they had already secured the partnership of a neighborhood community-based organization. According to Chioco, when he confronted groups like AVSI and WSUP, they realized their error and thereafter consulted with local leadership within the neighborhood. This allowed projects to run more smoothly. Critically, Chioco noted that it was also through the local administrative structure that families most in need of benefits that projects offered were locally identified:

> They [i.e., international partners] corrected the difficulties, apologized, said they didn't know that all these procedures had to be observed ... And from there, we started to coordinate, to meet together, followed these steps of the Advisory Council comprised of *chefes de quarteirões* and some older residents of the neighborhood who know the neighborhood's history ... We saw that they [i.e., international partners] had already carried out a survey to identify the most critical areas [for intervention], where there are many families with health problems. But already at the meeting of the advisory council, it was seen that priority had to be given to some *quarteirões* [blocks] which had more critical conditions. So the WSUP itself said, "You say where you think we should give priority." So we said *Quarteirão* 5, for example. It was the first block where the larger toilet was built. Because there were about forty families sharing the same space. So [they] listened to our wish and implemented it. From then on, from that moment, we have good relations.[1]

[1] Interview, January 16, 2015, Maputo. Translated from the Portuguese by the author.

While ultimately one could contest the *quarteirão* chosen as a priority by a number of measures and for the very real political and other power dynamics at play within the neighborhood's advisory council, what Secretary Chioco described was at the very least one take at prioritarianism through a locally-driven definition of the neediest households and blocks for intervention. The situatedness of Chioco's judgment within the specific context of Chamanculo was critical. It is this type of situated judgment that can bring a contextually informed ethics of equity into practice, as influential planning scholars like Campbell (2002), Flyvbjerg (2001), and Watson (2003) have argued. One could imagine a process by which different local groups define and identify what they consider to be priority spaces of intervention, so that various situated takes on prioritarianism could be mapped out, advocated, and negotiated. In negotiation, stakeholders might also consider the full extent of project benefits on the table. I was, for example, impressed with Chioco's insistence that international partners hire local youth in the neighborhood, instead of outside technicians, to help survey the neighborhood's households and familiarize everyone with the project. In other words, he was insisting that the project partners deploy a kind of participatory action that would benefit neighborhood residents in more ways than one, and would ensure that expertise and knowledge produced in surveying the community for the international cooperation project also stayed with the community. This too is a project benefit, though one not initiated by international partners, nor the type of benefit that showed up in project evaluations. However, it was a principle of engagement that I often found the most local-level administrators like Chioco in Chamanculo or Secretary Maria Botão in the Guachene neighborhood of KaTembe advocated.

Instead, internationally-led project reports and evaluations, like initial plans and contracts for work, share a concern and prioritization of logics of efficiency and accountability. JICA's 3Rs project completion report weighed in at 173 pages, not counting appendices, while a report approved by EWB and AMDEC on work in Maxaquene A stopped at twenty pages. Despite their differences in depth, both reports followed a general rationale of accountability, asking whether the objectives that had been set out were achieved. The reports also provided hints at what could have been better implemented or incorporated in projects—but these acknowledgments come too late to effect change. Another example comes from one of the most significant evaluation machines in the world—the World Bank's Independent Evaluation Group (IEG). The IEG provides a depth of assessment few other organizations can match. In addition to the evaluation reports authored by Bank staff on *ProMaputo*, the IEG conducted its own assessment of the Bank's programming in the city—a program that was a sort of leitmotif running across and occasionally connecting with cooperation projects I was researching in Maputo. In its assessment of *ProMaputo*, the IEG noted that:

> Transfer of skills from consultants to staff often did not work as envisioned, weakening the sustainability of capacity building efforts. The project had to rely on external consultants to accelerate project implementation and to help transfer knowledge through on-the-job training and mentoring. However, the disparities in remuneration between international consultants and local staff discouraged local staff from learning and performing operational tasks.
>
> (IEG–World Bank, 2020: x)

This finding is striking to me, not because it was unexpected but because it was well-known and understood by both domestic and international project practitioners from rather early on in international development projects across the city. Mozambican municipal staff—and their international partners—often relayed to me this same problem—of incentive, of crowding out local capacity-building, and more. What, then, if projects in Maputo had been co-designed and if their staff knew they would be ultimately evaluated for how effectively their project distributed benefits to locally identified priority areas or households? And what if local professionals' knowledge production—as well as the expertise acquired by partner organizations' staff—were just as valued and recognized in formal evaluations as the tonnage of trash collected or the costs of equipment?

We are starting to see examples of how material, procedural, and even epistemic equity is translating into the evaluations of work done by organizations involved in urban development elsewhere. In studying water affordability challenges across US cities, for example, I was pleasantly surprised to find that the city of Seattle now uses a template for evaluating equity—yes, equity—in its projects. And while the political economy and technological tools used by city of Seattle are different from those in Maputo, as I hope this book makes clear practices aiming to improve infrastructure development and maintenance on the ground are influenced by much more than geopolitical and technical categories. In this same study of US water affordability, I find myself often referring US urban water-utility executives to efforts at improving the accessibility and affordability of drinking-water systems forwarded in cities I have studied in

Mozambique, Brazil, and elsewhere. It is my own small effort to shift grand narratives and instead promote learning and equity across proximate peers.

While city managers can be more explicit about the kinds of international partnership that they have found to be productive and the kinds of cooperation project they would welcome, such positioning is delimited by financial needs and the autonomy of power afforded to them by national or state governments. As such, my own final thoughts and recommendations aim instead at the bilateral and multilateral partners claiming interest in advancing equity and infrastructural improvements through cooperation projects in cities like Maputo. Pay attention to whether hierarchy or heterarchy is institutionalized in the governance of cooperation projects supported—this matters for promoting all types of learning, but especially high-level knowledge production. In the co-design and evaluation of projects, give attention to the spatial distribution of benefits and how this translates across categories of prioritized communities, as defined by those communities themselves. Further, give space for reflective assessments by international and domestic staff about the kinds of knowledge and experience they valued. Avoid big, autonomous footprints within the cities where you work. Instead, embed and find ways of co-locating. Finally, advance practitioners who understand and value flexibility, and who recognize the epistemic value and knowledge they too will gain from interaction with project partners located at "beneficiary" sites. When such principles of project co-design and evaluation are combined and incorporated into international cooperation, let the community of practitioners and researchers then reassess, revise, and refine as necessary. As Nhachuchane from AMDEC noted, "We're not going to cross paths just once." Barcelona seems to understand this with its institutionalized budgetary commitment to cooperation work at the subnational level. International cooperation and movement toward equity on the ground therein will require iteration. Here I have argued that this commitment best translates among proximate, not necessarily "Southern," peers.

Bibliography

Abdenur, A. E., & Da Fonseca, J. M. E. M. (2013). The North's growing role in South–South cooperation: Keeping the foothold. *Third World Quarterly, 34*(8), 1475–1491. https://doi.org/10.1080/01436597.2013.831579

Acemoglu, D. (2010). Theory, General Equilibrium, and Political Economy in Development Economics. *Journal of Economic Perspectives, 24*(3), 17–32.

African Development Bank (2019). Building today, a better Africa tomorrow. Investor Presentation. Retrieved from https://www.afdb.org/fileadmin/uploads/afdb/Documents/Financial-Information/AfDB_Investor_Presentation_-_15_Mar_2019.pdf

Agarwal, M. (2012). South–South economic cooperation for a better future. In S. Chaturvedi, T. Fues, & E. Sidiropoulos (Eds.), *Development Cooperation and Emerging Powers: New Partners or Old Patterns?* (pp. 37–63). London and New York: Zed Books.

Agência Brasileira de Cooperação (n.d.). SENAI – Serviço Nacional de Aprendizagem Industrial.

Aguilar, D. (2018). Ganó el Sí en Ecuador: ¿Qué futuro le depara a la reserva del Yasuní? *Mongabay Latam*, February 5. Retrieved from https://es.mongabay.com/2018/02/areas-naturales-protegidas-referendum-petroleo-pueblos-indigenas/

AidData Research and Evaluation Unit (2017). Geocoding Methodology, Version 2.0. Williamsburg, VA: AidData at William & Mary. https://www.aiddata.org/publications/geocoding-methodology-version-2-0

Albrechts, L. (2013). Reframing strategic spatial planning by using a coproduction perspective. *Planning Theory, 12*(1), 46–63. https://doi.org/10.1177/1473095212452722

Alden, C. & Chichava, S. (Eds.). (2014). *China and Mozambique: From Comrades to Capitalists*. Auckland Park, South Africa: Fanele.

Alden, C., Chichava, S., & Roque, P. (2014). China in Mozambique: Caution, Compromise, and Collaboration. In C. Alden & S. Chichava (Eds.), *China and Mozambique: From Comrades to Capitalists* (pp. 1–23). Auckland Park, South Africa: Fanele.

Alden, C., Morphet, S., & Vieira, M. A. (2010). *The South in World Politics*. New York: Palgrave Macmillan.

Alden, C., & Schoeman, M. (2015). South Africa's symbolic hegemony in Africa. *International Politics, 52*(2), 239–254. https://doi.org/10.1057/ip.2014.47

Alden, C., & Vieira, M. A. (2005). The new diplomacy of the South: South Africa, Brazil, India and trilateralism. *Third World Quarterly, 26*(7), 1077–1095. https://doi.org/10.1080/01436590500235678

Alfredo, I. (2019). Um ano de transformações profundas e metas não atingidas. *O PAÍS*, November 10. Retrieved from https://www.opais.co.mz/um-ano-de-transformacoes-profundas-e-metas-nao-atingidas/

Alkin, M. (Ed.). (1990). *Debates on Evaluation*. Newbury Park, CA: Sage.

Allan, A., Warner, J., Sojamo, S., & Keulertz M. (Eds.), *Handbook of Land and Water Grabs in Africa*. New York: Routledge. https://doi.org/10.4324/9780203110942

Amanor, K. S., & Chichava, S. (2016). South–South Cooperation, Agribusiness, and African Agricultural Development: Brazil and China in Ghana and Mozambique. *World Development*, *81*, 13–23. https://doi.org/10.1016/j.worlddev.2015.11.021

Amin, A. (2004). Regions Unbound: Towards a new Politics of Place. *Geografiska Annaler: Series B, Human Geography*, *86*(1), 33–44. https://doi.org/10.1111/j.0435-3684. 2004.00152.x

Amin, A., & Cohendet, P. (2004). *Architectures of knowledge: firms, capabilities, and communities*. Oxford: Oxford University Press.

Amin, A. and Graham, S. (1997). The ordinary city. *Transactions of the Institute of British Geographers*, *22*(4), 411–429.

Amsden, A. H. (2001). *The Rise of "the Rest": Challenges to the West from Late-industrializing economies*. Oxford: Oxford University Press.

Anderson, L. W., & Krathwohl, D. R. (2001). *A taxonomy for learning, teaching, and assessing: A revision of Bloom's taxonomy of educational objectives*. New York: Longman.

Andreatta, V., & Magalhães, S. (2011). Relatório Sobre As Condições do Planejamento Infraestruturas Em Maputo. Retrieved from https://www.theigc.org/wp-content/uploads/2014/11/Andreatta-2011-Working-Paper.pdf

Andrews, M., Pritchett, L., & Woolcock, M. (2013). Escaping Capability Traps Through Problem Driven Iterative Adaptation (PDIA). *World Development*, *51*, 234–244. https://doi.org/10.1016/j.worlddev.2013.05.011

Aponte-Garcia, M. (2017). Regionalismos estratégicos, empresas nacionales y transnacionales de hidrocarburos en Estados Unidos y América Latina. *Problemas Del Desarrollo*, *48*(191), 27–54.

Arden McHugh, N. (2017). Epistemic Communities and Institutions. In I. J. Kidd, J. Medina, & G. Pohlhaus, Jr. (Eds.), *The Routledge Handbook of Epistemic Injustice* (pp. 270–278). London and New York: Routledge.

Arezki, R., & Sy, A. (2016). Financing Africa's Infrastructure Deficit: From Development Banking to Long-term Investing. *Journal of African Economies*, *25*(suppl 2), ii59–ii73. https://doi.org/10.1093/jae/ejw017

Argote, L. (2013). *Organizational Learning: Creating, Retaining and Transferring Knowledge*. Boston: Kluwer Academic. https://doi.org/10.1007/978-1-4614-5251-5

Argyris, C., & Schön, D. (1996). *Organizational learning II: Theory, method and practice*. Reading, MA: Addison-Wesley.

Asian Development Bank (2018). ADB Financial Report 2017.

Associated Press (2013). Yasuni: Ecuador abandons plan to stave off Amazon drilling. *The Guardian*, August 15. Retrieved from https://www.theguardian.com/world/2013/aug/16/ecuador-abandons-yasuni-amazon-drilling

Avril Consulting (2015). Maputo acolheu Fórum de cooperação industrial Moçambique-Coreia do Sul. Retrieved from http://www.avrilconsult.com/blog/forum-de-cooperation-industrielle-mozambique-coree-du-sud/?lang=pt

Bakker, K. (2007). The "Commons" Versus the "Commodity": Alter-globalization, Anti-privatization and the Human Right to Water in the Global South. *Antipode*, *39*(3), 430–455. https://doi.org/10.1111/j.1467-8330.2007.00534.x

Banerjee, T., & Verma, N. (2001). Probing the Soft Metropolis: Third World Metaphors in the Los Angeles Context. *Planning Theory & Practice*, *2*(2), 133–148. https://doi.org/10.1080/14649350120068768

Bardhan, P. (2013). LITTLE, BIG. *Boston Review*, *38*(3), 56.

Barkin, D., & Lemus B. (2014). Rethinking the Social and Solidarity Society in Light of Community Practice. *Sustainability*, *6*(9), 6432–6445. https://doi.org/10.3390/su6096432

Barros, C. P., Chivangue, A., & Samagaio, A. (2014). Urban dynamics in Maputo, Mozambique. *Cities, 36,* 74–82. https://doi.org/10.1016/j.cities.2013.09.006

Barthel, F., Neumayer, E., Nunnenkamp, P., & Selaya, P. (2014). Competition for export markets and the allocation of foreign aid: The role of spatial dependence among donor countries. *World Development, 64,* 350–365. https://doi.org/10.1016/j.worlddev.2014.06.009

Bassett, E. (2019). Reform and resistance: The political economy of land and planning reform in Kenya. *Urban Studies, 57*(6), 1164–1183. https://doi.org/10.1177/0042098019829366

Beard, V. A. (2002). Covert Planning for Social Transformation in Indonesia. *Journal of Planning Education and Research, 22*(1), 15–25.

Beard, V. A. (2003). Learning Radical Planning: The power of collective action. *Planning Theory, 2*(1), 13–35.

Beck, A. (2019). Water operator partnerships: Peer learning and the politics of solidarity in water and sanitation service provision. *Wiley Interdisciplinary Reviews: Water, 6*(1), e01324. https://doi.org/10.1002/wat2.1324

Beling, A. E., Vanhulst, J., Demaria, F., Rabi, V., Carballo, A. E., & Pelenc, J. (2018). Discursive Synergies for a "Great Transformation" Towards Sustainability: Pragmatic Contributions to a Necessary Dialogue Between Human Development, Degrowth, and Buen Vivir. *Ecological Economics, 144*(March), 304–313. https://doi.org/10.1016/j.ecolecon.2017.08.025

Bennaton, A., Oliveira, P., Cortes, A. C., & Cumbane, A. (2015). A cooperacao Descentralizada para Democratizar a Cidade: Projecto de melhora das capacidades de Autoridades Locais de Brasil e Moçambique como actores da cooperação decentralizada. Cidades e Governos Locais Unidos. Retrieved from https://issuu.com/uclgcglu/docs/libro_expo_brasil_moz-port-web

Berg, R. J. (2014). Interviewed by: Charles Stuart Kennedy. Initial interview date: August 15th, 2012. Arlington, VA.

Besharati, N. A. (2013). South African Development Partnership Agency (SADPA): Strategic Aid or Development Packages for Africa? Economic Diplomacy Programme Research Report No. 12.

Bhattacharya, S. B. (2011). The BRICS and Africa: Emerging Markets and South–South Cooperation. In R. Modi (Ed.), *South–South Cooperation: Africa on the Centre Stage* (pp. 96–115). New York: Palgrave Macmillan.

Bloom, B. S., Engelhart, M. D., Furst, E. J., Hill, W. H., and Krathwohl, D. R. (1956). *Taxonomy of educational objectives: The classification of educational goals; Handbook I: Cognitive Domain.* New York: Longmans, Green.

Bluhm, R., Dreher, A., Fuchs, A., Parks, B., Strange, A., & Tierney, M. J. (2018). Connective financing: Chinese infrastructure projects and the diffusion of economic activity in developing countries. AidData Working Paper #64. Williamsburg, VA: AidData at William & Mary.

Bolnick, J. (2016). Where will the money come from? SDI and local-level finance. IIED Working Paper No. December 2016. https://doi.org/10.1177/0002716283465001002

Bontenbal, M., & Lindert, P. van. (2009). Transnational city-to-city cooperation: Issues arising from theory and practice. *Habitat International, 33,* 131–133.

Booth, L. (2013). The 0.7% aid target. Information note to UK Members of Parliament. London.

Bradlow, B. (2015). City learning from below: Urban poor federations and knowledge generation through transnational, horizontal exchange. *International Development Planning Review, 37*(2), 129–142.

Branigan, T. (2015). Support for China-led development bank grows despite US opposition. *The Guardian*. March 13. Retreived from https://www.theguardian.com/world/2015/mar/13/support-china-led-development-bank-grows-despite-us-opposition-australia-uk-new-zealand-asia

Bratman, E. (2011). Development's Paradox: Is Washington DC a Third World City? *Third World Quarterly*, 32(9), 1541–1556. https://doi.org/10.1080/01436597.2011.620349

Brautigam, D. (2009). *The Dragon's Gift: The Real Story of China in Africa*. Oxford: Oxford University Press.

Braveboy-Wagner, J. A. (2008). *Institutions of the Global South*. London: Routledge. https://doi.org/10.4324/9780203018422

Brenner, N. (2004). *New State Spaces: Urban Governance and the Rescaling of Statehood*. Oxford: Oxford University Press.

Brenner, N. (2014). *Implosions/Explosions: Towards a Study of Planetary Urbanization*. Berlin: Jovis.

Brenner, N., & Schmid, C. (2015). Towards a new epistemology of the urban? *City*, 19(2–3), 151–182. https://doi.org/10.1080/13604813.2015.1014712

Broome, J. (1991). *Weighing Goods*. Oxford: Blackwell.

Broome, J. (2015). Equality versus priority: A useful distinction. *Economics and Philosophy*, 31(2), 219–228. https://doi.org/10.1017/S0266267115000097

Bunkenborg, M. (2014). Ethnographic Encounters with the Chinese in Mozambique. In C. Alden & S. Chichava (Eds.), *China and Mozambique: From Comrades to Capitalists* (pp. 50–66). Auckland Park, South Africa: Fanele.

Burtless, G. (1995). The Case for Randomized Field Trials in Economic and Policy Research. *The Journal of Economic Perspectives*, 9(2), 63.

Caldeira, A. (2019a). Zucula embolsou 135, Chang 250 mas PGR não revela quem ficou com os 215 mil restantes dos subornos. *Verdade*, March 19. Retrieved from http://www.verdade.co.mz/nacional/68197-zucula-embolsou-135-chang-250-mas-pgr-nao-revela-quem-ficou-com-os-215-mil-restantes-dos-subornos-pagos-pela-odebrecht?utm_source=feedburner&utm_medium=email&utm_campaign=Feed%3A+verdade+%28%40Verdade%29

Caldeira, A. (2019b). China destaca-se como maior credor Bilateral de Moçambique. *Verdade*, January 17. Retrieved from http://www.verdade.co.mz/tema-de-fundo/35-themadefundo/67757-china-destaca-se-como-maior-credor-bilateral-de-mocambique

Campbell, H. (2002). Planning: An idea of value. *Town Planning Review*, 73(3), 271–288.

Campbell, T. (2012). *Beyond Smart Cities: How cities network, learn, and innovate*. London and New York: Earthscan.

Campodónico, H., Carbonnier, G., & Tezanos Vázquez, S. (2017). Alternative Development Narratives, Policies and Outcomes in the Andean Region. *Revue Internationale de Politique de Développement*, 9(9), 3–15. https://doi.org/10.4000/poldev.2346

Carmody, P. R. (2013). *The rise of the BRICS in Africa: The geopolitics of South–South relations*. London and New York: Zed Books. https://doi.org/10.1080/09557571.2014.902632

Carolini, G. Y. (2017). Sisyphean Dilemmas of Development: Contrasting Urban Infrastructure and Fiscal Policy Trends in Maputo, Mozambique. *International Journal of Urban and Regional Research*, 41(1), 126–144. https://doi.org/10.1111/1468-2427.12500

Carolini, G. Y. (2021). Aid's urban footprint and its implications for local inequality and governance. *Environment and Planning A: Economy and Space*. 53(2), 389–409. doi:10.1177/0308518X20947099

Carolini, G. Y., & Cruxên, I. (2020). Infrastructure: The Harmonization of an Asset Class and Implications for Local Governance. In J. Knox-Hayes & D. Wójcik (Eds.), *The Routledge Handbook of Financial Geography*. New York and London: Routledge.

Carolini, G., Gallagher, D., & Cruxên, I. (2018). The promise of proximity: The politics of knowledge and learning in South–South cooperation between water operators. *Environment and Planning C: Politics and Space, 36*(7), 1157–1175. https://doi.org/10.1177/2399654418776972

Carolini, G. Y., & Raman, P. (2021). Why Detailing Spatial Equity Matters in Water and Sanitation Evaluations. *Journal of the American Planning Association, 87*(1), 101–107.

Castells, M. (1996). *The Rise of the Network Society*. Cambridge, UK: Blackwell Publishing.

Chase, H. (1906). Notes on municipal government: Municipal accounting. *Annals of the American Academy of Political and Social Science, 28*(95), 453–462.

Chaturvedi, S. (2012). Development cooperation: contours, evolution and scope. In S. Chaturvedi, T. Fies, & E. Sidiropoulos (Eds.), *Development Cooperation and Emerging Powers: New Partners or Old Patterns?* (pp. 13–36). London: Zed Books.

Chaturvedi, S., Fies T., & Sidiropoulos E. (Eds.). (2012). *Development Cooperation and Emerging Powers: New Partners or Old Patterns?* London: Zed Books.

Cheru, F. (2016). Emerging Southern powers and new forms of South–South cooperation: Ethiopia's strategic engagement with China and India. *Third World Quarterly, 37*(4). https://doi.org/10.1080/01436597.2015.1116368

Cheru, F., & Modi, R. (Eds.). (2013). *Agricultural Development and Food Security in Africa: The Impact of Chinese, Indian and Brazilian Investments*. London and New York: Zed Books.

Chichava, S. (2014). Assessing Chinese Investment in Mozambique. In C. Alden & S. Chichava (Eds.), *China and Mozambique: From Comrades to Capitalists* (pp. 24–38). Auckland Park, South Africa: Fanele.

Chivulele, F. M. (2017). Em Moçambique E a Sua Relação Com As Dinâmicas De Acumulação. In L. de Brito, C. Nuno Castel-Branco, S. Chichava & A. Francisco (Eds.), *Desafios para Moçambique 2016* (pp. 113–139). Maputo: IESE.

Christie, F., & Hanlon, J. (2001). *Mozambique & the great flood of 2000*. Oxford: International African Institute in association with James Currey; Bloomington: Indiana University Press.

Cirera, X. (2013). The Economic Engagement Footprint of Rising Powers in Sub-Saharan Africa: An Analysis of Trade, Foreign Direct Investment and Aid Flows. IDS Evidence Report 43.

Cities Alliance (2008). *Alagados: The Story of Integrated Slum Upgrading in Salvador (Bahia), Brazil*. Washington, D.C.: Cities Alliance.

CMM-JICA (2017). *Minutes of the Meeting of the 8th Joint Coordination Committee for the Project for the Promotion of Sustainable 3R Activities in Maputo, Republic of Mozambique*. Maputo.

Comaroff, J., & Comaroff, J. L. (2012). *Theory from the South: Or, How Euro-America is Evolving Toward Africa*. London and New York: Routledge.

Conselho Municipal de Maputo (2008). *Plano Director: Gestão de Residuos Solidos Urbanos na Cidade de Maputo*. Maputo.

Conselho Municipal de Maputo (2010). *Projecto de Cooperação Técnica Trilateral Brasil-Moçambique-Itália: Proposta de Plano de Implementação*. Maputo.

Coordenadoria de Relações Internacionais (2015). *Relatório Trilateral*. Guarulhos, Brazil.

Corkin, L. (2012). Redefining Foreign Policy Impulses toward Africa: The Roles of the MFA, the MOFCOM and China Exim Bank. *Journal of Current Chinese Affairs, 40*(4), 61–90.

COWI Moçambique (2013). *Report Card Sobre a Satisfação dos Municipes 2012*. Prepared for the Conselho Municipal de Maputo. Maputo.

Cracknell, B. E. (2000). *Evaluating development aid: Issues, problems and solutions*. New Delhi and Thousand Oaks, CA: Sage Publications.

Crewe, E., & Harrison, E. (1998). *Whose Development? An Ethnography of Aid*. London: Zed Books.

Cuna, A. (2004). *A Problematica de Lixo em Meio Urbano: Caso de Estudo Cidade de Maputo*. Maputo: Imprensa Universitária.

Cusack, A. K. (2019). Venezuela, ALBA, and the Limits of Postneoliberal Regionalism. In A. K. Cusack, Venezuela, ALBA, and the Limits of Postneoliberal Regionalism in Latin America and the Caribbean (pp. 191–212). New York: Palgrave Macmillan. https://doi.org/10.1057/978-1-349-95003-4_7

Dados, N., & Connell, R. (2012). The Global South. *Contexts, 11*, 12–13. https://doi.org/10.1177/1536504212436479

da Silva, R. (2016). Famílias insatisfeitas com indemnizações para a construção da ponte entre Maputo e Katembe. *Deutsche Welle*, June 29. Retrieved from https://p.dw.com/p/1JFv2

Davis, M. (2006). *Planet of Slums*. London: Verso.

De Bruyn, T. (2019). Analysing South–South Capacity Building. Comparing Six Flagship Projects of Brazil, India and China in Mozambique. *Forum for Development Studies, 46*(2), 249–275. https://doi.org/10.1080/08039410.2018.1525424

Deen, T. (2016). Perez-Guerrero Trust Fund Finances 278 Projects in Developing Nations. *Inter Press Service – Global Issues*, October 3. Retrieved from http://www.globalissues.org/news/2016/10/03/22521

de Haan, A., & Warmerdam, W. (2013). New Donors and Old Practices: The Role of China in the Multilateral System. In H. Besada & S. Kindornay (Eds.), *Multilateral Development Cooperation in a Changing Global Order* (pp. 215–240). London: Palgrave Macmillan. https://doi.org/10.1057/9781137297761_10

Dehejia, R. H., Pop-Eleches, C., & Samii, C. (2015). *From local to global: External validity in a fertility natural experiment*. Cambridge, MA: National Bureau of Economic Research.

Dehejia, V. (2016). The experimental turn in economics. Retrieved from http://www.livemint.com/Sundayapp/IM5bHpfFjniYIONzr1qJWJ/The-experimental-turn-in-economics.html

de Oliveira, H. A. (2012). *Brasil e China: cooperação Sul–Sul e parceria estratégica*. Belo Horizonte: Fino Traço Editora.

de Renzio, P., & Hanlon, J. (2007). Contested Sovereignty in Mozambique: The Dilemmas of Aid Dependence, Managing Aid Dependency Project No. 25. Oxford. Retrieved from https://www.econstor.eu/bitstream/10419/196288/1/GEG-WP-025.pdf

Desai, H., & Greenhill, R. (2017). Aid allocation within countries: Does it go to areas left behind? ODI Briefing Note. London: Overseas Development Institute.

de Sousa Santos, B. (2015). *Epistemologies of the South: Justice Against Epistemicide*. Boulder, CO and London: Paradigm Publishers.

de Sousa Santos, B., Nunes, J. A., & Meneses, M. P. (2008). Introduction: Opening Up the Canon of Knowledge and Recognition of Difference. In B. de Sousa Santos (Ed.), *Another Knowledge is Possible: Beyond Northern Epistemologies* (pp. xix–lxii). London and New York: Verso.

Dewey, J. (1916). *Democracy and education; an introduction to the philosophy of education*. New York, Macmillan.

DFID (2013). DFID Evaluation Policy.

DFID (2014). DFID Evaluation Strategy 2014–2019.

Direcção dos Serviços Municipais de Salubridade e Cemitérios (2012). Relatório de Visita Técnica à Guarulhos. Maputo.

Donaldson, R., Kotze, N., Visser, G., Park, J., Wally, N., Zen, J., & Vieyra, O. (2013). An Uneasy Match: Neoliberalism, Gentrification and Heritage Conservation in Bo-Kaap, Cape Town, South Africa. *Urban Forum*, *24*(2), 173–188. https://doi.org/10.1007/s12132-012-9182-9

Dreher, A. and Fuchs, A. (2011). Rogue aid? The determinants of China's aid allocation. Courant Research Centre Discussion Paper No. 93.

Dreher, A., Nunnenkamp, P., & Thiele, R. (2011). Are "New" Donors Different? Comparing the Allocation of Bilateral Aid Between nonDAC and DAC Donor Countries. *World Development*, *39*(11), 1950–1968. https://doi.org/10.1016/j.worlddev.2011.07.024

Dumontier, M. B., McDonald, D. A., Spronk, S., Baron, C., & Wartchow, D. (2016). Social efficiency and the future of Water Operators' Partnerships. MSP Occasional Paper - February 2016, No. 29.

Eduful, A., & Hooper, M. (2015). Urban Impacts of Resource Booms: The Emergence of Oil-Led Gentrification in Sekondi-Takoradi, Ghana. *Urban Forum*, *26*(3), 283–302. https://doi.org/10.1007/s12132-015-9257-5

Edwards, B., et al. (2015). Municipal finance for sanitation in African cities. Water and Sanitation for the Urban Poor (WSUP) Discussion Paper, *29*(2), 122–137. Retrieved from https://www.wsup.com/content/uploads/2017/08/DP007-Municipal-finance-for-sanitation-in-three-African-cities-PRINT-VERSION1.pdf

Elwood, S., Bond, P., Novo, C. M., & Radcliffe, S. (2016). Learning from postneoliberalisms. *Progress in Human Geography*, *41*(5), 676–695. https://doi.org/10.1177/0309132516648539

Emidio, F. (2018). Katembe: A cidade do futuro. *O PAÍS*, August 29. Retrieved from http://opais.sapo.mz/katembe-a-cidade-do-futuro

Enns, C. (2015). Knowledges in competition: Knowledge discourse at the World Bank during the Knowledge for Development era. *Global Social Policy*, *15*(1), 61–80. https://doi.org/10.1177/1468018113516968

Escobar, A. (2011). Sustainability: Design for the pluriverse. *Development*, *54*(2), 137–140. https://doi.org/10.1057/dev.2011.28

Eze, M. O. (2018). Menkiti, Gyekye and Beyond: Towards a Decolonization of African Political Philosophy. *Journal of African Philosophy, Culture and Religions*, 7 (2), 1–19.

Fainstein, S. S. (2014). The just city. *International Journal of Urban Sciences*, *18*(1), 1–18. https://doi.org/10.1080/12265934.2013.834643

Ferguson, J. (1994). *The anti-politics machine: "development," depoliticization, and bureaucratic power in Lesotho*. Minneapolis: University of Minnesota Press.

Findley, M. G., Powell, J., Strandow, D., & Tanner, J. (2011). The Localized Geography of Foreign Aid: A New Dataset and Application to Violent Armed Conflict. *World Development*, *39*(11), 1995–2009. https://doi.org/10.1016/j.worlddev.2011.07.022

Finnegan, W. (1992). *A Complicated War: The Harrowing of Mozambique*. Berkeley: University of California Press.

Flyvbjerg, B. (2001). *Making Social Science Matter*, Cambridge: Cambridge University Press.

Flyvbjerg, B., Bruzelius, N., & Rothengatter, W. (2003). *Megaprojects and risk: An anatomy of ambition*. Cambridge: Cambridge University Press.

Forester, J. (1988). *Planning in the Face of Power*. Berkeley and Los Angeles: University of California Press.

Forester, J. (2013). *Planning in the Face of Conflict: The Surprising Possibilities of Facilitative Leadership*. Chicago and Washington, D.C.: American Planning Association.

Fraser, N. (2000). Rethinking Recognition. *New Left Review*, May/June. Retrieved from https://newleftreview.org/issues/ii3/articles/nancy-fraser-rethinking-recognition

Fraser, N., & Honneth, A. (2004). *Redistribution or Recognition? A Political Philosophical Exchange*. New York: Verso.

Freire, P. (1968). *Pedagogy of the oppressed*. New York: Seabury Press.

Fricker, M. (2007). *Epistemic Injustice: Power and the Ethics of Knowing*. Oxford: Oxford University Press.

Fricker, M. (2017). Evolving concepts of epistemic injustice. In I. J. Kidd, J. Medina, & G. Pohlhaus, Jr. (Eds.), *The Routledge Handbook of Epistemic Injustice* (pp. 53–60). New York: Routledge. https://doi.org/10.4324/9781315212043

Friedmann, J. (1978). The epistemology of social practice. *Theory and Society*, 6(1), 75–92. https://doi.org/10.1007/BF01566158

Fuchs, A., Nunnenkamp, P., & Öhler, H. (2015). Why Donors of Foreign Aid Do Not Co-ordinate: The Role of Competition for Export Markets and Political Support. *The World Economy*, 38(2), 255–285. https://doi.org/10.1111/twec.12213

Fuchs, A., & Vadlamannati, K. C. (2013). The Needy Donor: An Empirical Analysis of India's Aid Motives. *World Development*, 44, 110–128. https://doi.org/10.1016/j.worlddev.2012.12.012

Gade, C. B. N. (2012). What is Ubuntu? Different Interpretations among South Africans of African Descent. *South African Journal of Philosophy*, 31(3), 484–503. https://doi.org/10.1080/02580136.2012.10751789

German, L., Schoneveld, G., & Mwangi, E. (2013). Contemporary processes of large-scale land acquisition by investors: Case studies from Sub-Saharan Africa. Occasional Paper 68. Bogor, Indonesia: CIFOR.

Gertler, P., Martinez, S., Premand, P., Rawlings, L., & Vermeersch, C. (2016). *Impact Evaluation in Practice* (2nd ed.). Washington, D.C.: Inter-American Development Bank and World Bank.

Gibson-Graham, J. K. (2006). *A Post-Capitalist Politics*. Minneapolis: University of Minnesota Press.

Gosovic, B. (2016). The resurgence of South–South cooperation. *Third World Quarterly*, 37(4), 733–743. https://doi.org/10.1080/01436597.2015.1127155

Gratius, S. (2018). Brazil and the European Union: From liberal inter-regionalism to realist bilateralism. *Revista Brasileira de Politica Internacional*, 61(1), 1–21. https://doi.org/10.1590/0034-7329201800103

Gruening, G. (2001). Origin and theoretical basis of new public management. *International Public Management Journal*, 4(1), 1–25. https://doi.org/10.1016/S1096-7494(01)00041-1

Grugel, J., Hammett, D., & Mohan, G. (2016). Emerging Powers in International Development: Questioning South–South Cooperation. In J. Grugel & D. Hammett (Eds.), *The Palgrave Handbook of International Development* (pp. 279–296). New York: Palgrave Macmillan. https://doi.org/10.1057/978-1-137-42724-3

Gudynas, E. (2011). Buen Vivir: Today's tomorrow. *Development*, 54(4), 441–447. https://doi.org/10.1057/dev.2011.86

Gudynas, E. (2016). Beyond varieties of development: Disputes and alternatives. *Third World Quarterly*. https://doi.org/10.1080/01436597.2015.1126504

GWOPA (2013). Global Water Operators' Partnerships Alliance Strategy 2013–2017. Barcelona.

Haifang, L. (2010). China's development cooperation with Africa: Historical and cultural perspectives. In F. Cheru & C. Obi (Eds.), *The Rise of China and India in Africa* (pp. 53–62). London and New York: Nordic Africa Institute and Zed Books.

Hall, D., Lobina, E., Corral, V., Hoedeman, O., Terhorst, P., Pigeon, M., & Kishimoto, S. (2009). Public-public partnerships (PUPs) in water. Retrieved from https://www.tni.org/files/download/pupinwater.pdf

Hanlon, J. (2004). Do donors promote corruption?: The case of Mozambique. *Third World Quarterly, 25*(4), 747–763. https://doi.org/10.1080/01436590410001678960

Hanlon, J. (2006). "Illegitimate" loans: Lenders, not borrowers, are responsible. *Third World Quarterly, 27*(2), 211–226. https://doi.org/10.1080/01436590500432283

Hanlon, J. (2010). Mozambique: "The war ended 17 years ago, but we are still poor." *Conflict, Security & Development, 10*(1), 77–102. https://doi.org/10.1080/14678800903553902

Hanlon, J. (2015). *A Decade of Mozambique: Politics, Economy and Society 2004–2013.* Leiden and Boston: Brill.

Haque, M. S. (2004). New Public Management: Origins, Dimensions, and Critical Implications. *Public Administration and Public Policy, 1*(1), 13–27.

Harmer, A., & Cotterrell, L. (2005). Diversity in donorship: The changing landscape of official humanitarian aid. Retrieved from https://cdn.odi.org/media/documents/333.pdf

Harrison, G. (2002). Mozambique: Development, Inequality, and the New Market Geography. In A. Lemon & C. M. Rogers (Eds.), *Geography and economy in South Africa and its neighbours* (pp. 252–272). New York: Ashgate Publishing.

Harrison, P. (2015). South–South relationships and the transfer of "best practice": The case of Johannesburg, South Africa. *International Development Planning Review, 37*(205–223). https://doi.org/10.3828/idpr.2015.16

Haslanger, S. (2017). Epistemic objectification and oppression. In I. J. Kidd, J. Medina, & G. Pohlhaus, Jr. (Eds.), *The Routledge Handbook of Epistemic Injustice* (pp. 279–290). New York: Routledge.

Hawkins, P., & Muximpua, O. (2015). *Developing business models for fecal sludge management in Maputo.* Maputo.

Healey, P. (1992). Planning through debate: The communicative turn in planning theory. *Town Planning Review, 63*(2), 143. https://doi.org/10.3828/tpr.63.2.422x602303814821

Healey, P., & Upton, R. (Eds.). (2010). *Crossing Borders: International exchange and planning practices.* London and New York: Routledge.

Herbert, R. (2012). Sixty years of development aid: Shifting goals and perverse incentives. In S. Chaturvedi, T. Fues, & E. Sidiropoulos (Eds.), *Development Cooperation and Emerging Powers: New Partners or Old Patterns?* (pp. 67–94). London and New York: Zed Books.

Hirschman, A. O. (1958). *The strategy of economic development.* New Haven: Yale University Press.

Hirschman, A. O. (2014 [1967]). *Development projects observed.* Washington, D.C.: Brookings Institution Press.

Hoffmann, A. M. (2019). *Regional Governance and Policy-Making in South America.* Cham, Switzerland: Palgrave Macmillan. https://doi.org/10.1007/978-3-319-98068-3

Holtug, N. (2010). *Persons, Interests, and Justice.* Oxford: Oxford University Press. https://doi.org/10.1093/acprof:oso/9780199580170.001.0001

Hood, C. (1991). A Public Management for all Seasons? *Public Administration, 69*(1), 3–19.

Horner, R. (2019). Towards a new paradigm of global development? Beyond the limits of international development. *Progress in Human Geography, 44*(3), 415–436. https://doi.org/10.1177/0309132519836158

Horner, R., & Hulme, D. (2017). Converging divergence? Unpacking the new geography of 21st century global development. Global Development Institute Working Paper No. 2017–010. Manchester.

Humphrey, C., & Michaelowa, K. (2013). Shopping for Development: Multilateral Lending, Shareholder Composition and Borrower Preferences. *World Development*, *44*, 142–155. https://doi.org/10.1016/j.worlddev.2012.12.007

Hurrell, A. (2013). Narratives of emergence: Rising powers and the end of the Third World? *Revista de Economia Politica*, *33*(2), 203–221.

IEG (2016). About Independent Evaluation Group.

IEG World Bank (2020). Mozambique – ProMaputo, Maputo Municipal Development Program (MMDP I and II). 146784. Retrieved from https://documents.worldbank.org/en/publication/documents-reports/documentdetail/777631588168466281/mozambique-promaputo-maputo-municipal-development-program-mmdp-i-and-ii

Innes, J. E., & Booher, D. E. (1999). Consensus Building and Complex Adaptive Systems. *Journal of the American Planning Association*, *65*(4), 412–423. https://doi.org/10.1080/01944369908976071

Instituto de Pesquisa Econômica Aplicada, & Agência Brasileira de Cooperação (2018). *Cooperação brasileira para o desenvolvimento internacional: levantamento 2014–2016.* Brasilia: IPEA/ABC.

Inter-American Development Bank (2019). Information Statement: Inter-American Development Bank. Washington, D.C. Retrieved from https://www.iadb.org/en/idb-finance/capital-and-funds-under-administration

International Development Statistics Database (2017). Detailed aid statistics: ODA commitments.

International Monetary Fund (2015). *Coordinated Direct Investment Survey Guide.* Washington, D.C.: IMF.

International Monetary Fund (2018). *Coordinated Direct Investment Survey Guide.* Washington, D.C.: IMF.

International Research & Exchanges Board (2016). *Falta tudo em Mahocha.* Mozambique: TV Moçambique.

Iskander, N. (2010). *Creative State: Forty Years of Migration and Development Policy in Morocco and Mexico.* Ithaca, NY: ILR Press.

Jackson, S. F. (1995). China's Third World Foreign Policy: The Case of Angola and Mozambique, 1961–93. *The China Quarterly*, *142*(June), 388–422.

James, R. C., Arndt, C., & Simler, K. R. (2005). Has Economic Growth in Mozambique Been Pro-Poor? *Journal of African Economies*, *15*(4), 571–602. Retrieved from http://papers.ssrn.com/abstract=1288836

Jenkins, P., & Andersen, J. E. (2011). Developing Cities in between the Formal and Informal. In ECAS 2011—4th European Conference on African Studies African Engagements: On Whose Terms? Uppsala, Sweden. Retrieved from http://www.nai.uu.se/ecas-4/panels/81-100/panel-85/Jenkins-and-Eskemose-Full-paper.pdf

JICA (2017). The Project for the Promotion of Sustainable 3R Activities in Maputo in the Republic of Mozambique.

Johnson, H., & Wilson, G. (2009). *Learning for Development.* London and New York: Zed Books.

Jones, G. A., & Corbridge, S. (2010). The continuing debate about urban bias: The thesis, its critics, its influence and its implications for poverty-reduction strategies. *Progress in Development Studies*, *10*(1), 1–18. https://doi.org/10.1177/146499340901000101

Jones, H. (2009). The "gold standard" is not a silver bullet for evaluation. London: Overseas Development Institute.

Jones, L., & Zeng, J. (2019). Understanding China's "Belt and Road Initiative": Beyond "grand strategy" to a state transformation analysis. *Third World Quarterly, 40*(8), 1415–1439. https://doi.org/10.1080/01436597.2018.1559046

Jones, N., Jones, H., & Datta, A. (2009). Improving impact evaluation production and use. ODI Working Paper. London: Overseas Development Institute.

Kerr, R. (2008). International development and the new public management: Projects and logframes as discursive technologies of governance. In S. Dar & W. Cooke (Eds.), *The New Development Management* (pp. 91–110). London and New York: Zed Books.

Killick, T., Castel-Branco, C. N., & Gerster, R. (2005). Perfect Partners? The performance of Programme Aid Partners in Mozambique.

Klinger, J. M., & Muldavin, J. S. S. (2019). New geographies of development: Grounding China's global integration. *Territory, Politics, Governance, 7*(1), 1–21. https://doi.org/10.1080/21622671.2018.1559757

Kogen, L. (2018). What have we learned here? Questioning accountability in aid policy and practice. *Evaluation, 24*(1), 98–112. https://doi.org/10.1177/1356389017750195

Kowsmann, P., Pearson, S., & Lewis, J. T. (2019). Brazil Probe Finds Vale Auditor, Employees Knew Dam Wasn't Stable. *The Wall Street Journal.* February 16. Retrieved from https://www.wsj.com/articles/brazil-police-arrest-8-vale-employees-in-dam-disaster-11550232619?reflink=desktopwebshare_permalink

Kragelund, P. (2008). The Return of Non-DAC Donors to Africa: New Prospects for African Development? *Development Policy Review, 26*(5), 555–584.

Kragelund, P. (2014). "Donors go home": Non-Traditional State Actors and the Creation of Development Space in Zambia. *Third World Quarterly, 35*(1), 145–162. https://doi.org/10.1080/01436597.2014.868994

Kragelund, P. (2015). Towards convergence and cooperation in the global development finance regime: Closing Africa's policy space? *Cambridge Review of International Affairs, 28*(2), 246–262.

Krapohl, S. (2019). Regionalism: In Crisis? In T. M. Shaw, L. C. Mahrenbach, R. Modi, & X. Yi-Chong (Eds.), *The Palgrave Handbook of Contemporary International Political Economy* (pp. 89–101). London: Palgrave Macmillan.

Kremer, M. (2003). Randomized Evaluations of Educational Programs in Developing Countries: Some Lessons. *The American Economic Review, 93*(2), 102.

Kühn, M. (2021). Agonistic planning theory revisited: The planner's role in dealing with conflict. *Planning Theory, 20*(2), 143–156. https://doi.org/10.1177/1473095220953201

Kumar, S., Leonard, A., Watkins, R., Vovides, Y., & Kerby, B. (2018). *The Art of Knowledge Exchange: A Results-Focused Planning Guide for Development Practitioners in the Social, Urban, Land, and Resilience Sectors.* Washington, D.C.: World Bank.

Lall, S. (1987). *Learning to industrialize: The acquisition of technological capability by India.* London: Palgrave Macmillan.

Lall, S. V., Henderson, J. V., & Venables, A. J. (2017). *Africa's Cities: Opening Doors to the World.* Washington, D.C.: World Bank.

Lee, C. K. (2017). *The Spectre of Global China: Politics, Labor, and Foreign Investment in Africa.* Chicago: University of Chicago Press.

Legacy, C., Metzger, J., Steele, W., & Gualini, E. (2019). Beyond the post-political: Exploring the relational and situated dynamics of consensus and conflict in planning. *Planning Theory, 18*(3), 273–281. https://doi.org/10.1177/1473095219845628

Lewis, D. (2015). Contesting Parallel Worlds: Time to Abandon the Distinction Between the "International" and "Domestic" Contexts of Third Sector Scholarship? *VOLUN-TAS: International Journal of Voluntary and Nonprofit Organizations, 26*(5), 2084–2103. https://doi.org/10.1007/s11266-014-9482-x

Lipton, M. (1977). *Why Poor People Stay Poor: Urban Bias in World Development.* Canberra: Australian National University Press.

Lubbock, R. (2019). The Social Contradictions of Regional Development in the ALBA-TCP: The Case of Food Production. *New Political Economy, 25*(2), 213–230. https://doi.org/10. 1080/13563467.2019.1586863

Lucci, P., Bhatkal, T., & Khan, A. (2016). Are we underestimating urban poverty? *World Development, 103,* 297–310.

Lucey, A., & O'Riordan, A. (2014). South Africa and aid effectiveness lessons for SADPA as a development partner. ISS Working Papers No. 252. Pretoria, South Africa. Retrieved from https://www.issafrica.org/uploads/Paper252.pdf

Macamo, E. (2006). Accounting for disaster: Memories of war in Mozambique. *Africa Spectrum, 41*(2), 199–219. Retrieved from http://www.jstor.org/stable/40175129

Macauhub (2012). First stone of Maputo-Catembe bridge due to be laid Thursday. Retrieved from https://macauhub.com.mo/2012/09/18/first-stone-of-maputo-catembe-bridge-due-to-be-laid-thursday/

Macauhub (2014). Empresa chinesa constrói novo Palácio Presidencial de Moçambique. Retrieved from https://macauhub.com.mo/pt/2014/01/26/portugues-empresa-chinesa-constroi-novo-palacio-presidencial-de-mocambique/

Macauhub (2018). Ponte Maputo-Catembe, em Moçambique, tem inauguração marcada para 10 de Novembro. October. Retrieved from https://macauhub.com.mo/pt/2018/10/ 30/pt-ponte-maputo-catembe-em-mocambique-tem-inauguracao-marcada-para-10-de-novembro/

Macauhub (2019). Debt woe continues for Mozambique. May. Retrieved from https:// macauhub.com.mo/feature/debt-woe-continues-for-mozambique/

McBain, H. L. (1921). The problem of governmental reorganization. *Proceedings of the Academy of Political Science in the City of New York,* 9 (3), 1–5. Retrieved from https://www.jstor.org/stable/117217

McCann, E., & Ward, K. (2011). *Mobile Urbanism: Cities and Policymaking in the Global Age.* Minneapolis: University of Minnesota Press.

McCarthy, D. (2017). The priority view. *Economics and Philosophy, 33*(2), 215–257. https:// doi.org/10.1017/S0266267116000225

McEwan, C., & Mawdsley, E. (2012). Trilateral Development Cooperation: Power and Politics in Emerging Aid Relationships. *Development and Change, 43*(6), 1185–1209. https://doi.org/10.1111/j.1467-7660.2012.01805.x

McFarlane, C. (2010). The Comparative City: Knowledge, Learning, Urbanism. *International Journal of Urban and Regional Research, 34*(4), 725–742. https://doi.org/10.1111/j. 1468-2427.2010.00917.x

McGranahan, G., & Mitlin, D. (2016). Learning from Sustained Success: How Community-Driven Initiatives to Improve Urban Sanitation Can Meet the Challenges. *World Development, 87,* 307–317. https://doi.org/10.1016/j.worlddev.2016.06.019

Magalhães, F., & Di Villarosa, F. (2012). *Slum Upgrading Lessons Learned from Brazil.* Washington, D.C.: Inter-American Development Bank.

Manning, R. (2006). Will "Emerging Donors" Change the Face of International Co-operation? *Development Policy Review, 24*(4), 371–385.

Marcondes, D., & Mawdsley, E. (2017). South–South in retreat? The transitions from Lula to Rousseff to Temer and Brazilian development cooperation. *International Affairs*, *93*(3). https://doi.org/10.1093/ia/iix076

Marcuse, P. (2009). From critical urban theory to the right to the city. *City*, *13*(2–3), 185–197. https://doi.org/10.1080/13604810902982177

Marra, M. (2004). Knowledge partnerships for development: What challenges for evaluation? *Evaluation and Program Planning*, *27*(2), 151–160. https://doi.org/10.1016/j.evalprogplan.2004.01.003

Martens, K. (2016). *Transport Justice: Designing fair transportation systems*. New York: Routledge.

Martin, W. G., & Palat, R. A. (2014). Asian Land Acquisitions in Africa: Beyond the "New Bandung" or a "New Colonialism"? *Agrarian South: Journal of Political Economy*, *3*(1), 125–150. https://doi.org/10.1177/2277976014530221

Mawdsley, E. (2010). Non-DAC donors and the changing landscape of foreign aid: The (in)significance of India's development cooperation with Kenya. *Journal of Eastern African Studies*, *4*(2), 361–379. https://doi.org/10.1080/17531055.2010.487345

Mawdsley, E. (2012). *From Recipients to Donors: Emerging Powers and the Changing Development Landscape*. London and New York: Zed Books.

Mawdsley, E. (2015). Development geography 1: Cooperation, competition and convergence between "North" and "South." *Progress in Human Geography*, *41*(1), 108–117. https://doi.org/10.1177/0309132515601776

Mawdsley, E. (2018). The "Southernisation" of development? *Asia Pacific Viewpoint*, *59*(2), 173–185. https://doi.org/10.1111/apv.12192

Mayaki, I. A. (2010). South–South Mutual Learning: A priority for national capacity development in Africa. *Development Outreach*, (October), 12 (2), 13–16.

Mbembe, A., & Nuttall, S. (2004). Writing the World from an African Metropolis. *Public Culture*, *16*(3), 347–372.

Melo, V. de P. (2016). The Production of Urban Peripheries For and By Low-Income Populations at the Turn of the Millennium: Maputo, Luanda and Johannesburg. *Journal of Southern African Studies*, *42*(4), 619–641. https://doi.org/10.1080/03057070.2016.1196955

Melo, V., & Jenkins, P. (2019). Between normative product-oriented and alternative process-oriented urban planning praxis: How can these jointly impact on the rapid development of metropolitan Maputo, Mozambique? *International Planning Studies*, *26*(1), 81–99. https://doi.org/10.1080/13563475.2019.1703654

Mertanen, S. T., Langa, J. J., & Ferrari, K. (2013). *Catadores de Lixo de Maputo*. Maputo.

Metz, T., & Gaie, J. B. R. (2010). The African ethic of Ubuntu/Botho: Implications for research on morality. *Journal of Moral Education*, *39*(3), 273–290. https://doi.org/10.1080/03057240.2010.497609

Mignolo, W. (2000). *Local Histories/Global Designs: Coloniality, Subaltern Knowledges, and Border Thinking*. Princeton, NJ: Princeton University Press.

Mignolo, W. (2010). Introduction: Coloniality of power and De-Colonial Thinking. In W. Mignolo & A. Escobar (Eds.), *Globalization and the Decolonial Option* (pp. 1–21). Hoboken, NJ: Taylor and Francis.

Ministério do Desenvolvimento Regional (2016). Trilateral: Brasil, Itália e Moçambique. Retrieved from https://antigo.mdr.gov.br/saneamento/proeesa/redes-de-aprendizagem/160-snh-secretaria-nacional/habitacao-cooperacao-internacional/4302-trilateral-brasil-italia-e-mocambique

Miraftab, F. (2009). Insurgent Planning: Situating Radical Planning in the Global South. *Planning Theory*, *8*(1), 32–50. https://doi.org/10.1002/9781119084679.ch24

Miraftab, F. (2016). *Global heartland: Displaced labor, transnational lives, and local place-making*. Bloomington: Indiana University Press.

Mitchell, T. (2002). *Rule of Experts: Egypt, Techno-Politics, Modernity*. Berkeley and Los Angeles: University of California Press.

Mitlin, D., & Satterthwaite, D. (2013). *Urban Poverty in the Global South: Scale and nature*. London and New York: Routledge.

Modi, R. (Ed.). (2011). *South–South Cooperation: Africa on the Centre Stage*. New York: Palgrave Macmillan.

Mohan, G. (2016). Emerging Powers in International Development: Questioning South–South Cooperation. In J. Grugel & D. Hammett (Eds.), *The Palgrave Handbook of International Development* (pp. 279–296). New York: Palgrave Macmillan.

Mohan, G., Lampert, B., Tan-Mullins, M., & Chang, D. (2014). *Chinese Migrants and Africa's Development: New Imperialists or Agents of Change?* London: Zed Books.

Mohan, G., & Power, M. (2009). Africa, China and the "new" economic geography of development. *Singapore Journal of Tropical Geography*, *30*(1), 24–28. https://doi.org/10.1111/j.1467-9493.2008.00352.x

Mondlane, E. (1969). *The Struggle for Mozambique*. Baltimore: Penguin Books.

Moodley, S. (2019). Defining city-to-city learning in southern Africa: Exploring practitioner sensitivities in the knowledge transfer process. *Habitat International*, *85*(January), 34–40. https://doi.org/10.1016/j.habitatint.2019.02.004

Morton, D. (2013). From racial discrimination to class segregation in post-colonial urban Mozambique. In F. W. Twine & B. Gardener (Eds.), *Geographies of Privilege* (pp. 231–262). New York and London: Routledge.

Morton, D. (2019). *Age of Concrete: Housing and the Shape of Aspiration in the Capital of Mozambique*. Athens, OH: Ohio University Press.

Mosse, D. (2005). *Cultivating Development: An ethnography of aid policy and practice*. London and Ann Arbor, MI: Pluto Press.

Mosse, D. (2013). The Anthropology of International Development. *Annual Review of Anthropology*, *42*, 227–246. https://doi.org/10.1146/annurev-anthro-092412-155553

Mozambique Liberation Front (1963). Why We Are Fighting. Maputo, Mozambique: Boletim de informação, FRELIMO, September, p. 4.

Muhr, T. (2011). Conceptualising the ALBA-TCP: Third Generation Regionalism and Political Economy. *International Journal of Cuban Studies*, *3*(2/3), 98–115. https://doi.org/10.2307/41945939

Muhr, T. (2016). Beyond "BRICS": Ten theses on South–South cooperation in the twenty-first century. *Third World Quarterly*, *37*(4), 630–648. https://doi.org/10.1080/01436597.2015.1108161

Mukhija, V., & Loukaitou-Sideris, A. (2014). *The informal American city: Beyond taco trucks and day labor*. Cambridge, MA: MIT Press.

Müller, T. (2010). "Memories of paradise"—Legacies of socialist education in Mozambique. *African Affairs*, *109*(436), 451–470. https://doi.org/10.1093/afraf/adq024

Müller, T. (2014). The rise of the BRICS in Africa: The geopolitics of south–south relations. *Cambridge Review of International Affairs*, *27*(2), 393–395. https://doi.org/10.1080/09557571.2014.902632

Mwase, N., & Yang, Y. (2012). BRICs' Philosophies for Development Financing and Their Implications for LICs. IMF Working Paper: Strategy, Policy, and Review Department No. 74. Retrieved from https://www.imf.org/external/pubs/ft/wp/2012/wp1274.pdf

Myers, G. (2005). *Disposable Cities: Garbage, Governance, and Sustainable Development in Urban Africa*. Aldershot, UK and Burlington, VT: Ashgate.

Myers, G. (2011). *African Cities: Alternatives Visions of Urban Theory and Practice*. London and New York: Zed Books.

Naidu, S. (2009). India's Engagement in Africa: Self-Interest or Mutual Partnership? In R. Southall & H. Melber (Eds.), *A New Scramble for Africa? Imperialism, Investment, and Development* (pp. 111–138). Scottsville, South Africa: University of KwaZulu-Natal Press.

Ndikumana, L., & Pickbourn, L. (2017). The Impact of Foreign Aid Allocation on Access to Social Services in Sub-Saharan Africa: The Case of Water and Sanitation. *World Development*, *90*, 104–114. https://doi.org/10.1016/j.worlddev.2016.09.001

Neuwirth, R. (2005). *Shadow Cities*. London and New York: Routledge.

Ngulela, D. (2019). Lixeira De Hulene "Ganha" Mais Tempo De Vida. *O PAÍS*, February 27. Retrieved from https://www.opais.co.mz/lixeira-de-hulene-ganha-mais-tempo-de-vida/

Nhampossa, T., Mandomando, I., Acacio, S., Nhalungo, D., Sacoor, C., Nhacolo, A., Alonso, P. (2013). Health care utilization and attitudes survey in cases of moderate-to-severe diarrhea among children ages 0–59 months in the district of Manhica, southern Mozambique. *American Journal of Tropical Medicine and Hygiene*, *89*(SUPPL.1), 41–48. https://doi.org/10.4269/ajtmh.12-0754

Nielsen, J. (1993). *Usability Engineering*. Boston: AP Professional.

Nielsen, M. (2010). Mimesis of the State. *Social Analysis*, *54*(3), pp. 153–173.

Nielsen, M. (2014). How Not to Build a Road: An Analysis of the Socio-economic Effects of a Chinese Infrastructure Project in Mozambique. In C. Alden & S. Chichava (Eds.), *China and Mozambique: From Comrades to Capitalists* (pp. 67–83). Auckland Park, South Africa: Fanele.

Nonaka, I. (1994). A Dynamic Theory of Organizational Knowledge Creation. *Organization Science*, *5*(1), 14–37. http://www.jstor.org/stable/2635068

Noticias (2017). Distrito Municipal Katembe: Falta mercado para colocar a produção. *Noticias*, August 25. Retrieved from https://jornalnoticias.co.mz/index.php/capital/70827-distrito-municipal-katembe-falta-mercado-para-colocar-a-producao.html

Novick, D. (1968). The Origin and History of Program Budgeting. *California Management Review*, *11*(1), 7–12.

Nyerere, J. K. (1980). Unity for a New Order. In K. Haq (Ed.), *Dialogue for a New Order*. New York: Pergamon Press.

O País (2018). Maputo Sul reage às manifestações dos trabalhadores da ponte Maputo - Ka Tembe. *O PAÍS*. July 20. Retrieved from http://opais.sapo.mz/maputo-sul-reage-as-manifestacoes-dos-trabalhadores-da-ponte-maputo-ka-tembe

OECD (1993). *A History Of The DAC Expert Group Aid Evaluation*. Paris.

OECD (2013). *Evaluating Development Activities: 12 Lessons from the OECD DAC*. Paris.

OECD (2019). *OECD International Development Statistics (database)*. Retrieved from https://www.oecd.org/dac/financing-sustainable-development/development-finance-data/idsonline.htm

OECD/UNDP (2016). *Making Development Co-operation More Effective: 2016 Progress Report*. Paris.

Palat, R. A. (2008). A new Bandung? *Futures*, *40*(8), 721–734. https://doi.org/10.1016/j.futures.2008.02.004

Parks, B. (2015). 10 Essential Facts about Chinese Aid in Africa. *The National Interest*. Retrived from https://nationalinterest.org/feature/10-essential-facts-about-chinese-aid-africa-14456

Patel, C. (2011). Challenges and Opportunities of Regional Trading Agreements in Africa. In R. Modi (Ed.), *South–South Cooperation: Africa on the Centre Stage* (pp. 138–153). New York: Palgrave Macmillan.

Patel, N. (2011). India to create central foreign aid agency. *The Guardian*, July 26. Retrieved from https://www.theguardian.com/global-development/2011/jul/26/india-foreign-aid-agency

Patton, M. Q. (1978). *Utilization-focused evaluation*. Beverly Hills, CA: Sage.

Peck, J. (2011). Geographies of policy. *Progress in Human Geography*, *35*(6), 773–797. https://doi.org/10.1177/0309132510394010

Penvenne, J. M. (1983). "Here We All Walked with Fear": The Mozambican Labor System and the Workers of Lourenço Marques, 1945–1962. In F. Cooper (Ed.), *Struggle for the City: Migrant Labor, Capital, and the State in Urban Africa* (pp. 131–166). Beverly Hills, CA: Sage.

Penvenne, J. M. (2011). Two tales of a city: Lourenco Marques, 1945–1975. *Portuguese Studies Review*, *19*(1–2), 249–271.

Penvenne, J. M. (2015). Women, Migration & the Cashew Economy in Southern Mozambique. Woodbridge, UK: Boydell & Brewer. https://doi.org/10.7722/j.ctt17mvj7x

Pereira, E. M. B. (2017). Análise dos principais desafios e entraves para a cooperação técnica internacional em saúde Brasil–Moçambique. *Ciência & Saúde Coletiva*, *22*(7), 2267–2276. https://doi.org/10.1590/1413-81232017227.03502017

Pieterse, J. N. (2011). Global Rebalancing: Crisis and the East–South Turn. *Development and Change*, *42*(1), 22–48. https://doi.org/10.1111/j.1467-7660.2010.01686.x

Pila, E. (2019). Comiche promete construir um Parque Industrial na Katembe. *Magazine Independente*, November. Retrieved from http://www.magazineindependente.com/www2/comiche-promete-construir-um-parque-industrial-na-katembe/

Pitcher, M. A. (2002). *Transforming Mozambique*. Cambridge: Cambridge University Press. https://doi.org/10.1017/CBO9780511491085

Poindexter, C. C. (1969). Planning-Programming-Budgeting Systems for Education. *The High School Journal*, *52*(4), 206–217. http://www.jstor.org/stable/40366054

Polanyi, M. (1962).Tacit Knowing: Its Bearing on Some Problems of Philosophy. *Reviews of Modern Physics, 34* (4), 601–616.

Polanyi, M. (1967). *The Tacit Knowledge Dimension*. London: Routledge & Kegan Paul.

Pollard, J., McEwan, C., Laurie, N., & Stenning, A. (2009). Economic geography under postcolonial scrutiny. *Transactions of the Institute of British Geographers*, *34*(2), 137–142. https://doi.org/10.1111/j.1475-5661.2009.00336.x

Portes, A., & Sassen-Koob, S. (1987). Making it Underground: Comparative Material on the Informal Sector in Western Market Economies. *American Journal of Sociology*, *93*(1), 30–61. https://doi.org/10.1086/228705

Porto de Oliveira, O. (2017). *International Policy Diffusion and Participatory Budgeting Ambassadors of Participation, International Institutions and Transnational Networks*. London: Palgrave Macmillan.

Power, M. (1999). *The audit society: Rituals of verification* (2nd ed.). Oxford: Oxford University Press.

Power, M., & Mohan, G. (2010). Towards a critical geopolitics of China's engagement with African development. *Geopolitics*, *15*(3), 462–495. https://doi.org/10.1080/14650040903501021

Power, M., Mohan, G., & Tan-Mullins, M. (2012). *China's Resource Diplomacy in Africa: Powering Development?* London: Palgrave Macmillan.

Prashad, V. (2007). *The Darker Nations: A people's history of the Third World. Race & Class* (Vol. 50). New York: The New Press. https://doi.org/10.1177/03063968090500040702

Prashad, V. (2012). *The Poorer Nations: A Possible History of the Global South*. London and New York: Verso.

Prebisch, R. (1950). The Economic Development of Latin America, and Its Principal Problems. Lake Success, NY: United Nations Department of Economic Affairs. Retrieved from http://hdl.handle.net/11362/29973

Price, G. (2004). India's aid dynamics: from recipient to donor? Chatham House, Asia Programme Working Paper.

Prichard, W. (2009). The Mining Boom in Sub-Saharan Africa: Continuity, Change, and Policy Implications. In R. Southall & H. Melber (Eds.), *A New Scramble for Africa? Imperialism, Investment, and Development* (pp. 240–273). Scottsville, South Africa: University of KwaZulu–Natal Press.

Pritchett, L., & Woolcock, M. (2004). Solutions When *the* Solution is the Problem: Arraying the Disarray in Development. *World Development, 32*(2), 191–212. https://doi.org/10.1016/j.worlddev.2003.08.009

PTI (2015). Benefits for Africa as India expands ITEC programme. *The Economic Times*, November 30. Retrieved from https://economictimes.indiatimes.com/news/economy/foreign-trade/benefits-for-africa-as-india-expands-itec-programme/articleshow/49982822.cms

Qobo, M. & Nyathi, N. (2016) Ubuntu, public policy ethics and tensions in South Africa's foreign policy. *South African Journal of International Affairs, 23*(4), 421–436. DOI: 10.1080/10220461.2017.1298052

Radcliffe, S. A. (2015). Development Alternatives. *Development and Change, 46*(4), 855–874. https://doi.org/10.1111/dech.12179

Rafael, A. (2011). Moçambique para todos. *O PAÍS*, August 8. Retrieved from http://www.opais.co.mz/index.php/analise/92-adelson-rafael/16099-o-neocolonialismo-brasileiro-em-mocambique.html

Rajagopal, B. (2003). *International Law from Below: Development, Social Movements, And Third World Resistance*. Cambridge: Cambridge University Press.

Rapoport, E., & Hult, A. (2017). The travelling business of sustainable urbanism: International consultants as norm-setters. *Environment and Planning A: Economy and Space, 49*(8), 1779–1796.

Ravallion, M. (2009). Should the Randomistas Rule? *Economists' Voice, 6*(2), 1–5.

Rawls, J. (1971). *A Theory of Justice*. Cambridge, MA: Belknap Press.

Rawls, J. (2001). *Justice as fairness: A restatement*. Cambridge, MA: Harvard University Press.

Redação (2019). Moradores da Katembe queixam-se ao Parlamento, ponte beneficia aos turistas. *Verdade*, May 27. Retrieved from http://www.verdade.co.mz/nacional/68591-moradores-da-katembe-queixam-se-ao-parlamento-ponte-beneficia-aos-turistas

Redacção (2017). Presidente da Turquia inicia hoje visita oficial a Moçambique. *O PAÍS*, January 23. Retrieved from http://opais.sapo.mz/index.php/politica/63-politica/43308-presidente-da-turquia-inicia-hoje-visita-oficial-a-mocambique.html

Riggirozzi, P. (2014). Regionalism through social policy: Collective action and health diplomacy in South America. *Economy and Society, 43*(3), 432–454. https://doi.org/10.1080/03085147.2014.881598

Riggirozzi, P., & Tussie, D. (Eds.) (2012). *The Rise of Post-Hegemonic Regionalism in Latin America*. Dordrecht: Springer Netherlands. https://doi.org/10.1007/978-94-007-2694-9_1

Robinson, J. (2006). *Ordinary Cities: Between Modernity and Development*. London and New York: Routledge.

Robinson, J. (2008). Developing ordinary cities: City visioning processes in Durban and Johannesburg. *Environment and Planning A, 40*(1), 74–87. https://doi.org/10.1068/a39127

Robinson, J. (2011a). Cities in a World of Cities: The Comparative Gesture. *International Journal of Urban and Regional Research, 35*(1), 1–23. https://doi.org/10.1111/j.1468-2427.2010.00982.x

Robinson, J. (2011b). The Spaces of Circulating Knowledge: City Strategies and Global Urban Governmentality. In E. McCann & K. Ward (Eds.), *Mobile Urbanism: Cities and Policymaking in the Global Age.* Minneapolis: University of Minnesota Press.

Roque, P., & Alden, C. (2012). China em Moçambique: Prudência, Compromisso e Colaboração. In S. Chichava & C. Alden (Eds.), *A Mamba e o Dragão. Relações Moçambique-China em perspectiva* (pp. 11–32). Maputo: IESE.

Rosenberg, L. J., Posner, L. D., & Hanley, E. J. (1970). Project Evaluation and the Project Appraisal reporting System: Volume One: Summary.

Roskam, C. (2015). Non-Aligned Architecture: China's Designs on and in Ghana and Guinea, 1955–92. *Architectural History, 58,* 261–291. https://doi.org/10.1017/S0066622X00002653

Roy, A. (2006). Praxis in the time of empire. *Planning Theory, 5*(1), 7–29. https://doi.org/10.1177/1473095206061019

Roy, A. (2009). The 21st-Century Metropolis: New Geographies of Theory. *Regional Studies, 43*(6), 819–830. https://doi.org/10.1080/00343400701809665

Roy, A. (2011a). Commentary: Placing Planning in the World—Transnationalism as Practice and Critique. *Journal of Planning Education and Research, 31*(4), 406–415.

Roy, A. (2011b). Postcolonial Urbanism: Speed, Hysteria, Mass Dreams. In A. Roy & A. Ong (Eds.), *Worlding Cities: Asian Experiments and the Art of Being Global* (pp. 307–335). Malden and Oxford: Blackwell Publishing.

Roy, A. (2011c). Slumdog Cities: Rethinking Subaltern Urbanism. *International Journal of Urban and Regional Research, 35*(2), 223–238. https://doi.org/10.1111/j.1468-2427.2011.01051.x

Russo, G., de Oliveira, L., Shankland, A., & Sitoe, T. (2014). On the margins of aid orthodoxy: The Brazil–Mozambique collaboration to produce essential medicines in Africa. *Globalization and Health, 10*(1), 1–8. https://doi.org/10.1186/s12992-014-0070-z

Sambo, M. G. (2016). O Desafio da Gentrificação na Cidade de Maputo: Reflexões sobre o sistema habitacional, a política social de habitação e a exclusão social. In L. de Brito, C. N. Castel-Branco, S. Chichava, & A. Francisco (Eds.), *Desafios para Moçambique 2016* (pp. 355–372). Maputo: IESE.

Sandercock, L. (2003). Out of the closet: The importance of stories and storytelling in planning practice. *Planning Theory and Practice, 4*(1), 11–28. https://doi.org/10.1080/1464935032000057209

Saraiva, J. F. S. (2012). *África parceira do Brasil atlântico: relações internacionais do Brasil e da África no início do século XXI.* Belo Horizonte: Fino Traço Editora.

Sato, J., Shiga, H., Kobayashi, T., & Kondoh, H. (2011). "Emerging donors" from a recipient perspective: An institutional analysis of foreign aid in Cambodia. *World Development, 39*(12), 2091–2104.

Savedoff, W., Levine, R. & Birdsall, N. (2006). When will we ever, learn? Improving lives through impact evaluation. Report of the Evaluation Gap Working Group. Centre for Global Development, Washington.

Savoie, D. J. (1994). *Thatcher, Reagan, Mulroney: In search of a new bureaucracy.* Pittsburgh: University of Pittsburgh Press.

Schick, A. (1973). A Death in the Bureaucracy: The Demise of Federal PPB. *Public Administration Review, 33*(2), 146.

Schön, D. A. (1994). Hirschman's elusive theory of social learning. In L. Rodwin & D. A. Schön (Eds.), *Rethinking the development experience: Essays provoked by the work of Albert O. Hirschman* (pp. 67–96). Washington, D.C.: Brookings Institution.

Schultz, T. P. (2004). School subsidies for the poor: Evaluating the Mexican Progresa poverty program. *Journal of Development Economics, 74*(1), 199–250.

Scott, A. J. (2001). *Global City-Regions: Trends, Theory, Policy*. Oxford: Oxford University Press.

Seers, D. (1969) The Meaning of Development. IDS Communication 44, Brighton: IDS

Selemane, A. (2015) Inicia reassentamento dos afectados [Resettlement of affected people begins]. *Jornal Domingo*, March 8. http://www.jornaldomingo.co.mz/index.php/sociedade/4945-inicia-reassentamento-dos-afectados

Sen, A. (1999). *Commodities and capabilities*. New Delhi: Oxford University Press.

Sexta, H. X. (2010). Há 35 anos economicamente dependentes. *Verdade*. June 25. Retrieved from http://www.verdade.co.mz/destaques/economia/ha-35-anos-economicamente-dependentes.html

Shankland, A., & Gonçalves, E. (2016). Imagining Agricultural Development in South–South Cooperation: The Contestation and Transformation of ProSAVANA. *World Development, 81*, 35–46. https://doi.org/10.1016/j.worlddev.2016.01.002

Sheppard, E., Leitner, H., & Maringanti, A. (2013). Provincializing global urbanism: A manifesto. *Urban Geography, 34*(7), 893–900. https://doi.org/10.1080/02723638.2013.807977

Sidaway, J. D. (1993). Urban and Regional Planning in Post-independence Mozambique. *International Journal of Urban and Regional Research, 17*(2), 241–259. https://doi.org/10.1111/j.1468-2427.1993.tb00479.x

Sihlongonyane, M. F. (2015a). Empty Signifiers of Transformation in Participatory Planning and the Marginalization of Black People in South Africa. *Planning Practice and Research, 30*(1), 83–100. https://doi.org/10.1080/02697459.2015.1008803

Sihlongonyane, M. F. (2015b). The challenges of theorising about the Global South—a view from an African perspective. *Africa Insight, 45*(2), 59–74. Retrieved from https://journals.co.za/content/afrins/45/2/EJC185949

Silva, C. N. (Ed.). (2015). *Urban Planning in Sub-Saharan Africa: Colonial and Post-Colonial Planning Cultures*. New York and London: Routledge.

Simone, A. (2004). *For the City Yet to Come: Changing African Life in Four Cities*. Durham, NC and London: Duke University Press.

Simone, A., & Pieterse, E. (2017). *New Urban Worlds: Inhabiting Dissonant Times*. Cambridge, UK: Polity Press.

Singer, H. (1950). The Distribution of Gains between Investing and Borrowing Countries. *American Economic Review, 40*, 473–485.

Singley, M. K. & Anderson, J. R. (1989). *Transfer of Cognitive Skill*. Cambridge, MA: Harvard University Press.

Sklair, L. (2005). The Transnational Capitalist Class and Contemporary Architecture in Globalizing Cities. *International Journal of Urban and Regional Research, 29*(3), 485–500. https://doi.org/10.1111/j.1468-2427.2005.00601.x

Smith, N. (2002). New Globalism, New Urbanism: Gentrification as Global Urban Strategy. *Antipode, 34*, 427–450.

Soja, E. (2001). *Postmetropolis: Critical Studies of Cities and Regions*. Oxford: Basil Blackwell.

Sorensen, J. S. (2010). *Challenging the Aid Paradigm: Western Currents and Asian Alterna-tives*. London: Palgrave Macmillan UK.

South Africa Department of International Relations and Cooperation (2018). Annual Financial Report.

South Commission (1990). *The Challenge to the South: The Report of the South Commission Under the Chairmanship of Julius Nyerere*. Oxford: Oxford University Press.

Spivak, G. C. (1996). Subaltern Talk, an Interview with the Editors. In G. C. Spivak, D. Landry, & G. M. MacLean (Eds.), *The Spivak reader: Selected works of Gayatri Chakravorty Spivak* (pp. 287–308). New York: Routledge.

State Council of the People's Republic of China (2019). Premier Li stresses importance of co-operation at Boao Forum. Retrieved March 28, 2019, from http://english.gov.cn/premier/video/2019/03/28/content_281476584197692.htm

Stiglitz, J. E., & Greenwald, B. C. (2014). *Creating a Learning Society*. New York: Columbia University Press.

Storper, M., & Scott, A. J. (2016). Current debates in urban theory: A critical assessment. *Urban Studies*, 53(6), 1114–1136. https://doi.org/10.1177/0042098016634002

Strange, A., Parks, B., Tierney, M. J., Fuchs, A., & Dreher, A. (2015). Tracking Under-Reported Financial Flows: China's Development Finance and the Aid-Conflict Nexus Revisited. *SSRN*, 935–963. https://doi.org/10.2139/ssrn.2611110

Sunstein, C. (2018). *The Cost-Benefit Revolution*. Cambridge, MA: MIT Press.

Taneja, K. (2012). India sets up global aid agency. *The Sunday Guardian*, July 1. Retrieved from http://www.sunday-guardian.com/news/india-sets-up-global-aid-agency

Taylor, I. (2011). South African "imperialism" in a region lacking regionalism: A cri-tique. *Third World Quarterly*, 32(7), 1233–1253. https://doi.org/10.1080/01436597.2011.596743

Taylor, I. (2012). India's rise in Africa. *International Affairs*, 88(4), 779–798.

Taylor, I. & Williams, P. (2004). The "all-weather friend"? Sino-African interaction in the twenty first century. In *Africa in International Politics: External Involvement on Africa* (pp. 83–101). London and New York: Routledge.

Tegel, S. (2018). A referendum in Ecuador is another defeat for South America's left-wing populists. *The Washington Post*, February 5. Retrieved from https://www.washingtonpost.com/news/worldviews/wp/2018/02/05/a-referendum-in-ecuador-is-another-defeat-for-south-americas-left-wing-populists/?utm_term=.ce04224f2cb9

Tendler, J. (1997). *Good government in the tropics*. Baltimore: Johns Hopkins University Press.

Thakur, R. (2014). How representative are BRICS? *Third World Quarterly*, 35(10), 1791–1808.

Thompson, D. (2013). Constructing a History of Independent Mozambique, 1974–1982. *Kronos*, 39, 158–184. Retrieved from http://www.jstor.org.libproxy.mit.edu/stable/26432414

Tierney, M. J., Nielson, D. L., Powers, R. M., Parks, B., Wilson, S. E., & Hicks, R. L. (2011). More Dollars than Sense: Refining Our Knowledge of Development Finance Using Aid-Data. *World Development*, 39(11), 1891–1906. https://doi.org/10.1016/j.worlddev.2011.07.029

Tosey, P., Visser, M., & Saunders, M. N. (2011). The origins and conceptualisations of "triple-loop" learning: A critical review. *Management Learning*, 43(3), 291–307. https://doi.org/10.1177/1350507611426239

Tvedten, I., & Candiracci, S. (2018). "Flooding our eyes with rubbish": Urban waste management in Maputo, Mozambique. *Environment and Urbanization*, 30(2), 631–646. https://doi.org/10.1177/0956247818780090

Ul Haq, M. (1980). Beyond the slogan of South–South co-operation. *World Development*, 8(10), 743–751. https://doi.org/10.1016/0305-750X(80)90001-7

UN (2018). *World Urbanization Prospects—The 2018 Revision*. New York.

UNCTAD (2019). *World Investment Report*. Geneva: United Nations.

UNDP (2016). *Monitoring and Evaluation Mechanisms for South–South and Triangular Development Cooperation: Lessons from Brazil for the 2030 Agenda*. New York.

UN-ECA (2017). *Economic Report on Africa 2017: Urbanization and Industrialization for Africa's Transformation. United Nations Economic Commission for Africa*. Addis Ababa.

UN-Habitat and IHS-Erasmus University Rotterdam (2018). *The State of African Cities 2018: The Geography of African Investment*. Nairobi, Kenya: United Nations Human Settlements Programme (UN-Habitat).

UN Millennium Project (2005). *A Home in the City*. London: Earthscan.

USAID (2011). *Evaluation: Learning from Experience*. Washington, D.C.

van Ewijk, E., Baud, I., Bontenbal, M., Hordijk, M., van Lindert, P., Nijenhuis, G., & van Westen, G. (2015). Capacity development or new learning spaces through municipal international cooperation: Policy mobility at work? *Urban Studies, 52*, 756–774.

Vieira, M. (2012). Rising States and Distributive Justice: Reforming International Order in the Twenty-First Century. *Global Society, 26*(3), 311–329. https://doi.org/10.1080/13600826.2012.682276

Villalba, U. (2013). Buen Vivir vs Development: A paradigm shift in the Andes? *Third World Quarterly, 34*(8), 1427–1442.

Wagstaff, A. (2012). So what exactly is a "Knowledge Bank"? on World Bank Blog: *Let's Talk Development*. https://blogs.worldbank.org/developmenttalk/so-what-exactly-is-a-knowledge-bank-1

Watson, V. (2002). The Usefulness of Normative Planning Theories in the Context of Sub-Saharan Africa. *Planning Theory, 1*(1), 27–52.

Watson, V. (2003). Conflicting rationalities: Implications for planning theory and ethics. *Planning Theory and Practice, 4*(4), 395–407. https://doi.org/10.1080/1464935032000146318

Watson, V. (2006). Deep Difference: Diversity, Planning and Ethics. *Planning Theory, 5*(1), 31–50. https://doi.org/10.1177/1473095206061020

Watson, V. (2008). Down to Earth: Linking Planning Theory and Practice in the "Metropole" and Beyond. *International Planning Studies, 13*(3), 223–237. https://doi.org/10.1080/13563470802521408

Watson, V. (2009). Seeing from the South: Refocusing Urban Planning on the Globe's Central Urban Issues. *Urban Studies, 46*(11), 2259–2275.

Watson, V. (2014). African urban fantasies: Dreams or nightmares. *Environment and Urbanization, 26*(2), 561–567.

Watson, V. (2016a). Planning mono-culture or planning difference? *Planning Theory and Practice, 17*(4), 663–667. https://doi.org/10.1080/14649357.2016.1230364

Watson, V. (2016b). Shifting approaches to planning theory: Global North and South. *Urban Planning, 1*(4), 32–41. https://doi.org/10.17645/up.v1i4.727

Watson, V., & Odendaal, N. (2012). Changing Planning Education in Africa: The Role of the Association of African Planning Schools. *Journal of Planning Education and Research, 33*(1), 96–107.

Weiner, M. L. (2002). Institutionalizing the evaluation function at the World Bank. Operations Evaluation Department (OED) working paper series. Washington D.C.

Weinstein, J. M., & Francisco, L. (2005). The Civil War in Mozambique: The Balance Between Internal and External Influences. In P. Collier & N. Sambanis (Eds.), *Understanding Civil War, Volume 1* (pp. 157–192). Washington, D.C.: World Bank.

Weiss, T. G. (2009). Moving Beyond North–South Theatre. *Third World Quarterly*, *30*(2), 271–284. https://doi.org/10.1080/01436590802681033

Wethal, U. (2017). Workplace regimes in Sino-Mozambican construction projects: Resentment and tension in a divided workplace. *Journal of Contemporary African Studies*, *35*(3), 383–403. https://doi.org/10.1080/02589001.2017.1323379

White, L. (2013). Emerging powers in Africa: Is Brazil any different? *South African Journal of International Affairs*. https://doi.org/10.1080/10220461.2013.781257

WHO/UNICEF (2017). Progress on drinking water, sanitation and hygiene: 2017 update and SDG baselines. Geneva. https://doi.org/10.1371/journal.pone.0164800

Winkler, T. (2018). Black texts on white paper: Learning to see resistant texts as an approach towards decolonising planning. *Planning Theory*, *17*(4), 588–604. https://doi.org/10.1177/1473095217739335

Wolford, W., & Nehring, R. (2015). Constructing parallels: Brazilian expertise and the commodification of land, labour and money in Mozambique. *Canadian Journal of Development Studies/Revue Canadienne d'études Du Développement*, *36*(2), 208–223. https://doi.org/10.1080/02255189.2015.1036010

Woods, N. (2008). Whose Aid? Whose Influence? China, Emerging Donors and the Silent Revolution in Development Assistance. *International Affairs (Royal Institute of International Affairs 1944–)*, *84*(6), 1205–1221. Retrieved from http://www.jstor.org/stable/25144989

World Bank (2010). World Bank – Investing in South–South knowledge exchange | LenCD. World Bank.

World Bank (2012). *Implementation Competition and Results Report – ProMaputo: The Maputo Municipal Development Program*. Washington, D.C.

World Bank (2016). *i2i Annual Report: Transforming Development through Impact Evaluation*. Washington, D.C.

World Bank (2018). *Management's Discussion & Analysis and Condensed Quarterly Financial Statements December 31, 2018* (Vol. Financial). Washington, D.C. Retrieved from http://siteresources.worldbank.org/EXTABOUTUS/Resources/29707-1280852909811/IBRD_Dec_18.pdf

World Bank (2019). *Mozambique Urban Sanitation Project* (Vol. 1). Washington, D.C. https://documents1.worldbank.org/curated/pt/556331558836037864/pdf/Mozambique-Urban-Sanitation-Project.pdf

WSUP – Water and Sanitation for the Urban Poor (2018). An integrated approach to peri-urban sanitation and hygiene in Maputo: Working with city authorities to improve services and practices. Retrieved from https://www.wsup.com/content/uploads/2018/02/02-2018-An-integrated-approach-to-peri-urban-sanitation-and-hygiene-in-Maputo.pdf

Yiftachel, O. (1999). "Ethnocracy": The politics of judaizing Israel/Palestine. *Constellations*, *6*(3), 364–390.

Young, I. M. (1999). Justice and the Politics of Difference. Princeton, NJ: Princeton University Press.

Index

Note to Index: names of persons discussed in the text are given *in full*: citations of authors have their forenames as *initials*
italic letters *f* and *t* denote figures and tables; (fn) indicates foot-note